T0194653

J. R. R. Tolkien, Owen Barfield and the Cosmic Christ

LUIGI MORELLI

J. R. R. TOLKIEN, OWEN BARFIELD AND THE COSMIC CHRIST

Editor: Kristine Hunt
Image source: Adobe Stock
Book Cover: Megan Pugh

iUniverse books may be ordered through booksellers or by contacting:

iUniverse
1663 Liberty Drive
Bloomington, IN 47403
www.iuniverse.com
1-800-Authors (1-800-288-4677)

ISBN: 978-1-5320-8073-9 (sc)

Print information available on the last page.

iUniverse rev. date: 08/21/2019

Contents

Introduction

This book follows on the heels of *Tolkien, Mythology, Imagination, and Spiritual Insight: The Enduring Power of* The Lord of the Rings. In that earlier book I was trying to reveal the general archetypal dimensions of Tolkien's work, which were the reasons I asserted for the enduring power and appeal of the trilogy. I purposefully framed the earlier book within a phenomenological approach, in which I let Tolkien's imaginations speak for themselves. From there I moved to the most general and accessible concepts of spiritual science: knowledge of the threefoldness of the human being in body, soul, and spirit; the four temperaments; and the ascent to the spiritual world through the elemental world and the lower and higher spiritual worlds. This was possible because of the clarity of the images in Tolkien's work and all the subsequent, extensive scholarly work about it, which creates a bridge to an understanding of Tolkien's opus.

As I was writing the book, it became clear that there is another very coherent element in Tolkien's work that can be noticed once we stop looking at the constitutive elements of his trilogy and instead apprehend it as a whole. What Tolkien weaves within his *Silmarillion* and *The Lord of the Rings* emerges as a specific cosmology linked to the West as it continued the inheritance of the Mysteries of Atlantis and took new forms in the westernmost part of Europe.

The comprehension of Tolkien's deeper individuality moves in the same direction as what emerges from the theme he treats. Tolkien shows in his personality the connection to these Mysteries; his work articulates this spiritual legacy. Tolkien carries in his soul the desire, an almost lifelong obsession, of transmitting and translating these Mysteries of the past into the present.

After completing my immersion in Tolkien's literary legacy, I realized that I could address another question around which I had formulated a wish, and which up to then I thought impossible to realize. When I completed *Aristotelians and Platonists: Towards a Convergence of the Michaelic Streams in the Third Millennium*, I had what felt like the clear contrast of the work of Aristotelians and Platonists in natural science, psychology, and social sciences. I also repeatedly felt that this contrast can be lived and experienced in art forms that I am familiar with, as well as in the way artists relate to these and how they present their work. I felt this tendency more strongly than anywhere else in artistic workshops, especially when I could compare a very similar artistic experience (painting and music most strongly comes to mind) presented by various individuals. However, the artistic realm of experience lies so far from my field of expertise that I did not feel qualified to pursue it even in the simplest terms. Thus I had no way to confirm what I felt.

My present work on Tolkien offered me a foothold into the artistic realm that lies closest to my realm of experience: working with biographies and myths, albeit "modern myths." This exploration started to give me also a deeper understanding of Tolkien's place in the frame of reference of the Michaelic Movement as a whole.

Tolkien was part of one of the most well-known and explored literary circles of the twentieth century, that of the Inklings. Here again I had the good fortune of an already thoroughly explored field of inquiry. The four most celebrated authors of the Inklings have left an abundant legacy and have themselves been studied from an abundant variety of scholarly perspectives.

When I turn my mind's eye upon the literary foursome, two individuals form a stark and most interesting contrast in their being and literary styles: J. R. R. Tolkien and Owen Barfield. I felt it was an interesting contrast to pursue in light of my previous interests. I sensed that here too we have a Platonic/Aristotelian polarity, and I wanted to pursue it further.

To pursue this comparison/contrast, I found I had to penetrate Barfield's biography and work as completely as I had previously done with Tolkien. To this end I followed four overlapping strands: what Barfield and others say about the author's life, what Barfield's most autobiographical fiction reveals about his soul journey, the content of Barfield's worldview, and finally, and most importantly, the qualities at work in Barfield's most purely fictional work.

It would be impossible to fully give life to this contrast without acquainting myself with the whole living reality of the two individuals (their biographies and the whole range of literary output), but I limited the focus of my inquiry on the contrast between their works of fiction. And among those, I focus on the ones in which the imagination reaches its highest manifestation, or those which are most accessible to my understanding. These are Tolkien's *The Lord of the Rings* and Barfield's *The Silver Trumpet* and *The Rose on the Ash-Heap*. No need to anticipate here what the work tries to bear out in its results. Let it suffice to say that here are two individuals who pursue similar or parallel aims in diametrically polar ways. One example: both Tolkien and Barfield expressed the reality of the Cosmic Christ, but their perspectives could not have been more different. Both perspectives combined are crucial for an understanding of the Christ being in our time.

This study addresses another additional perspective to the ones mentioned above. Tolkien and Barfield, in dramatically different ways, stand out as two literary giants of the twentieth century. They offer us complementary perspectives to the needs of the West, or more broadly the needs of the people of the consciousness soul.

As much as I have gathered from experience, it is rare for any given individual to perceive the global dimension of both authors' work. People often take sides behind one without being able to recognize the work and validity of the other. And at times the difference becomes even stronger, a certain antipathy and aversion. It may take the form of dismissal or complete lack of appreciation.

When it comes to completion, this work purports to be an affirmation of both authors. However, it did not start this way. I read Tolkien when I was twenty-six, and it was an immediately transformative experience. It gave me a deeper feeling for historical reality.

I felt impelled to read Barfield upon suggestion from friends and worked through *Saving the Appearances* with inner reticence. Only later did I return to Barfield with the aim of looking at his most imaginative work. As part of a research project, I felt motivated to look deeper into all aspects of his work. Reading him became "interesting" as a research project, before it grabbed me. Over time I gained a deeper and deeper appreciation for Barfield's biography and the context in which his work arose. There were little moments of transformation: the impact of reading the *Silver Trumpet* or *The Rose on the Ash-Heap*; Barfield's characterization of the mission of the West in relation to central Europe; what he believes is required from Anthroposophy for the spirit of the West and of the consciousness soul; the inner coherence of all his work, particularly Barfield's articulation of the importance of achieving imaginative consciousness, of showing us how this was accomplished in himself, and what this leads to in the artistic field.

By the end of the research, I have become enthusiastic about the depth and reach of Barfield's work, as much as I have been of Tolkien's legacy, particularly of his trilogy, his *Silmarillion*, *Leaf by Niggle*, and *Smith of Wootton Major*, among others. Seeing more fully the two Inklings in perspective emboldened me to invite the reader to integrate the work of both authors. The challenge of rising above possible inner antipathies is well worth the trouble. It will offer a larger view on art and imagination, and will reveal itself fruitful in other aspects of our inner life.

PART I

J. R. R. Tolkien

Chapter 1

JRRT: Initiate of Old?

Each of us is an allegory, embodying in a particular tale and clothed
in the garments of time and place, universal truth and everlasting life.
—Tolkien in a 1955 letter to W. H. Auden

Both Tolkien's and Barfield's biographies will here be explored from
symptomatic and imaginative perspectives. Both authors were very
critical of the modern critical perspective that sees in a literary work
the mere reflection of the author's psychological make-up. Tolkien
put it succinctly: "I should not suppose that artistic work proceeded
from the weaknesses that produced them, but from other and still
uncorrupted regions of my being."[1] Beyond this, both were also skeptical
of a literary criticism that does not see the fundamental importance of
ideas that permeate an author's life. In Tolkien's case, this would be
the importance of Christianity; in Barfield's it would make no sense
whatsoever to omit spiritual science as a formative experience for his
work and art; nor can his work and art be understood if the reader is not
willing to rebuild the world of ideas in the way Barfield did. Otherwise
he would in effect remain an enigma.

As for what were the most critical factors and influences
in his life, Tolkien lists:

---

[1] Carpenter, *Letters of J. R. R. Tolkien*, 288.

1

- really significant facts: his four early years in "the Shire" (cottage in Sarehole) his Catholic faith; the importance of his mother also in relation to his faith
- significant facts: his natural interest in languages; his philological vocation

BIOGRAPHICAL TURNING POINTS

Tolkien's early life is replete with all the themes of a dramatic Dickens novel. We could not ask for more tests to the earthly personality prior to reaching the turning point of age twenty-one and shortly after. The very trials that could have broken other individuals were somehow the preconditions for freeing the enduring from the passing, for relating Tolkien's personality to the universal human condition.

Tolkien was born in Bloemfontein, South Africa, on January 3, 1892, and was christened John Ronald Reuel. Destiny could not have awakened Tolkien to his mission in a more emblematic place. No other place than South Africa could have symbolized English imperialism more fully: not only was there the obvious clash of cultures between the English occupants and the local population, as in any other place of the British Empire. In addition here the First Boer War had been fought between the English and the Dutch-descendant Afrikaners for the first time in 1880–81, which had resulted in a British defeat. The Afrikaners had formed the South African Republic, or Republic of Transvaal, to the north of the country, which lasted from 1852 to 1902. Thus, at the time, in Bloemfontein, which is situated a good distance to the south of Transvaal, the Afrikaners mostly kept apart from the English-speaking population. This unique situation created competing colonial interests and an intriguing cultural mix, to say the least.

Tolkien's father, who had chosen emigration in order to build a career, soon found himself in poor health. While the family returned to England, he died of rheumatic fever early in 1896. The meager inheritance he left could not go a long way in supporting a mother with two boys.

Nature, with its appeal and even some mild dangers, had been around Tolkien in his South African days. Now Tolkien spent the next four years in the hamlet of Sarehole, immediately south of Birmingham, a place that he remembered fondly throughout his life as "the longest seeming and the most formative part in my life."[2] Here he could roam the countryside at will. Soon after, industrialism entered the child's consciousness when the family moved to Moseley, closer to the city's center.

Tolkien had the fortune of shaping his literary tastes from very early on. His mother, Mabel, who had teaching and linguistic skills, decided to expose her children to Latin, French, and German and to the world of fairy tales and fantasy. Among these Tolkien already had clear preferences. At the top of the list stood *Alice in Wonderland* by Lewis Carroll, and *The Princess and Curdie* and *The Princess and the Goblin* by George MacDonald. But most of all he had been impacted by the tale of Sigurd, the slayer of the dragon Fafnir, in the fairy books by Andrew Lang, which later led him to conclude that "the world that contained even the imagination of Fafnir was richer and more beautiful, at whatever cost or peril."[3] Around the same age, not only did literature enter deeply into his life but so did the whole question of language, anticipating the future Lit-Lang (Literature-Language) dichotomy of his Oxford days. Having undertaken to write his own dragon story, he was informed by his mother that he could only say "a great green dragon" instead of what he wrote, "a green great dragon." It is deeply indicative of Tolkien that he felt the need to stop writing to better understand this new matter, inaugurating a leitmotif of his life.

Another seemingly innocent but quite fateful choice led his mother away from her Anglican faith to Catholicism. Even before her official conversion in 1900, Mabel started bringing her children to a Catholic church in the slums of Birmingham. This choice, soon engulfing also Mabel's sister, provoked the ire of the Anglican family and the withdrawal of further financial help. Under the shock of these events, Mabel contracted a serious form of diabetes and was hospitalized. The condition worsened, and she died after a coma in 1903.

---

[2] Carpenter, *Letters of J. R. R. Tolkien*, 32.
[3] Carpenter, *Tolkien: A Biography*, 22–23.

An important karmic encounter had preceded the tragic fate of Mabel. In a matter of a few years the mother formed a strong friendship with Father Xavier Morgan of the Birmingham Oratory. At her death she appointed him guardian of the two boys. Even before Mabel's death the Oratory had become Tolkien's second home. And all the more so, after the death, Tolkien was exposed to a strict regime of Mass and daily Communion. Together with a sense that his mother had died for her convictions, this shaped a strong religious faith in Tolkien. Father Xavier contributed to the lives of the two children out of his own resources and ensured they would live with their aunt Beatrice, not far from the Oratory. He thus played a formative role in Tolkien's life, until he went to college and to war.

Tolkien's education took a turn for the best thanks to a grant that made it possible for him to attend the prestigious King Edward's School from 1903 to 1911. It is here that Tolkien created the first of many literary informal clubs: the later-famous TCBS (Tea Club Borrovian Society) with Christopher Wiseman, Robert Q. Gilson, and Geoffrey Bache Smith. The friendship was fashioned and deepened around a common knowledge of Latin and Greek literature, to which Tolkien soon added his interests for English medieval literature such as *Beowulf*, *The Pearl*, and *Sir Gawain and the Green Knight*, all of which he later explored in depth in his academic life.

In looking at the TCBS a few things stand out in terms of karmic significance. It was here that Tolkien fashioned the first understanding of his life mission. The friendships were to be sorely tested by the world events that engulfed England in World War I.

Immediately after King Edward's, Tolkien enrolled in Oxford and graduated magna cum laude in English language and literature. He could then no longer postpone the draft and was called to serve in 1915 at age twenty-three. This was to prove another critical trial of destiny and awakening of soul.

The college years revealed the most permanent traits of Tolkien's personality. Carpenter describes him as a "cheerful almost irrepressible person with a great zest for life,"[4] accompanied by long spells of deep despair from which the youth felt there was no way out. What tempered

---

[4] Carpenter, *Tolkien: A Biography*, 31.

the extremes was a keen, self-deprecating sense of humor, accompanied by an ease in striking friendships. Added to this was a deep earnestness that kept him out of any cynicism. Tolkien simply could not help taking things at heart and commit fully to what mattered most. These are the elements of what I would call the "epic mood" that accompanies well the style of his writings.

War brought Tolkien to what he later called the experience of "animal horror." The English and Germans were engulfed in trench warfare in the Battle of the Somme. The endless battle for yards of mud, now made famous by books and movies, lasted for months and devastated both European landscape and consciousness. Evil was made graphic to an extreme and Europe was never to be the same; witness the artistic impact that the Battle of the Somme left particularly in the works of painters. It may have marked the beginning of a collective crossing of the threshold.

The war experience marked Tolkien in more than one way. In a war zone where both British and German suffered around 600,000 casualties, Tolkien had a firsthand experience of the primeval and archetypal nature of human cruelty and evil, seeing despair and death all around him. Many of his acquaintances and much of his generation suffered death in the front lines; none could touch him as deeply as the deaths of Gilson and Smith of the TCBS. Death had brought devastation once more in his immediate circles. And Tolkien himself suffered from the very common trench fever, whose symptoms are similar to typhus and influenza. His battle with the illness went on and off for some eighteen months.

A closer look at the effects of the TCBS will highlight how important these short destiny encounters were to be in the awakening of Tolkien the writer. In 1914, after a short Christmas weekend spent together, he had formally decided to "kindle a new light" and become a poet. He later claimed, "I have always laid that [to write poetry] to the credit of the inspiration that even a few hours with the four brought to us."[5]

Shortly before his death Bache Smith had written to Tolkien, "The T.C.B.S. is not finished and never will be."[6] Soon after he restated:

---

[5] Carpenter, *Tolkien: A Biography*, 73.
[6] Carpenter, *Tolkien: A Biography*, 84.

There will still be a member of T.C.B.S to voice what
I dreamed and what we all agreed upon. . . . Death
can make us loathsome and helpless individuals, but it
cannot put an end to the immortal four! *A discovery I am
going to communicate to Rob before I go off tonight.* . . . Yes,
publish. You, I am sure, are chosen, like Saul among
the children of Israel. . . . May God bless you, my dear
John Ronald, and *may you say the things I have tried to
say* long after I am not there to say them, if such be my
lot.[7] (emphasis added)

Note that this is more than a hunch for Smith: he calls it a "discovery."
About what Bache Smith himself wanted to say, we have a witness
among one of his poems that Tolkien published posthumously in 1918.
In the poem, reminiscent of Tolkien's own *The Sea-Bell*, Smith brings
to the surface themes, such as the longing for the true West and the
memory of the island to the West (Atlantis), that will form the mainstay
of Tolkien's literary opus:

Now the old winds are wild about the house,
And the old ghosts cry to me from the air
Of a far isle set in the western sea,
And of the evening sunlight lingering there.
Ah! I am bound here, bound and fettered,
The dark house crumbles, and the woods decay,
I was too fain in life, that bound me here;
Away, old long-loved ghosts, away, away![8]

War played an important part in awakening Tolkien to his literary
task, as he acknowledged in a 1938 Andrew Lang lecture: "A real taste
for fairy stories was wakened by philology on the threshold of manhood,
and quickened to full life by war."[9] Although the first traces of his future
The Silmarillion collection of tales saw its genesis as early as 1912–13,

---

7 Carpenter, *Tolkien: A Biography*, 86.
8 Flieger, *Interrupted Music*, 223.
9 Tolkien, "On Fairy-Stories," in *The Monsters and the Critics and other Essays*, 135.

it was during his inner fight with the demons of animal horror and trench fever, between 1915 and 1918, that Tolkien brought out of his deeper layers of consciousness most of the contents of Middle-earth's so-called First Age.

The emergence of these contents is itself very revealing. The following is the order in which the stories of *The Silmarillion* presented themselves to the author:

1. "Lay of Eärendel" (Chapter XXIV of *The Silmarillion*)
2. "The Fall of Gondolin" in 1917 (chapter XXIII)[10]
3. the story that later evolved into "The Children of Hurin" (Chapter XXI)[11]
4. the legend that eventually became the story of "Beren and Lúthien / Tinúviel" (Chapter XIX).[12]

As we can see, the stories were revealed in the reverse order of their chronological sequence. When Tolkien "received" the story of the Fall of Gondolin, he saw in it the initial, missing part of the story of Eärendel, the main hero to escape Gondolin and later known as Eärendil. All the above are stories of *The Silmarillion*'s First Age. Something similar occurred in relation to the Second Age.

When later in time Tolkien wrote his "Akallabêth," relating to the Second Age of Middle-earth, the so-called Númenor [Tolkien's term for Atlantis], he put to rest another inner demon, the Great Wave dream—about the Flood of Atlantis—that he shared with his son Michael. Something further had been called up from the depth of his consciousness, another important step in the history of the "true West." Referring to the dream in a letter to W. H. Auden, he wrote: "I mean the terrible recurrent dream (beginning with memory) of the Great Wave, towering up, and coming in ineluctably over the trees and green fields. (I bequeathed it to Faramir.) I don't think I have had it since I wrote 'Downfall of Númenor' as the last of the legends"[13] The theme

---

[10] Carpenter, *Tolkien: A Biography*, 92.
[11] Carpenter, *Tolkien: A Biography*, 96.
[12] Carpenter, *Tolkien: A Biography*, 97.
[13] Carpenter, *Letters of J. R. R. Tolkien*, 213.

of the end of Atlantis is central to *The Lost Road* and *The Notion Club Papers*; when these literary efforts were discarded, Atlantis emerged centrally in *The Lord of the Rings* in the figure of Faramir, or more widely in the figures of the Rangers.

A review of Tolkien's biography before reaching age twenty-six (1918) highlights his full encounter with the Saturnian spirit of the West, at its worst, with all its external death-causing effects; from the bewildering effects of colonialism on the social structure of South Africa, to the ecological devastation that industrialism wreaked upon nature in England, and the most obvious and extreme atrocities of war that one could have witnessed at the time. All these themes will reappear at the archetypal level in Tolkien's mythology. The Saturnian imprint was present as well in the most personal tenor of the biography, through poverty and lack to the death of his parents and his closest friends.

In the midst of these trials, Tolkien's love for the Word and for the true West had both been awakened. He had developed great clarity of purpose. It seems that the tragic part of his karma had awakened him to the great purpose he was to fulfill. What an initiate of old experienced in the soul trials of the Mysteries, now life brings about through seemingly fortuitous circumstances, through external trials, until the individuality reclaims the strength of previous incarnations.

ART AND NATURE

From early on Tolkien also developed an interest and skill in painting. Many of the later illustrations of his work do in fact come from his own hand, as do some of the early book covers.

Tolkien took to painting in his adolescent years and continued in his years in college and later on. There was a definite evolution in his artistic expression. It went roughly from a purely naturalistic trend; to the development of the "symbolic/archetypal," seemingly abstract themes; to the portrayal of the imaginations that peopled his inner world. Let us see how.

As has been brought up before, the young Tolkien experienced nature very closely. He observed it keenly, as we know from some of his notes even in his later years. He would pay attention to how the same plant grew in different environments, how certain plants marked a transition between a genus and another, and kept precise observations of how soon trees would leaf out and grow, noticing differences and anomalies over the years.[14] In one of his drawings Tolkien portrays an eagle, taking care to exactness in the details by borrowing from a book of natural science. Tolkien was able to immerse himself in nature with both in detached observation and in warm interest. With his usual insight Carpenter comments, "And though he liked drawing trees he liked most of all to be *with* trees."[15]

The second phase, following his portrayals from nature, is of the greatest interest here. It may seem the most mysterious, since it addresses what looks like abstract themes. Among these are some visionary paintings that Tolkien gathered and labeled "Earliest Ishnesses," executed between 1911 and 1913, hence preceding the phases of writing the first *Silmarillion* drafts. Such are: *Before* and *Afterwards*; *Undertenishness*, in which one can see both a forest and the outline of a symmetrical butterfly, with its companion, *Grownupishness*; *Other People*, which refers to Tolkien's feelings of being prevented from walking one's own path, paired with the painting of a figure happily walking off a cliff towards a shining sun, stars, and moon (*End of the World*). With these pairings it is quite clear that Tolkien is exploring polarities in artistic fashion. Other Ishnesses include *Wickedness* and *Thought*. The latter is represented as a mythical being, leading Hammond and Scull to hypothesize this is the Valar that Tolkien calls Manwë, which has many of the characteristics of a Michael figure in *The Silmarillion*.[16]

We can complete the exploration of these purely archetypal themes, and their possible origin, from the recollections of Tolkien's son, Christopher: "My father once described to me his dream of 'pure

---

[14] See examples in Carpenter, *Letters of J. R. R. Tolkien*, 402, 403, 408, 414.

[15] Carpenter, *Letters of J. R. R. Tolkien*, 22.

[16] In *The Lost Road* we are told that "Manwë, greatest of the Valar, sat now long in thought, and at length he spoke to the Valar, revealing to them the mind of the Father." Quoted in Hammond and Scull, *J. R. R. Tolkien*, 37.

Weight,' but I do not remember when that was; probably before this time."[17] A similar experience is conveyed by Ramer in the drafts of *The Lost Road*, a projected book of autobiographical nature, in the examples of dreams about Speed or Fire (Elemental Fire, "a mode or condition of physical being") and Endlessness (or Length, applied to Time). The latter is expanded upon thus: "Time; unendurable length to mortal flesh. In that kind of dream you can know about the feeling of aeons of constricted waiting."[18] All of the above seems to indicate that Tolkien's Ishnesses originate in direct soul experiences.

The later paintings gather archetypal experience arising from inner life and what could have an objective grounding in previous life memories. Here the natural scientific and symbolic paintings, that were a mere preparation, seem gathered at a higher level. And these are closely associated to Tolkien's legendarium.

The painting entitled *Tanaqui*, according to Hammond and Scull, is closely linked to the poem "Kôr," written in 1915, which refers to the city of Tirion built upon the hill Túna. The names, however, were only given by Tolkien later in the elaboration of *The Silmarillion*.

Likewise, the painting *Water, Wind and Sand* of 1915 is closely associated to the poem "Sea Song of an Elder Day," which underwent two successive changes. Externally, it arose during Tolkien's visit to Cornwall's Lizard peninsula—the most southwesterly point of the British mainland—which left a deep imprint on his soul. The second version was titled "Sea Chant of an Elder Day." The third, "The Horns of Ylmir [Ulmo]," became the song that Tuor sings to his son Eärendil in their exile from Gondolin.[19] Not to be missed is a clue given at the base of a painting of a person enclosed in a white sphere, evoking someone as if transported out of his body and present to the re-creation of the event. Could this be Tolkien himself? From all of the above Hammond and Scull conclude, "Tolkien's creativity sometimes worked in advance of his consciousness, and the painter occasionally preceded the poet."[20]

[17] Hammond and Scull, *J. R. R. Tolkien*, 215.
[18] Hammond and Scull, *J. R. R. Tolkien*, 182.
[19] Hammond and Scull, *J. R. R. Tolkien*, 46.
[20] Hammond and Scull, *J. R. R. Tolkien*, 47.

One could wonder if Tolkien both saw and heard simultaneously the elements of his mythology, and then had to engage in interpretation.

All of the above points out to how Tolkien carried a consciousness that is far from common in present times. It is to be remembered that many of the later experiences—and those that led to the creation of his legendarium—were ushered in by the emergence of literary material from the depths of his unconscious, after the maturation of time in which he explored artistically the polarities, intended as real soul experiences.

That some of the sources of Tolkien's inspiration could have been a previous-life memory is affirmed by Tolkien's deep knowledge of spontaneous previous-life memories that he expressed most fully in his unpublished *The Lost Road* and *The Notion Club Papers*. Among elements of these spontaneous recalls we can list xenoglossy, the ability to speak in languages not consciously known; the retrieval of memories closest to the time of death (as in Tolkien's Atlantis dream); confusion upon returning from a previous life experience; remembering facts alien to one's present culture; and being fully engulfed in emotions from another time and space. All of these elements are commonly found in the reports of spontaneous experiences of previous-life memories published ever since the 1980s.[21] These experiences often occur in moments of illness, as was the case for Tolkien. The inspirations reached him most often during his episodes of trench fever during World War I.

Note in all of the above that Tolkien seems to have had a degree of what Barfield would call "participatory consciousness" that is quite unlikely for his time, in fact what amounts to some holdover natural clairvoyance. Not only did he commune more fully with nature than his fellow human beings; he also lived in the reality of ancient myths and legends almost as a matter of fact, and marveled that few around him could do the same. We turn to this aspect next.

---

[21] See Morelli, *A Revolution of Hope*, Chapter 2.

LANGUAGE AND LITERATURE

Tolkien intuited that words once had meaning and magic that are no longer present in them. He strongly felt that our early ancestors had an altogether richer experience of the word, that they "savoured words like meat and wine and honey in their tongues. Especially when declaiming. They made a scrap of verse majestically sonorous: like thunder moving on a slow wind, or the tramp of mourners at the funeral of a king."[22]

Another form of consciousness reigned in ancient times in which the human being was much more closely united with the natural world and with the sources of his own culture. Looking further back to the ancient times of his legendarium, Tolkien expresses it thus: "The light of Valinor (derived from light before any fall) is the light of art undivorced from reason, that sees things both scientifically (or philosophically) and imaginatively (or subcreatively) and 'says that they are good'—as beautiful"[23]

In his philological essays Tolkien demonstrates his love of even a single word, witness his essay on Sigelwara Land. Under these premises it is less surprising to see him say in his letters, "To me a name comes first and the story follows. I should have preferred to write in Elvish."[24] In a footnote he explains that this is exactly what happened with his "Hobbit inspiration." First came the word *Hobbit*, then followed the story.

A concrete example of the above has been gathered by Tolkien's biographer Humphrey Carpenter, in the instance of the impact that the name Earendel in two lines of the Old English poem *Crist* had upon Tolkien: "Hail Earendel, brightest of angels / above the middle-earth sent unto men." Returning to this moment, Tolkien commented, "There was something very remote and strange and beautiful behind these words, if I could grasp it, far beyond ancient English."[25] No doubt these words from the past echoed as a memory in Tolkien's mind; they gave the impetus for Tolkien's own *Lay of Eärendel*. They give us an idea

---

[22] Tolkien, *Sauron Defeated*, 242.
[23] Carpenter, *Letters of J. R. R. Tolkien*, 148.
[24] Carpenter, *Letters of J. R. R. Tolkien*, 219.
[25] Carpenter, *Tolkien: A Biography*, 64.

of how the past continuously reverberated in Tolkien's present. Some of these echoes entered his consciousness from the archives of legends and myths; others were brought back to consciousness through dreams and visions.

In his largely autobiographical *The Lost Road*, Alboin—the character who most closely resembles the author—tells his father, "But I got a lot of jolly new words a few days ago: I am sure *lomelinde* means *nightingale*, for instance, and certainly *lome* is *night* (though not *darkness*)."[26] The above is applicable to how Tolkien related to his "artificially created" languages of Sindarin and Quenya. It seems that, at least in his later stages of his invented languages, Tolkien took a detective approach to what he inwardly heard. He looked at what presented itself to his consciousness as a riddle to be solved. From the above we are far from advancing the thesis that Tolkien's invented languages are wholly, coherently re-created ancient languages. They probably were only partly so.

Verlyn Flieger, a dedicated Tolkien scholar, confirms, "Language came first, and his development of it forced him to realize that there can be no language without a people who speak it, no people without a culture which expresses them, no culture without a myth which informs and shapes it."[27]

Under the cover of fictitious events and characters, Tolkien is revealing something more about the nature of his lifelong quest: "Surveying the last thirty years, he felt he could say that the most permanent mood, though often overlaid or suppressed, had been since childhood, the desire to go back. To walk in Time, perhaps, as men walk on long roads."[28] Echoes of the past constantly illuminate the present and the future, in Tolkien's life as in his opus.

Tolkien's philological work formed a departure from many tendencies of the time. Tolkien the scientist allied great precision with imaginative insight. Carpenter characterizes Tolkien's philological writing as "forceful in its imagery, . . . however abstruse or unpromising the subject might seem."[29] Tolkien was able to ally uncompromising

---

[26] Carpenter, *Tolkien: A Biography*, 41.
[27] Flieger, *Splintered Light*, 60.
[28] Tolkien, *The Lost Road and Other Writings*, 45.
[29] Carpenter, *Tolkien: A Biography*, 134.

and scrupulous intellectual precision with an imagination able to detect patterns and relationships. In this regard the young Tolkien owed a debt of gratitude to Barfield.

Tolkien and Barfield mostly communicated through the intermediary of C. S. Lewis, the social glue of the Inklings. For the most part they lived in vastly different worlds and could not find immediate common ground. With the benefit of hindsight, this is one of the finest ironies of history, because Barfield too was a creator of fantasy—the first one of the Inklings to do so—and built his worldview around his understanding of language in relation to the evolution of consciousness. Barfield's early books—*Poetic Diction* at least—had an immediate and lasting impact on Tolkien.

C. S. Lewis indicates this connection in a letter to Barfield:

> You might like to know that when Tolkien dined with me the other night he said, *a propos* of something quite different, that your conception of the ancient semantic unity had modified his whole outlook, and that he was always [*sic*] just going to say something in a lecture when your concept stopped him in time. "It is one of those things," he said, "that when you've once seen it there are all sorts of things you can never say again."[30]

On the other hand, Barfield recognized that Tolkien's idea of sub-creation closely resembled his "poet as world-maker," placing him closer to Tolkien than to C. S. Lewis.

Carpenter argues that, had Tolkien not devoted most of his energy to fiction, he could have started a school of thought in philology. In proof of this, Oxford University awarded him an honorary Doctorate of Letters in 1972, not for his already acclaimed work of fiction, but for his academic philological work. Many of these views emerge in Tolkien's essay "On Fairy Stories."

"On Fairy Stories" posits theses that at the time were strongly countercultural, standing strongly in contrast with luminaries of his time: Max Müller, George Dasent, and Andrew Lang. They

---

[30] Flieger, *Splintered Light*, 35–36.

indicate a different understanding of the relationship between myths and language, whose closest counterpart could be found in German romanticism, particularly in the work of the Grimm brothers. Most strikingly, Tolkien countered Müller's famous assertion that mythology was a disease of language by arguing that "Mythology is not a disease at all. . . . It would be more near the truth to say that languages, especially modern European languages, are a disease of mythology."[31] By this he meant that our modern, prosaic languages derived from the far more poetic ones, closely associated with myths and legends, a view Barfield would no doubt have echoed.

Tolkien stood against Dasent's cultural perspective on fairy tales by shifting the focus from the cultural element to an almost phenomenological perspective on the content of the story itself. Andrew Lang, shocked by what he saw as savage elements, envisioned fairy tales as the content that humanity could share at a stage corresponding to its infancy. Tolkien countered that these stories still had a lot to offer to adults of our time, not only to children.

Finally, Tolkien went further in linking fairy tales and myths with similar modern work, not the least of which was his own. Tolkien saw that what appears as a flight from reality is actually a deeper understanding of it; that what most of his contemporaries criticized as "escape" was not a denial of pain, sorrow, or failure, but a reconciliation at a higher level, which does not deny any of these but sees beyond them to their redemption.

It is not difficult to concur once more with Verlyn Flieger's insight:

> Research into early forms and uses of words, the search after lost meanings and nuances—a scientific study in the truest sense of the word—led [Tolkien] through science into art, and from art into an almost spiritual realm wherein the word was the conveyer of primal truth, the magic vehicle not just of communication but of genuine communion. As such, words were for Tolkien not just a window onto the past but the key to

---

[31] Tolkien, "On Fairy Stories" in *The Monsters and the Critics and Other Essays*, 121–22.

that lost relationship between man and God of which
our sense of the Fall is our only memory.[32]

Through the study of words Tolkien returned to the original Word/
Logos and to the archetypal relationship between the human being and
God of biblical tradition.

C. S. Lewis recognized Tolkien's "unique insight at once into the
language of poetry and into the poetry of language," and came thus to
argue that "[Tolkien] had been inside of language."[33] One of Tolkien's
Oxford students, Simonne d'Ardenne, herself a philologist, once asked
Tolkien, "You broke the veil [of the word], didn't you and passed
through?"[34] Tolkien recognized this assertion as true, indicating that
through the word he could reach to a level of perception of supersensible
reality. This is what leads Flieger to the insight that the "word was the
light through which he saw."[35]

IMAGINATION AND INSPIRATION

We have already seen Tolkien at work with the dimension of imagination
in paintings of ideas (*Thought*) or polarities (among his Ishnesses
paintings). Unlike Barfield who could raise these imaginations to
conscious awareness, Tolkien remains in the purely artistic realm, be
it in his fiction or in his paintings. We could say that Tolkien arrives
the closest in these examples to what is Imagination in the real sense
of the word.

When we come to the whole content of his legendarium, we enter
another dimension of consciousness. Tolkien did not remain completely
silent about these experiences either. In his unpublished fiction—
particularly in his *Notion Club Papers*—he offers us a precious amount
of insights.

---

[32] Flieger, *Splintered Light*, 9.
[33] Carpenter, *Tolkien: A Biography*, 133–34.
[34] Quoted in Flieger, *Splintered Light*, 9.
[35] Flieger, *Splintered Light*, 9.

In a way similar to Barfield, Tolkien wrote, or attempted, some very closely autobiographic fiction; his took the form of time travel. *The Notion Club Papers* re-creates in a hypothetical future the findings of papers in which a group very much like Oxford's Inklings explored unusual states of consciousness among its members. A few of the characters in the projected book bear some resemblance to Tolkien: Ramer, a professor of Finno-Ugric philology; Alwin Arundel Lowdham, a scholar of Anglo-Saxon, Icelandic, and comparative philology; Wilfrid Trewin Jeremy, an author who explores time travel and imaginary lands.

In the book draft the climax is reached when external weather conditions bring some members of the group to relive memories from an earlier time in history, through veiled references to "ancestral memory," "serial longevity," or even through envisioning the possibility of reincarnation, through which some souls can carry knowledge of earlier times pertaining to their culture. The earlier time in history, to all practical intents, pertains to Tolkien's Great Wave dream of Númenor/Atlantis.

The book is a treasure trove of insights that Tolkien safely kept to himself. They could not fit the life of an Oxford don, or of an orthodox Catholic. We will quote at length from the book. The first line of inquiry for Tolkien is the relationship between the conscious mind and what lives immediately below the surface of consciousness. This is done by him in a way far different than the psychology of his time.

"Minds can be lazy on their own account. Even for the energetic ones sleep is largely a rest. But of course, for a mind rest is not oblivion, which is impossible for it," says Lowdham. Tolkien then leads us deeply into what this kind of activity could be:

> If it has by nature, or has *acquired, some dominant interest*—like history, or languages, or mathematics—it may at times work away at such things, while the old body is recuperating. . . . I fancy that all *waking art* draws a good deal on this sort of activity. Those *scenes that come up complete and fixed* that I spoke of before, for

instance; though some of them, I believe, are *visions of real places*. (emphasis added)[36]

The hints to Tolkien himself are unmistakable; it is very likely that the author realized that what surfaced in his consciousness at particular times in his life belonged to "other time" and "other space."

Tolkien understood that what is revealed to the conscious mind is mediated by the spirit and has to enter the human mind, encountering then the challenge of interpretation; that "beings make us hear and see them in some appropriate form, by producing a direct impression on the mind. The clothing of this naked impression in terms intelligible to your incarnate mind is, I imagine, often left to you, the receiver. Though no doubt they can cause you to hear words and to see shapes of their own choosing, if they will."[37]

The character called Ramer warns us of the peculiarities and dangers of the world that comes to us in dreams. He notes that some minds that we encounter in dreams can be malicious, and that the fear that arises in dreams can warn us of something that goes beyond the life of dreams. Tolkien draws a list of distinctions, without, however, deepening the significance of these. Among the various ones are *perceiving*, as in visiting real scenes; *apparitions*, in which what is experienced comes to us from "another mind"; and *reading*, in which we perceive, as it were, the records of someone else's experiences. Most telling of all is what Ramer calls *lying*: "There's lying in the universe, some very clever lying. I mean some very potent fiction is specially composed to be inspected by others and to deceive, to pass as record; but it is made to the malefit of Men."[38] The above denotes that Tolkien is aware of the worlds of imagination and artistic inspiration to a high degree.

Among the unpublished essays of Tolkien is one about one of his latter fairy tales, *Smith of Wootton Major*, in which the author reflects on the nature of artistic inspiration, and, in a way, mourns the loss of inspiration in his later days: "A time comes for writers and artists, when invention and vision cease and they can only reflect on what they have

[36] Tolkien, *The Lost Road and Other Writings*, 189.
[37] Tolkien, *The Lost Road and Other Writings*, 202.
[38] Tolkien, *The Lost Road and Other Writings*, 196.

seen and learned," adding further that "that is not the whole point of the tale. Which includes sacrifice, and the handing on, with trust and without keeping a hand on things, of power and vision to the next generation."[39]

Couched in this mildly pessimistic perspective is the deeply perceptive, though artistically veiled, insight that this need not be the ultimate necessity. In the tale Smith [Tolkien's representative] meets with Alf, the king of Faery, who travels between worlds at will, and is himself the grandson of "first Cook," a great "traveler between worlds." Thus in the depth of his being Tolkien makes room for fully conscious converse with the spirit.

In a story that is a bit of Tolkien's testament, Faery is seen as the essential bridge to our deeper human nature, a bringer of health.

> Faery represents at its weakest a breaking out (at least in mind) from the iron ring of the familiar, still more from the adamantine ring of belief that is known, possessed, controlled, and so (ultimately) all that is worth being considered—a constant awareness of the world beyond these rings. More strongly it represents love. . . . This Faery is as necessary for the health and complete functioning of the Human as sunlight for physical life.[40]

Tolkien lived undoubtedly in the dimension of imagination, an imagination of artistic nature, not yet made conscious to the waking mind. He also received what amounts to artistic inspiration in the content of legends and myths that had no relationship to anything within the author's environment. And in his conscious life Tolkien fully lived in artistic imagination. Letter after letter shows how Tolkien addresses a matter of relationships, a social question, questions of faith or science with an artistic imaginative analogy. Had Tolkien embraced a phenomenological, or spiritual-scientific worldview, he would no doubt have crossed the threshold that lay so close to his consciousness.

---

39. Unpublished fol. 36r. in Flieger, *Green Suns and Faërie*, 236.
40. Flieger, *Green Suns and Faërie*, 247.

Of particular interest to our explorations is Tolkien's unique relationship to Christianity. We will return to it in a larger appraisal of Tolkien's individuality, when we will compare the world of his imaginations to that of Barfield. Suffice to say here that Tolkien saw Christianity not unlike his beloved legends and myths; however, here he saw myth made history. While becoming a historical event, the deed of Golgotha retained the quality of myth:

> The Gospels contain a fairy-story, or a story of a larger kind which embraces all the essence of fairy-stories. They contain many marvels—peculiarly artistic, beautiful, and moving: "mythical" in their perfect, self-contained significance. . . . But this story has entered History and the primary world; the desire and aspiration of sub-creation has been raised to the fulfillment of Creation. The Birth of Christ is the eucatastrophe [contrary of catastrophe] of Man's history. The Resurrection is the eucatastrophe of the story of the Incarnation. This story begins and ends in joy. It has pre-eminently the "inner consistency of reality."[41]

---

[41] Tolkien, "On Fairy-Stories," *The Monsters and the Critics and other Essays*, 155–56.

Chapter 2

Introduction to
The Lord of the Rings

In order to turn to the deeper aspects of Tolkien's legacy—particularly in relation to *The Lord of the Rings*—I will present here in a condensed fashion an overview of the trilogy's plot, which incorporates the insights that were presented in *Tolkien, Mythology, Imagination and Spiritual Insight: The Enduring Power of The Lord of the Rings*, particularly in Part II.

The overview will introduce a variety of themes and indicate how these are interconnected with various parts in the rest of the trilogy. This is possible in great part thanks to the work of Richard C. West and Randel Helms concerning the structure of *The Lord of the Rings*.[42]

We will refer to the six original book titles, which were: Book 1: The First Journey; Book 2: The Journey of the Nine Companions; Book 3: The Treason of Isengard; Book 4: The Journey of the Ring-Bearers; Book 5: The War of the Ring; Book 6: The End of the Third Age. Books I and II are part of *The Fellowship of the Ring*, Books III and IV form *The Two Towers*, and Books V and VI *The Return of the King*.

---

[42] See West, "The Interlace Structure of The Lord of the Rings," and Helms, *Tolkien's World*, chapter 5: "Tolkien's World: The Structure and Aesthetics of the Lord of the Rings."

PREMISES

It is necessary to offer some background about both Sauron and the Ring in order to understand some of the central motifs of *The Lord of the Rings*.

Sauron and the Rings

Sauron is "a being of Valinor [the realm of the immortal Valar of the West] perverted to the service of the Enemy [Melkor] and becoming his chief captain and servant." He retreats in haste when he sees the defeat of his master Melkor [the first opponent of the Gods and a clearly Luciferic figure], only to become "a reincarnation of Evil, and a thing lusting for Complete Power."[43] As Men multiply and the Elves start to fade, the Shadow of evil grows from the East. The two themes are treated in "Akallabêth" (the fall of Númenór, or Tolkien's Atlantis) and in "Of the Rings of Power and the Third Age," two episodes of *The Silmarillion*.

In "Akallabêth" we are told of the "fall" or "error" of the Elves. They are torn between retaining the memory of the eternal West and their high standing in Middle-earth where they tower above Men, Dwarves, and Hobbits. They are obsessed with "fading," want to prevent or slow down change that is viewed as a regrettable thing, and want to preserve what is desired or loved.[44] The Elves of the Second Age have maintained some lingering kingdoms such as Rivendell, Eregion at the feet of the Misty Mountains (close to the mines of Moria, which is the major realm of the Dwarves in the Second Age), and Lórien. Both Rivendell and the mines of Moria appear in the trilogy's first volume, *The Fellowship of the Ring*.

Many Elves will gradually start to listen to Sauron ("he was still fair in this early time") who lures them into making Western Middle-earth as beautiful as Valinor, to create a sort of independent and separate paradise, and with his help they forge the Rings of Power. This is what Tolkien calls "nearest to falling to 'magic' and machinery." Only the Elves Gil-galad and Elrond resist the temptation. The Rings prevent or

---

43 Tolkien, *The Silmarillion*, xxiv–v.
44 Tolkien, *The Silmarillion*, xxiv–v.

slow the natural decay and enhance the natural power of the possessor, approaching "magic." Sauron himself endows the Rings with the power of invisibility.

The Elves of Eregion crafted three rings directed to the preservation of beauty, which did not confer invisibility. Sauron built a Ring in his own domain that allowed him to "see the thoughts of all that used the lesser rings."[45] The Elves, aware of his secret purpose, hid the three rings, and tried to destroy the others—the nine given to Men and the seven of the Dwarves. There ensued a war between the Elves and Sauron in Middle-earth, and the West suffered further destruction. Sauron destroyed Eregion and captured many Rings of Power, through which he could enslave those who accepted them out of greed or ambition. Such were the Ringwraiths, Men who succumbed to the temptation of black magic. The Elves survived in secret places, such as the last Elf-kingdom of Gil-galad on the extreme western shores, or Elrond's enchanted sanctuary of Rivendell "on the extreme eastern margin of the western lands."

Sauron ruled a growing empire from the tower of Barad-dûr in Mordor to the east. In crafting the Ring, Sauron had to let some of his power pass into it. While he wore it, his power was enhanced, but if it came into someone else's hands, the possessor could challenge Sauron, overthrow him, and usurp his throne. But that was tempered by the reality that the Ring enslaved to its will the one who wore it. The above was the weakness Sauron had accepted in his effort to enslave the Elves. The other danger was that of the Ring being unmade in the fires of Mount Doom, but that could be thought of as a very unlikely matter.

The last of the Elven kings of Middle-earth, Elendil of Westernesse and Gil-galad, overthrew Sauron but perished in the deed; Elendil's son Isildur cut the Ring from Sauron's finger and took it for his own. The spirit of the defeated Sauron fled and hid many long years, until it took shape anew in the forest of Mirkwood. Isildur could not resist the pull of the Ring and would not listen to those who asked him to cast it into the fires of Orodruin. The Ring was lost by him in the waters of the Anduin River. Isildur himself died in the nearing Gladden Fields, and his esquire brought back the shattered Narsil sword to Rivendell.

---

[45] Tolkien, *The Silmarillion*, xxv.

Gollum and the Ring

Gollum will form an integral part of Frodo Baggins's path of redemption. The two are both alike and very different. To start with, they both are Hobbits.

Before receiving the nickname that made him famous, Gollum was known as Sméagol, a descendent of a Stoor branch of the Hobbits, those that liked to live close to the waters, in his case the waters of the great River Anduin. Sméagol had an early inquisitive mind and was quick and strong. In his youth he was a close friend to the Hobbit Déagol, and together they swam and fished on the river. It was during one of these fishing adventures that Déagol caught a big fish that pulled hard at the line and drew him deep into the water. At the bottom of the river he espied a shining ring and got hold of it. It happened to be Sméagol's birthday, and the Hobbit caught a glance of the Ring, instantly coveting it to the point of murdering his friend and immediately wearing it.

The Ring completely altered Sméagol's behavior. It gave him invisibility and the power to understand people's secrets for his evil ends. It also altered his behavior: in his attachment to the Ring, he started to speak of his "Precious," stealing and speaking to himself, gurgling in such a way as to gain the nickname of Gollum. Shunned by his people, he was sent far away and wandered off towards the Misty Mountains. Thus it was that the Ring disappeared with its owner inside the mountain, hidden from Sauron himself.

The Ring further altered Gollum's behavior and being. He was now constantly obsessed by having it and by the fear of losing it. It caused a split in Gollum's soul. He hated the darkness in which he lived but could not endure the light; he hated and loved the Ring as he hated and loved himself. The Ring prolonged his life, but gave him an appearance closer to that of an animal than of a Hobbit.

The real Sméagol survived in some remote recesses of his soul, Tolkien tells us in *The Fellowship of the Ring*: "There was a little corner of his mind that was still his own, and light came through it, as through a chink in the dark: light out of the past." Living under the mountain, Gollum did not need to wear the Ring; but even so he had become obsessed, practically possessed by it. After losing the Ring to Bilbo, he was turning old but also starting to revive.

In *The Hobbit* Bilbo Baggins, Frodo's uncle, accidentally recovered the Ring that Gollum left unguarded in the waters of a lake in a dark cave. Bilbo discovered that wearing the Ring rendered him invisible, but knew nothing of its origin. The Ring did not exert as strong a pull on Bilbo's soul as it did on Gollum. Nevertheless he grew an attachment towards it and did not want to relinquish it to Frodo at Gandalf's request.

The Ring travels from Hobbit to Hobbit on the days of their birthdays. Sméagol acquires it on his birthday by force. Bilbo inherits it from Sméagol and bequeaths it to Frodo on the day that is the birthday of both.

When we arrive at the part of the story published in *the Fellowship of the Ring*, Gandalf has learned from Gollum that the Ring has been found in the Anduin River. Then he reveals what he read after setting the Ring in the fire. He first reads in the original language: "One Ring to rule them all, One Ring to find them, One Ring to bind them all and in the Darkness bind them."

After escaping Elven captivity, Gollum goes to Mordor and Sauron now knows about the fate of the Ring. Gandalf foretells that "[Gollum] may play a part yet that neither he nor Sauron have foreseen."

BOOK I: THE FIRST JOURNEY

The narrative will be given here in the chronological order of the events. This means that events that in the books are only related after the facts are brought forth here at the time of their occurrence. This concerns mainly the two ordeals of the wizard Gandalf at the hand of Saruman first, and of his confrontation with the Balrog in the mines of Moria later.

The events take their departure from Gandalf's visit to the Shire on the occasion of Bilbo's 111th birthday celebrations. At this time the wizard, who is still called Gandalf the Grey, has become aware of the danger that the Ring presents for the Hobbits' Shire and for the whole of Middle-earth. He feels charged of the task of persuading Bilbo to take leave of the Ring and of encouraging Frodo to take it out of the

Shire. He knows that Sauron's nine Ringwraiths are hot on the tracks of the talisman of power and that time presses. The Ringwraiths have taken the shape of Black Riders atop black horses.

Frodo is joined in his quest by his most faithful Hobbit friends— Sam, Merry, and Pippin. Together they manage to leave the Shire and elude the pursuit of the Ringwraiths. The germs of the fellowship are thus formed and the gauntlet is thrown against Sauron and his minions. The Hobbits are first rescued from their pursuers by fellow Hobbit Farmer Maggot, and from a party of Elves, led by Gildor. The companions are being steeled to the trials that will follow. And their first ones are those they will visit in Tom Bombadil's domain.

The Elemental World: Tom Bombadil's Domain

The first trials that the Hobbits face place us directly in the world of the soul; first in the oppressive heat of the Old Forest to the north, later in the bleak desolation and cold of the Barrow-downs to the south. The two realms of experience are divided by Tom Bombadil's house, which stands at the border between the two.

The atmosphere of the Old Forest is heavy and oppressive, the air hot and stuffy. Everything seems to be alive, and much of it holds a hostile presence. Every movement, even singing, seems to exact a great dose of effort from the Hobbits; they experience hardly being able to resist sleep. The narrative tells us, "Everything in it is very much more alive, more aware of what is going on, so to speak, than things are in the Shire."[46] Much as they try to resist the forces of the Old Forest, the Hobbits are inexorably drawn towards the place that they want to avoid, the Withywindle River, "the queerest part of the whole wood" where they meet the Old Man Willow.

In a short time Merry and Pippin are rendered captives of the malignant tree. Sam and Frodo cannot resist much longer. The companions are providentially saved by the enigmatic figure of Tom Bombadil, who has a general appearance not too different from that of the Hobbits but who is said to be the "oldest being of Middle-earth" and who holds authority over the beings of this strange land, and the land

---

[46] Tolkien, *Fellowship of the Ring*, 108.

just to the south of it, the Barrow-downs. The rescued Hobbits spend the night in the house of Tom Bombadil and Goldberry, his companion, and here have significant dreams, particularly Frodo.

The Barrow-downs present us with a situation that is a polar opposite to that of the Old Forest. The air is once again heavy, but here reign coldness and fog, and the whole tends to darkness. The climax of the ordeal is the Hobbits' encounter with a Barrow-wight, a spectral figure reminiscent in character to an earthbound soul. "[Frodo] thought there were two eyes, *very cold* though lit with a pale light that seemed to come from some remote distance. Then a grip *stronger and colder* than iron seized him. The *icy touch froze* his bones and he remembered no more" (emphasis added).[47]

Other symptomatic elements are added to the experience both before the confrontation and after the Hobbits' rescue. At first we are told that Frodo sees his companions dressed as men of arms of older times. The Barrow-wight attacks Frodo as an enormous hand and Frodo hears a song changing into a chilly incantation, "*Cold* be hand and heart and bone, and *cold* be sleep under stone: never more to wake on stony bed, never till the Sun fails and the Moon is dead, . . . till the dark lord lifts his hand over dead sea and withered land" (emphasis added).[48]

Frodo finds new courage surging through him at the sight of his captive companions. Nevertheless, it is at this point that Frodo remembers Tom Bombadil's promise to come to their rescue if so invoked. Bombadil rescues the companions and calls the ghosts, of which the Barrow-wight is one, "sons of forgotten kings wailing in loneliness, guarding from evil things folk that are heedless."[49] The companions in a sort of dream state behold a vision of bygone times with warriors with swords led by a shining leader (with a star on his brow). The whole corresponds to a previous-life memory, and Merry awakes from it retelling some details of these times and speaking in an archaic English.

Tom Bombadil's being and his domain reveal the character of the Hobbits' trial. Gandalf qualifies Bombadil as "oldest and fatherless."

---

[47] Tolkien, *Fellowship of the Ring*, 137.

[48] Tolkien, *Fellowship of the Ring*, 138.

[49] Tolkien, *Fellowship of the Ring*, 142.

The experience of the forest and the encounter with the two sides of his domain lead the hobbits beyond the confines of the senses. In Tom and Goldberry's house the companions drink regular water, "yet it went to their hearts like wine and set free their voices. The guests became suddenly aware that they were singing merrily, as if it was easier and more natural than talking."[50]

Tom sings, dances, speaks of himself in the third person, and goes in and out of the sleeping condition. And dreams acquire particular importance for Frodo. While Merry and Pippin have what are essentially nightmares, Frodo's two dreams stand out as unique. In the first one he beholds an event in another place: he sees the figure of one made captive on top of a tower, but quite indicatively he cannot elucidate what this event portends. Only later will he realize that he has seen Gandalf, as the wizard confirms to him in Rivendell. In the other he has a vision that leads us to the conclusion of the fellowship's quest: the sailing off from the Grey Havens, which concludes the trilogy with Frodo's departure from the Shire. It is clear that it is thanks to Frodo that the other three companions are let past the threshold.

Tom Bombadil's domain is what spiritual science knows as the astral or elemental world; a world in which images are produced in the same way as in the physical world an object produces a sensation. It is the world in which our consciousness rises to Imagination. Though the perceptions are enhanced sense perceptions, and more real than physical ones, the pupil faces new trials: he is like one who loses firm ground under his feet. The images he perceives are manifestations of the qualities of spiritual beings, but at first their meaning is not revealed.

In this new world the soul has an enhanced experience of sympathy and antipathy, and this is palpable in the two sides of the experience: the Old Forest with its warmth and excessive growth and the Barrow-downs with cold and decay. Both realms conceal experiences that can be terrifying and are often associated with malevolent beings, another of the tests one has to face in the elemental world.

As Pia Skogemann perceives from a Jungian perspective, Tom is a figure that creates a bridge between two levels of reality; she calls him

---

[50] Tolkien, *Fellowship of the Ring*, 123.

a "trickster" working between consciousness and the unconscious.[51] In spiritual scientific terms we have come to the figure called the Lesser Guardian of the Threshold, which not surprisingly takes on a form close to that of a Hobbit. It is the first spiritual figure that the pupil meets in his rise through the spiritual worlds.

In the Lesser Guardian's domain lie on one side abundant growth related to the natural processes, and on the other the cold, death, and decay associated with the earthbound souls deceased in times past. And another aspect of the crossing of this first threshold lies in the Lesser Guardian revealing to the pupil that the blows experienced in this life are echoes and consequences of deeds committed in earlier lives. This element too appears with the imagination of the confrontation with the Barrow-wight, which Tolkien both builds up and veils in a way that can be dismissed. However, all the elements are there that unequivocally point to the experience of a previous lifetime.

After passing the threshold and its trials, Tom Bombadil essentially blesses the Hobbits on their quest and offers them weapons. They become the equivalent of knights on a spiritual quest. It is the Lesser Guardian's task to hold us to this side of the threshold until we have control over our fears and are ready to assume our spiritual tasks. In effect, before passing this threshold we were carried in the lap of the spirits of our family, folk soul, and race; past this point they can relinquish their task and we can take it in hand, having acquired new spiritual freedom.

The Hobbits' Meeting with Aragorn

Though the companions have been allowed past the Lesser Guardian of the Threshold, they still have to overcome a certain level of naivete. Once more providential help comes to their rescue. In the inn of the town of Bree, first Pippin, who speaks about Bilbo, and then Frodo, who inadvertently slips in the Ring and disappears from sight of the assembled guests of the inn, risk jeopardizing their mission.

They would be easy prey of the Black Riders were it not for the presence of Strider, a Ranger who roams the lands of Middle-earth

---

[51] Skogemann, *Where the Shadows Lie*, 82.

and who has witnessed Frodo's disappearance caused by his wearing of the Ring. In him is concealed the figure of the future king, heir of the kings of Westernesse (Atlantis) who had ruled over the kingdoms of Arnor to the north and Gondor to the south. It is Aragorn who will guide the companions to the Elven oasis of Rivendell, after receiving a letter from Gandalf that offers this recommendation. On their way to Elrond's enclave, the companions have to face five of the Ringwraiths at Weathertop hill.

Gandalf has not been able to join the companions so far because he was made captive in Saruman's domain. During the attack, Frodo again wears the Ring. He beholds the spectral forms of the wraiths and is wounded by a magic weapon that bears the spell of Sauron. He is in critical condition, kept alive by the healing skills of Aragorn. However, the king cannot fully restore him to his health and longs to reach Rivendell and entrust Frodo's full healing in the hands of Elrond.

The Ringwraiths set after the companions, particularly Frodo. It is only through the magic skills of Glorfindel and Elrond, who come to the companions' rescue, that the Ringwraiths are repelled at the Ford of Bruinen and drowned in the rising waters of the river. The companions can now cross into the safe haven of Rivendell.

Gandalf's Captivity in Orthanc

Gandalf has not appeared at Bree because he has been detained by Saruman. As a member of the White Council at whose head Galadriel has placed Saruman (after Gandalf declined), Gandalf fell to Saruman's reassurance that the Ring would never be found in Middle-earth.

Gandalf feels himself compelled to report to Saruman of his research about the Ring, even though he harbors some reservations about Saruman's behavior. Immediately upon meeting Saruman Gandalf notices that the title "Saruman the White" seemed to anger him. Saruman indicates that he is "Saruman the Wise, Saruman Ring-Maker, Saruman of Many Colours." His robes, which had seemed white, were in reality woven of all colors. "I liked white better," says Gandalf. He replies to Saruman's sneer: "It serves as a beginning. White cloth may be dyed. The white page can be overwritten; and the white light can be broken. . . . In which case it is no longer white. . . . And he that breaks a thing to find out what it is has left the path of wisdom."[52]

Saruman has basically fallen into the Luciferic temptation of leading a humanity deprived of freedom toward what he perceives as its highest good; to act paternalistically on behalf of the human being in whom he has lost hope. He wishes to enlist Gandalf to his aims, enticing him with the prospect of great power and the rewards of striving for "knowledge, rule and order." This is a proposition that Gandalf cannot accept, nor the subtle coaxing of Saruman to give him access to the Ring. The disappointed Saruman keeps Gandalf captive for a time on top of the tower of Orthanc, until Gwaihir, Lord of Eagles, comes to the rescue of the wizard. Gandalf reconnects with the companions in Rivendell after having lost precious ground and time. The arrival of Aragorn providentially rescues the Hobbits and the quest of the Ring.

The above is the first part of Gandalf's initiation. At this stage Tolkien still calls him Gandalf the Grey; only later, after the test at the mines of Moria, will he become Gandalf the White. Gandalf sees his counterpart Saruman, an Istari or wizard like him, succumb to the temptation of black magic and press him to do likewise. In captivity Gandalf surrenders completely to his fate because in effect he is in a situation seemingly without escape.

BOOK II: THE JOURNEY OF THE NINE COMPANIONS

The Oasis of Rivendell

In Rivendell have assembled all those individuals who carry the future of Middle-earth in their hearts, and those among them who are ready to take a stand. At their head stands Gandalf who wears the red Ring of Fire on his hand, and Elrond with the blue Ring of Air. Those gathered gain new strength before entering the fray of one of the decisive battles of the Third Age. Frodo is the one in most need of healing, and that is what only Elrond can do.

After Frodo's recovery a council is held in Middle-earth in which is presented to all a comprehensive view of the forces that stand for

---

[52] Tolkien, *Fellowship of the Ring*, 252–53.

and against the progressive evolution of Middle-earth. Chief among the deliberations are the plans of Sauron, the fate of the Ring, and the presence of the one entitled to be the future king, Aragorn/Strider.

An audacious plan is devised of taking the Ring to Mordor and cast it into the fire from which it originated, thus annulling its power. Frodo finds the courage, much to his surprise, to take on such a daunting task for which he seems ill prepared, and he is gifted a magic *mithril* coat by Bilbo. What Gandalf has foreseen as Frodo's task is confirmed by Elrond's inner feeling. To Frodo the other three Hobbits are naturally joined in fellowship. To the four are added Aragorn and Gandalf, the Elf Legolas, the Dwarf Gimli, the human Boromir; nine in total to counter the nine Ringwraiths.

Rivendell forms a progression, a step beyond Tom Bombadil's domain. Master Elrond, the bearer of the Ring of Air, has lived through all three ages of Middle-earth. His knowledge spans the great themes concerning Men and Elves.

Elrond and Gandalf have invited the assembled guests to a festival of knowledge in the Elven enclave. They know of all the threads of the past and can lift the curtain over the events of the present to let people perceive the forces that are shaping the future of Middle-earth: the role of Sauron, of the high Elves, and of the wizards; the betrayal of Saruman; the ambitions of the empire of Sauron; the pervading threat posed by the Ring.

In Rivendell the meaning of prophecies and dreams is revealed. Boromir understands his dream of the sword that was broken and that shall be reforged. Frodo understands the truth of the dream he had in Rivendell that referred to the man at the top of the tower of Orthanc; he now knows it was Gandalf. Together the nine realize that the future of Middle-earth requires audacity and daring. This deeper knowledge allows the Hobbits and their allies to recover a fuller sense of self, to say yes to their destiny, no matter how daunting it may look.

Time flows differently in Rivendell, even more so than in Tom Bombadil's domain. The companions are relieved of their fears and cares, because evil cannot enter the Elves' domain; nor can Gollum follow Frodo there.

This is no longer a place of dream as was the house of Tom Bombadil. Rather than prophetic dreams, Frodo is exposed to the magic power of stories of bygone times and visions of times to come as they are expressed in poetry and song in the Hall of Fire. Frodo is as if engulfed in a living dream that causes rapture but also overwhelms his consciousness, such is the request it places upon him.

In Rivendell we have moved from the elemental world into the spiritual world proper, the lower Devachan. Here we rise from Imagination to Inspiration. The archetypes of the spiritual world reveal themselves more fully. The companions learn to apprehend the powers that move behind the veils of sense appearances.

After Rivendell the nine companions have been steeled for their task by the providential help of spiritual powers. But their spiritual instruction has not been fully completed yet.

Leaving Rivendell the fellowship aims at crossing the Misty Mountains, choosing first what seems like the easiest route: the pass of Caradhras. They are repelled by the ill will of the mountain fighting them with an unusual blizzard. The test of Caradhras amounts to a repetition of the ordeal of the Old Forest at a new level.

Gandalf and Aragorn know of another way through the mountains, but that is a fearful choice that they have left as a last resort: the dangerous passage through the mines of Moria, where encounters with Orcs and other enemies are to be feared.

The company resists the onslaught of the Orcs thanks to the guidance of Gandalf and Aragorn, though Frodo receives a blow in his right side at the hand of an Orc. The nine are then confronted by the menacing Balrog, a supernatural being of fire, which threatens to destroy the fellowship. "Its streaming mane kindled, and blazed behind it. In its right hand was a blade like a stabbing tongue of fire; in its left hand it held a whip of many thongs."[53] Only Gandalf, keeper of the sacred fire, can hope to resist his onslaught. Gandalf protects the company at his own peril and is drawn into the chasm of Khazad-dûm by the fierce creature. The eight manage to cross the bridge before it collapses.

---

[53] Tolkien, *Fellowship of the Ring*, 321.

Soon past the bridge Frodo is hit by an arrow that bounces against the *mithril* coat that Bilbo gifted him in Rivendell. Aragorn now takes the lead of the company and helps Frodo in his healing. The ordeals of Moria form a further stage of the trial of the Barrow-wight in Book 1.

Gandalf's Initiation

Gandalf and the Balrog are two equal Maiar spirits. However, in days of old the Balrog joined Melkor, a Luciferic rebel figure of the beginnings of creation. Gandalf proclaims, "I am a servant of the Sacred Fire, wielder of the flame of Anor [the Sun deity],"[54] indicating that he serves another power. When the Balrog nevertheless leaps onto the bridge, he falls downwards, managing to pull the wizard along.

Gandalf, deadlocked with the Balrog, falls into the abyss wrapped in the fire of his enemy. Then he plunges into icy water and darkness that feel like death. The fight continues down into the bowels of the earth, "beyond light and knowledge" in a place "where time is not counted," before reemerging and ascending a seemingly never-ending spiral leading to Durin's Tower, high up above the world.

Gandalf manages to hurl his enemy against the mountain where he runs to his ruin. When he recounts his experiences later, he says, "The darkness took me, and I strayed out of thought and time, and I wandered far on roads that I will not tell." And further:

> Naked I was sent back—for a brief time, until my task is done. And naked I lay upon the mountain-top. . . . I was alone, forgotten, without escape upon the hard horn of the world. There I lay staring upward, while the stars wheeled over, and each day was as long as a life-age of the earth. Faint to my ears came the gathered rumours of all lands: the springing and the dying, the song and the weeping, and the slow everlasting groan of overburdened stone.[55]

---

[54] Tolkien, *Fellowship of the Ring*, 344.
[55] Tolkien, *The Two Towers*, 111.

Gwaihir, Lord of Eagles, rescues Gandalf, carrying him to Lórien where Galadriel can complete his healing. The wizard can now truly be called Gandalf the White. Unlike Saruman of Many Colors, Gandalf has passed the formidable test.

After the great ordeal of Moria comes the welcome regeneration of the Elven realm of Lórien, the forest of the Galadhrim Elves, led by Galadriel, the bearer of the white Ring of Water. Galadriel submits Frodo and Sam to the test of the water mirror in which the Hobbits can behold events from past and future, which will offer them some guidance at the appropriate times. In the test Galadriel herself has to overcome the temptation of the Ring that she detects at Frodo's neck, and which Frodo would eagerly give her. Galadriel's presence will continue to inspire the Hobbit's major pair in their time of need. She also offers them important gifts for the pursuit of their journey: the phial with the light that was taken from the original Silmarils of the First Age; the Elven waybread, or *lembas*, which will offer sustenance and spiritual strength in ways that no other food could; the Elven cloaks that will allow the Hobbits to merge with their environment and remain unseen.

Lórien

Lórien's heart is the hill of Cerin Amroth with a big *mallorn* tree at its center, on top of which lives the lady of the land with her consort Celeborn. Frodo feels as if "he had stepped over a bridge of time into a corner of Elder Days, and was now walking in a world that was no more. In Rivendell there was memory of ancient things; in Lórien the ancient things still lived on in the waking world. Evil had been seen and heard there, sorrow had been known ... but on the land of Lórien no shadow lay."[56] In Lórien is no illness, no winter, no suffering or death.

The experiences in Lórien deepen in relation to what they had been in Rivendell. Here Frodo can experience being at one with nature around him. In laying his hands on a tree, he perceives the life that flows through it and the delight that comes from the tree itself. In the

---

[56] Tolkien, *Fellowship of the Ring*, 340.

experience he hears the calls of the sea birds and of the sea for which he has been longing since the beginning of his quest.

Time itself flows differently from the rest of Middle-earth, an experience that was more common in the early ages of Middle-earth. Frodo cannot tell whether he has spent three nights or a month in the enchanted realm. Nor can he remember the moon, nor having any dreams. Lórien itself is a land of dream. In fact the narrative specifies "no sound or dream disturbed their slumber." Whereas in Rivendell Frodo is instructed about the Mysteries of ages past, in Lórien he can travel in time himself. His consciousness expands, however partially, beyond the confines of time.

While Rivendell is the spiritual realm in which Inspirational consciousness holds sway, in Lórien Frodo has an inkling of the experience of Intuition, described in his state of union with the tree. Whereas the other Hobbits struggle to retain the memory of Lórien once they are back into their quest, this consciousness still holds true for Frodo, who must conclude that what he has just experienced is part of a fuller reality and that everything after Lórien resembles a dream and pales in comparison.

Galadriel is a Higher Guardian of the Threshold figure. She is one of the oldest Elves of Middle-earth. She has witnessed all the ages of Middle-earth and travels to the past and the future. She is furthermore the one who called the White Council and who wished to place Gandalf at its head.

The companions feel that Galadriel is either offering them a way out of their trials or tempting them. This is a reflection of their stages of development. Boromir, who has not overcome his lower nature and the pull of the Ring, senses evil in the Elven lady, but this is the evil that he carries with him. Frodo and Sam are tempted in another way; they need to develop their fervent desire to place their spiritual discipleship to the service of the needs of Middle-earth, knowing that the choice will accrue to sustained sacrifice.

In Lórien we have entered the higher spiritual world, or higher Devachan, past the sphere of Saturn; Galadriel is the image of the Higher Guardian of the Threshold on the way to the macrocosm. At the threshold of the higher spiritual world lies the terrible temptation of black magic; in the book this is portrayed by Saruman, the one who wants to keep all higher knowledge for his own exclusive benefit.

In leaving Lórien the companions also receive Elven boats that will take them speedily down the great River Anduin. Gollum, who could not have entered Lórien, now resumes following the fellowship at a distance, and some are aware of his presence, particularly Aragorn and Frodo. Once arrived at the Falls of Rauros the company is split about what course to follow. Some want to go to the east towards Mordor, the Enemy's stronghold; others, Boromir in particular, want to lend a hand to the besieged city of Minas Tirith in Gondor. Frodo goes through one of his hardest trials. In a state of confusion about what choices to make, he reaches the seat of Amon Hen, from which he can see to great lengths all around. But that means also being seen by the Eye of Sauron, attracted by the power of his Ring. When the confrontation reaches a climax, Frodo nearly succumbs to the adversary power and cannot resist for a time the temptation of wearing the Ring. In a way this is a parallel test to the one Frodo experienced at Weathertop, where he effectively wore the Ring and was wounded. This time he saves himself in time with a great exertion of will.

Boromir has not understood and integrated the Lórien experience. He shows a lack of maturity in the belief that he can place the power of the Ring to his service; he first coaxes Frodo into yielding it to him, then readies to use force. Frodo can slip away unseen by wearing the Ring. The recent test has shown him that he is the only one who can do something about the Ring, and he has strengthened his resolve to go his way alone and not put others at risk. Thus he returns to the company's campsite and sets off in an Elven boat. Sam, who has witnessed the incredible scene of a boat seemingly moving away on its own, recognizes the hand of Frodo and decides to join him for the greater fortune of the quest. Together they head straight into danger, towards Mordor, east of the River Anduin.

Frodo, who has left behind much naivete in his earlier adventures, is now completely deprived of help apart from Sam, and knows what it means to stand on his own against impossible odds in assuming responsibility for the fate of the Ring, all the more so considering he believes Gandalf dead.

BOOK III: THE TREASON OF ISENGARD

In one of the many twists of fate, the minor Hobbit pair—Merry and Pippin—is attacked by Orcs and defended by Boromir, eager to redeem himself after he has understood how much the power of the Ring blinded him previously. He valiantly defends the Hobbits, who are captured by the Orcs and taken on a forced march towards Isengard, the enclave of Saruman, who covets the Ring. Aragorn, Gimli, and Legolas are hot on their heels through the plains of Rohan, west of the River Anduin, but can barely keep up with them.

Before catching up with the Orcs, the three pursuers meet with a band of the Riders of Rohan, led by Éomer, son of the sister of Théoden, king of the land. The two Hobbits find themselves object of rival interests among the Orcs, divided between those loyal to Saruman and those loyal to Sauron. Before their three companions, allied to the Riders of Rohan, arrive to encircle and destroy the party of Orcs, Pippin and Merry have managed to escape captivity and directed themselves towards the forest of Fangorn. Not long after they come across Treebeard, also called Fangorn, an Ent and protector spirit of the forest. Fangorn offers them shelter and protection and takes them to an Ent gathering—an Entmoot.

Fangorn has learned from the Hobbits the extent of the plans of Saruman, and he intends to rouse his fellow Ents against the one who has been cruel against the beings of the forest. The Ents leave the shelter of the forest, ready for open battle against the magician.

The Tests of Pippin and Merry (the Minor Hobbit Pair)

Aragorn, Legolas, and Gimli follow what they manage to recognize as the Hobbits' tracks up to the place where Treebeard has carried them. They are confronted by a test with two facets; the encounter with two magicians. At first they find an elderly figure who crosses their path and sows confusion by letting their horses loose. This is Saruman. Soon after they meet an unknown white figure, dazzling with light. They know it's a being of power but don't know whether to trust him. One by one they come to the realization that it is Gandalf, who has now reached a new stage of power after his ordeal with the Balrog. He has known death and no longer fears human weapons since he is Gandalf the White.

The reconstituted party now rides in the direction of Edoras, the golden hall of King Théoden, lord of the Rohirrim of Rohan. It is Gandalf's turn to show his newly acquired powers. King Théoden has been beguiled by his counselor Gríma Wormtongue, who is at the service of Saruman and feigns fealty to the king. Gandalf unmasks him and forces him to flight in a dramatic confrontation. King Théoden is awakened in the ordeal, and realizes the stupor under which he has been operating for a long spell under the influence of his counselor. He is ready to regain consciousness and power and lead his people into battle against Saruman first, Sauron later. The king's awakening brings a reconciliation with Éomer, whom Wormtongue had estranged from the king. Merry, who feels a great affinity for the king, is moved to swear him loyalty.

The Test of Théoden

The newly gathered forces under the leadership of Aragorn and Théoden are now facing a formidable foe of Orcs and Men, allies of Saruman, at the fortress of Helm's Deep. The battle stands long in the balance and is resolved in great part thanks to the valiance of Aragorn and Théoden, and to the providential arrival of Gandalf with new forces. The Huorns, younger versions of the Ents, manage to seal the fate of all escaping Orcs.

The victors now decide to direct their forces against Saruman's stronghold, only to find upon arrival, that the Ents have already completed the task and laid Isengard to waste. The magician and his ally, Wormtongue, have taken refuge in the impregnable fortress of Orthanc. Gandalf, impelled by inner duty, attempts to reach Saruman's heart and offer him a second chance. The magician predictably turns it down, not before testing the assembled company through the power of his beguiling voice. It is only under the firm guidance of Gandalf that they can resist the spell of Saruman's deception.

In the hope of hurting or killing Gandalf, Wormtongue throws an unknown heavy object in the direction of the wizard. Gandalf, unscathed, recovers what he knows to be a *palantír*, a seeing stone of old, which conceals hidden powers not totally known to Gandalf. The kings of old used the seven original *palantír* to communicate with each other from a distance.

The *palantír* reveals its nature through the unwitting and curious Pippin, who cannot resist peeking into the stone, unbeknownst to Gandalf. Unprepared, he comes close to revealing himself to Sauron's eye and comes out of the narrow escape traumatized. Good comes out of the ordeal inasmuch as Gandalf avoids revealing himself to the enemy and gains new insight about how Saruman and Sauron communicated with each other. The link is now broken, and suspicion is growing between the two uneasy allies.

BOOK IV: THE JOURNEY OF THE RING-BEARERS

Book IV returns to the fates of Sam and Frodo, who are now moving deeper into the enemy's territory. At first they are lost in the labyrinthine nature of the Emyn Muil mountains that seem to have a will to disorient the Hobbits, much as did the Old Forest in the Hobbits' first trial. Frodo wonders where help could possibly come from, intuiting that the two of them cannot manage the ordeal alone.

It is Gollum who answers Frodo's preconscious question. He has been following the two Hobbits, until a reversal of fate delivers him into the hands of his enemies. Frodo exacts obedience from Gollum and asks him to lead the way into the marshes. It is obvious that Gollum only follows because he pursues the Ring, which he wants to subtract from Sauron. Through his keen sight and dislike of sunlight, Gollum helps the two friends take advantage of darkness to travel unseen. He and Sam rescue Frodo from the danger of the ghosts of the dead warriors of ancient times that call him to the bottom of the Dead Marshes. In the test of the Dead Marshes we can sense an echo of the Barrow-downs in Tom Bombadil's domain.

Out of the marshes the three move into the direction of the Black Gate, where massive forces are gathering in preparation of an attack against Gondor. Frodo and Sam realize that the way through is blocked and decide to trust in Gollum's knowledge of a hidden, little-guarded passageway further south from where they are. At the Black Gate they recognize those who are called Nazgûl, the large and ominous bird forms now taken by the reborn Ringwraiths as their vehicle. The Nazgûl spread terror wherever they go.

On their way south the three Hobbits witness the build-up of forces coming to reinforce Sauron's armies. They are providentially rescued and temporarily placed under the custody of Faramir, Boromir's brother. The Gondorian prince is at first suspicious that the Hobbits may have played a part in his brother's death; later he realizes that Boromir went to his own death because he was incapable of resisting the allurement of the Ring, and decides to support his captives.

Gollum has been in hiding and is later made captive by Faramir's men. The pleading Frodo barely manages to convince Faramir to grant clemency towards the Hobbit, because he knows that Gollum is the only one who can still lead him to Mordor.

The captivity delays the Hobbits in what later will turn out to be providential ways. Faramir will be able to convey the news of the Hobbits' survival and their planned expedition towards Mordor. Gollum takes the two guarded Hobbits towards the pass of Cirith Ungol. In one of the long tunnels through the rock he intends to deliver them to the giant spider Shelob and take possession of the Ring, which presents no interest to her.

In the encounter with the spider, Frodo is stung by her poison and Sam fights against her, courageously inflicting her a serious wound. Frodo is stunned by the poison that the spider uses to put to sleep her prey before devouring it, and Sam, mistaking him for dead, decides to take the Ring and pursue Frodo's task. Only later does he realize that the Orcs know Frodo is alive and have captured him to take him into the fortress of Cirith Ungol. Wearing the Ring, Sam can devise a plan to come to the rescue of his master, now more alone and terrified than ever. He can count on the power of the Ring that renders him invisible. That advantage, however, comes at a price for his soul, from which Sam will be all the more able to appreciate the tremendous weight Frodo is under. He will share in his fate as a Ring-bearer.

Books III and IV lead us into two parallel ordeals: that of Pippin and Merry through Rohan and Fangorn; and that of Frodo and Sam through the Emyn Muil and the marshes. Just as Emyn Muil presents a challenge similar to the pulling and hypnotizing power of the Old Forest, so do the Dead Marshes haunt Frodo and Sam with the presence of ghosts of old, just like the Barrow-downs did in Tom Bombadil's domain. Merry and Pippin have traveled at record speed to strengthen the resistance against Saruman, and for that they have Saruman to thank. Frodo and Sam have managed to reach the back door to Mordor and for that they can be grateful to their adversary, Gollum.

The parallels continue. While Pippin and Merry have contributed to the downfall of the tower of Orthanc, Sam and Frodo are moving towards the tower of Barad-dûr in Mordor territory. The minor pair has met the providential Ents who both helped them and played a role in Saruman's demise; Sam and Frodo meet with Faramir, who will play a crucial role in allowing the coordination of efforts inside and outside of Mordor for the downfall of Sauron.

BOOK V: THE WAR OF THE RING

Book V returns to the deeds of the minor Hobbit pair: Merry and Pippin. Gandalf intuits the urge of preparing the defense of Minas Tirith and tries to enlist the help of Denethor, Gondor's regent and Boromir and Faramir's father. Clearly he knows that it is late at this stage, because Denethor has turned delusional and antagonistic towards the wizard. Pippin, in remembrance and gratitude for Boromir's heroic defense of himself and Merry, in a gesture parallel to the duo Merry-Theoden, offers his loyalty to Denethor, who knights him.

The Nature of Aragorn's Initiation

Sauron advances towards Gondor and Minas Tirith with the help of his own created darkness that plunges people into terror and despair. Still in Rohan, Aragorn realizes that the time presses if he wants to come to the help of Minas Tirith. He knows that another threat looms to the south of the city and he wants to address it first. The only way left is to tread the underground, dreaded Paths of the Dead, which none have dared to take before him.

Followed by Legolas and Gimli and the Rohirrim, he embarks on the perilous journey into the cold and dread of the caves, tested by the souls of the dead who infuse terror in the company. Aragorn shows true leadership and mastery over the souls of the dead. They pledge alliance to him in overcoming an old curse that befell them in the past for serving Sauron. They promise help in the coming battle in exchange for their being freed from the curse immediately after the first victory.

Aragorn takes the route to the south of the city, towards the River Anduin, countering the threat of the Corsairs of Umbar. Armed by the fear implanted in their souls by the dead, the Corsairs are overcome, and Aragorn takes possession of their fleet and sails north towards the besieged city, offering hope at a critical juncture of the battle.

Sauron's Defeat

Denethor, in his madness and vengefulness towards his younger son, sends Faramir to an impossible sortie to recover possession of the city of Osgiliath to the east. It is an impossible mission, and Faramir barely manages to return past the city's wall, seriously wounded by the poisoned arrow of a Nazgûl.

As Minas Tirith seems to be hopelessly overcome by a superior foe, the Rohirrim, led by Théoden, sound the charge to the city's walls. Théoden, completely renewed in courage, challenges the Black Captain, Lord of the Nazgûl. He meets his death, and his challenge is continued by his daughter Éowyn, who previously joined the ranks of the Rohirrim disguised as a man. She receives a deadly blow and is rescued by Merry who is also wounded, but only after inflicting a deadly blow on the captain, obliged to leave his physical form behind. At this time Aragorn injects new courage into the battle when he is seen bringing a fleet to the help of Minas Tirith.

Inside the city Pippin struggles between his loyalty to Denethor and his realization of his madness. He calls on the help of Gandalf, who arrives at the scene where Denethor, having erected a pyre, is setting fire to it intending to meet his son's and his own death. Gandalf and Pippin cannot refrain Denethor from committing suicide but manage to rescue Faramir.

Meanwhile, Aragorn has come to the city in disguise, wanting to offer help through his healing skills, in the first place to Faramir, Éowyn, and Merry. People remember the old prophecy of the healer king and recognize in him Gondor's future sovereign.

Gandalf knows that this victory is only a respite in Sauron's onslaught, and that only by being able to cast the Ring into the fire can the peril of the age be overcome. He needs to protect Frodo and Sam and attract Sauron's attention outside of Mordor. Drawn into this impossible gamble, he leads a clearly insufficient force of six thousand against the masses arrayed behind the Black Gate. He wants Sauron to believe that the Ring-bearer is among them, and the ambition caused by the Ring's possession blinds Sauron completely. At the gates Sauron wants to undermine all hope left in Gandalf and sends his lieutenant to show the wizard a grey cloak, an Elven brooch, the *mithril* coat worn by Frodo, and Sam's sword, leading Gandalf to believe for a moment that all resistance has been in vain. Deeply affected in his self-assurance, Gandalf takes a stand against Sauron, even when all hope seems lost.

In Book V Merry and Pippin continue their mission in relation to their newly adopted sovereigns. After Theoden's death, Merry rescues Éowyn; Pippin rescues Faramir from the delusional and suicidal Denethor. These events are providential for the future of the kingdom, since Faramir will end up marrying Éowyn and strengthening the links between Gondor and Rohan.

BOOK VI: THE END OF THE THIRD AGE

Book VI follows the crucial confrontation of Frodo and Sam with the forces of Mordor. Sam has gone into the tower of Cirith Ungol and has managed to rescue Frodo, taking advantage of the strife between two bands of Orcs who have decimated each other. The two wear Orc vestments to blend with their environment. But now they have to confront the dry and hot landscape of Mordor with nothing more than a few pieces of *lembas*, the Elven bread, and a little water. In reaching for Mount Doom they have to circumambulate first to the north, then to the east, and finally to the south in order to avoid the forces amassed in the plain below them. Meanwhile Frodo is tested to all limits of endurance by the growing weight of the Ring at his neck.

On their way east the hobbits have been captured by a band of Orcs who round off those who they believe to be deserters. Protected by their Elven cloaks at the moment of their escape, they now face the harshest part of their pursuit. In scorching heat and with little shade or water left, they have to tread in the open towards the mountain. Gollum is following them at a distance. In the last stages of the ascent, a spent Frodo can only go on because Sam has decided to carry him. At the edge of the volcano, Frodo cannot bring himself to part from his possession. It is Gollum who somehow rescues the quest. In a mad wrestle with Frodo made invisible by the Ring, Gollum manages to bite off the finger with the Ring. In his exultation at the recovery of his Precious, Gollum loses his balance and falls into the molten lava, taking the Ring to its undoing, the long-sought goal of the quest. The darkness of Sauron starts to dissipate.

The spiritual helpers have assisted Frodo and Sam in matters of timing by accelerating their arrival at Mount Doom in order to coincide with the critical moment of the battle of the Captains of the West at the Black Gate. When the Ring is cast into the fire, the armies of Sauron act as if dispirited and panic takes over them. Gandalf, realizing the synchronicities of the moment, knows there is no time to lose and sends Gwaihir, Lord of Eagles, to rescue Frodo and Sam from the erupting volcano. The Third Age has come to an end; the new age has begun.

The Captains of the West can now return to Minas Tirith, where Aragorn, crowned the new king of Gondor, marries the Elf Arwen. Faramir marries Éowyn.

Meanwhile Saruman has not been idle. Preceding the Hobbits he has taken possession of a deteriorating situation in the Shire to take control of the land and pillage its resources. After a small battle, the Hobbits, led by Merry and Pippin, defeat the intruders and start the slow process of rebuilding of the land. Frodo pardons the defeated Saruman and protects him from vengeful intentions. However, his subjugated Wormtongue, unable to contain his dose of daily humiliation, stabs Saruman and kills him.

For Frodo the time in the Shire offers no consolation. He suffers from his wounds and longs for another home, following the same longing that set him on the quest. Arwen, in deciding to marry Aragorn, has relinquished her immortality and can now offer Frodo the possibility to sail from the Grey Havens to the Undying Lands of the West, together with Bilbo and the ring-bearers, Elrond, Galadriel, and Gandalf.

OF SPIRIT, SOUL, AND BODY

Before turning to the themes of initiation in *The Lord of the Rings*, I will review briefly the relationship between the three main characters in the trilogy: Gandalf, Aragorn, and Frodo.

Throughout the book something emerges over and over again: the work of the three is equally crucial to the success of the quest. The deeds of wizard, Ranger/king, and Hobbit are cleverly interlocked at all the stages of the events. It is as if we had three facets of a larger individuality. And another theme is of equal importance: Aragorn and Frodo subordinate themselves willingly to the leadership of Gandalf; this is never put in doubt a single moment. When Gandalf leaves the company after the ordeal in the mines of Moria, Aragorn naturally assumes leadership. But when all seems lost, Frodo takes responsibility for the quest completely on his own, not having any idea of the fate of his companions.

Complete coordination and union goes hand in hand with clear separation of roles and willing delegation of power. Here are at play some archetypes that are basic to spiritual science.

Gandalf is by far the most exalted of the three individuals. He is more than human, being an emissary from the realm of the Valar, the servants of Ilúvatar, the One God. He is a wizard sent to guide humanity at a crucial turning point of its history. He carries a higher wisdom and power, and can link things of the spirit with the events on earth that he apprehends in his mind with complete clarity and certainty. He is in more than one way the representative of the spirit in the human being, the self. And yet he cannot confront the power of Sauron alone, since the Ring would present too much of a temptation for him; he needs to delegate this task to Frodo. At the end of the journey he reveals: "The Third Age was my age. I was the Enemy of Sauron: and my work is finished. I shall go soon. The burden must lie now upon you and your kindred."

Aragorn is next in power and glory after Gandalf. In his soul makeup he carries Elven elements and therefore what is associated with deathlessness, and the human element, although not just any human element. He is a heir of the Númenorean (Atlantean) kings, accessing their vast knowledge, inherited traits, and capacities, and is a king by right. Aragorn shows an intimate connection with the earth as a living organism; at crucial times he can sense that something in the aura of the earth has changed and can recognize what its new qualities are. He is also the one of the three to whom belong the art of healing; in this realm Gandalf delegates to him. Aragorn is a healer because, apart from the knowledge of herbs, he can follow the journey of the human soul between one world and another, as he clearly shows in the healings of Éowyn, Faramir, and Merry. He can sense the struggle of the soul between one world and another, and call it back to its unfinished earthly task. Aragorn is clearly the representative of the soul element in the human being. He bridges what is of the spirit with the earthly.

Frodo is the humblest of the three individuals, having in himself the purely Hobbit element, which makes him very earthly and earthy, even more so than the human being. He is the most at home with the earth element, like his fellow Hobbits, who like to garden and to eat. Frodo is constantly reminded of his limitations; he enters the quest as if in spite of himself. He is constantly wounded and hammered by the elements, constantly pressured by his Double, Gollum. Even in his success he cannot willingly throw the Ring into the fire. As the one closest to the limitations of the physical element, Frodo stands as the representative of the human body.

Between Frodo and Gandalf, Aragorn plays the role of the mediator, he who belongs fully to the earthly but has a greater awareness of the spirit than Frodo does. Both Aragorn and Frodo are pupils of Gandalf, but Aragorn has been so for a much longer time. Whereas Gandalf apprehends matters of the spirit and can enlighten and motivate his pupils, it is Aragorn and the Rangers who are able to defend the inhabitants of Middle-earth against the evils that threaten them. They have to disguise their intentions because they want to defend without spreading premature knowledge of those threats and fear upon those they protect—once more, a mediating role.

When the quest is launched, it is Gandalf who sets Frodo on his new task. But Gandalf pledges to continuously follow and protect him. And throughout the adventures of the fellowship, Gandalf is present at Frodo's side in spiritual terms. In the first instance Frodo is constantly remembering the words of the wizard and asking himself what Gandalf would do. And Gandalf follows his pupil spiritually, subordinating his task to that of Frodo as is the case in the last assault of the Captains of the West against the Black Gate. And we can sense that it is Gandalf who sends Frodo reassurances as in his most vivid dreams, and in his subconscious when his clarity of mind is weakened in the last stages of the quest.

Aragorn subordinates himself completely to Gandalf, and enters the scene as soon as Gandalf is delayed; he takes command when Gandalf is tested at the bridge of Khazad-dûm. He keeps Frodo alive through his healing skills, and renders possible the continuation of the quest by carrying Frodo to Rivendell.

We see a symbolic summing up of these webs of relationships, when at the beginning of the Fourth Age, on the occasion of his crowning, Aragorn gives back the crown to Faramir who had brought it to him, saying "By the labour and valour of many I have come into my inheritance. In token of this I would have the Ring-bearer bring the crown to me, and let Mithrandir set it upon my head, if he will; for he has been the mover of all that has been accomplished and this is his victory."

Chapter 3

Initiations into the Macrocosm and Microcosm

The Light of Valinor (derived from light before any fall) is
the light of art undivorced from reason, that sees things both
scientifically (or philosophically) and imaginatively (or subcreatively) and "says that they are good"—as beautiful.
—J. R. R. Tolkien

We have outlined in the previous chapter how Gandalf, Aragorn, and
Frodo represent the whole human being of spirit, mind (soul), and
body. Their paths of initiation are strikingly different, but wonderfully
complementary. And each of them has one or two counterparts through
which the path can better be understood.

One great step of Gandalf's initiation before the encounter with
the Balrog comes at the hand of Saruman who keeps him captive in
the tower of Orthanc. Saruman is what Gandalf himself could have
turned into, and vice versa. Gandalf does not tire to repeat it. Frodo's
path into Mordor would not be possible without the presence at his side
of Gollum/Sméagol, himself a Hobbit. Here too Frodo is an image of
what Gollum could have turned into, and vice versa. So where do we
find the polarity to Aragorn? None is discernable in the immediate
path of the future king. However, two key figures show here too in
which ways Aragorn could have strayed under the power of Saruman

or Sauron: Théoden and Denethor. Let us look at one after the other of these pairings.

GANDALF AND SARUMAN

Five wizards, or Istari, were sent to Middle-earth in the Third Age (around a thousand years after its inception); the Elves thought they were sent from Valinor. We know of three of them, each associated with a color: Gandalf Greyhame or Gandalf the Grey, Saruman the White, Radagast the Brown. They were forbidden to use anything else than persuasion in order to influence human affairs, not their magic. The Hobbits awaken to their own role around the same time as the Istari.

As Pia Skogemann points out, Gandalf is initiated through his confrontation with the Balrog, first through the sphere of the elements in the underworld—fire and heat, water and cold, earth—and second in the ascent into the air that involves all the elements anew: fire and air in the lightning, water in the ice and rain, earth in the rock.[57]

Gandalf and the Balrog are both Maiar spirits. So is Sauron. The Maiar served the Valar, the intermediaries of Ilúvatar, the creator god. Gandalf and the Balrog are thus equal. However, the Balrog served the rebellious Melkor already in olden times. In defiance of the Balrog Gandalf proclaims, "I am a servant of the Sacred Fire, wielder of the flame of Anor." Anor is a name for the Sun, indicating the nature of Gandalf's allegiance.

That Gandalf is sent back into the world naked means that he has been able to transform his physical body. This is why Gwaihir calls him "light as a swan's feather." However, he still needs healing, and that is why Galadriel calls him to Lórien. Later Gandalf can say that no weapon can hurt him because his physical body is like none other. In battle "He wore no helm nor mail. His snowy hair flew free in the wind, his white robes shone dazzling in the sun."[58]

Gandalf has a strong likeness to the spiritual Sun: his eyes are "bright, piercing as the rays of the sun." His horse, Shadowfax,

---

[57] Skogemann, *Where the Shadows* Lie, 64.
[58] Tolkien, *The Two Towers*, 513.

emphasizes the new qualities of the wizard's body, its ability to move like the wind from one place to another. It is of great interest that after his transformation Gandalf can hardly remember his name. Indeed, he declares in earnest that he is like Saruman, or rather he is what Saruman could have become. This revelation is central to the whole book.

Galadriel wished Gandalf to be the leader of the White Council in the year 2463. Those who came were: Elrond, Cirdan, Gandalf, Saruman, and some other Elf lords. Gandalf refused to assume leadership because he saw himself bound solely to those who sent him; hence, the mantle fell upon Saruman, who progressively sought to increase his power.

In Elvish language Saruman means "he who can"; potentially he is one who seeks and serves truth and knowledge. But Saruman over time variously calls himself "Saruman the Wise," "Saruman the Ring-maker," or "Saruman of Many-Colors." In him knowledge is developed at the expense of wisdom.

Gandalf respects Saruman, even though he has growing doubts. Upon coming to Isengard he is suddenly afraid, though he knows not why. Immediately upon meeting his peer, Gandalf notices that his robes, which had seemed white, were in reality woven of all colors. Gandalf points out the symbolism in this, that "white light can be broken. . . . And he that breaks a thing to find out what it is has left the path of wisdom."[59]

When Aragorn, Gimli, and Legolas meet the Rohirrim of Rohan, Éomer reveals that Saruman walks the land as an old man hooded and cloaked, and looks similar to Gandalf. In fact when the party, with everyone except Frodo and Sam, meets with Gandalf again, they first confuse him with Saruman. Legolas is the first to shout "Mithrandir," Gandalf's Elvish name. Then Aragorn recognizes him too, and Gandalf replies "'Gandalf,' . . . as if recalling from old memory a long disused word. 'Yes, that was the name. I was Gandalf.'" And he tells them "'Yes, I am white now, said Gandalf. . . . I have passed through fire and deep water since we parted. I have forgotten much that I thought I knew, and

---

[59] Tolkien, *The Fellowship of the* Ring, 252.

learned again much that I had forgotten. I can see many things far off, but many things that are close I cannot see."[60]

When talking about Saruman, even Aragorn is keen in recognizing his past greatness, the breadth of his knowledge, skills of his hands, but also the power he had over other minds.[61] This already indicates that he has transformed knowledge into a tool of power, that which the Valar had expressly forbidden the Istari to exert over the inhabitants of Middle-earth. Such is in fact the power of Saruman's voice that Aragorn wagers that only Gandalf, Elrond, and Galadriel—the Ring-bearers—would be able to resist him once they are in his presence. The chapter that treats of this matter is so important that it took Tolkien by surprise. In his words: "[The Voice of Saruman] was growing out of hand, and revealing endless new vistas."[62]

Gandalf asserts to the curious Gimli: "Saruman could look like me in your eyes, if it suited his purpose with you." And he challenges him thus: "Are you yet wise enough to detect all his counterfeits?"[63] Soon after a sobered Gimli recognizes that Saruman is, yes, like Gandalf, but also very unlike him. Such is the importance of the power of Saruman through his voice that it forms one of the most penetrating parts of the narrative of the entire epic, worth quoting in full:

> Suddenly another voice spoke, low and melodious, its very sound an enchantment. *Those who listened unwarily to that voice could seldom report the words that they heard*; and if they did, they wondered for little power remained in them. *Mostly they remembered only that it was a delight to hear the voice speaking, all that it said seemed wise and reasonable*, and desire awoke in them by swift agreement to seem wise themselves. When *others* spoke they seemed harsh and uncouth by contrast; and *if they gainsaid the voice, anger was kindled in the hearts of those under the spell. For some the spell lasted only while the voice spoke to them,*

[60] Tolkien, *The Two Towers*, 484.
[61] Tolkien, *The Two Towers*, 553.
[62] Carpenter, *Letters of J. R. R. Tolkien*, 321.
[63] Tolkien, *The Two Towers*, 562–63.

and when it spoke to another they smiled, as men would do who see through a juggler's trick while others gape at it. *For many the sound of his voice alone was enough to hold them enthralled*; but *for those whom it conquered the spell endured when they were far away, and ever they heard that soft voice whispering and urging them.* But *none were unmoved; none rejected its pleas and its commands without an effort of mind and will*, so long as its master had control of it.[64] (emphasis added)

Such is the power of his voice that it leads Saruman to heights of boldness. To Théoden, whom he has betrayed through Gríma, Saruman audaciously claims that he is the only one who can help him. Théoden cannot find words to respond to Saruman. Gandalf's followers are seduced by the words of Saruman, and the previous words of the former to Théoden pale in comparison. It seems to the people gathered in his presence that Saruman is throwing them a lifeline, whereas Gandalf is leading them to their doom. The experience that Galadriel has upon her listeners is here echoed and amplified though in a mirror image. Saruman the tempter flatters everyone's lower nature; he offers comfort and ease. Gandalf, or Galadriel, calls on people's higher nature; hence, they call them to confront their weaknesses and, as a result, they feel uncertain, angry, fearful.

Buoyed by his success, Saruman believes he can seduce Gandalf away from the others, calling to the pride of their order and to a supposed superiority the two share over "lesser folk." Just when the others start to fear Gandalf's betrayal, the wizard unmasks and mocks Saruman's megalomania, and reminds him that he was once his prisoner in Orthanc. At this point, backed against a wall, Saruman's pride and scorn come to the surface, and when he speaks again, his voice bears the deep imprint of both.

Regardless of the above, Gandalf is bound by his newfound self to give even Saruman a last chance. He wants to offer him real inner freedom, but asks of him first the Key of Orthanc and Saruman's staff. Saruman reacts with rage. When he tries to leave, he is dragged back

---

[64] Tolkien, *The Two Towers*, 564.

by the commanding voice of Gandalf. He rebukes him for his hard heart and his folly, then he lets him know that he is no longer Gandalf the Grey, but Gandalf the White who has returned from death, and that he is casting Saruman out of the order and the Council. Then he commands Saruman's staff broken.

Where did Saruman fall? The word *palantíri* means "that which look far away." Seven of them were wrought by the Noldor Elves. Saruman fell under the spell of one of them. Gandalf concludes: "Alas for Saruman! It was his downfall, as I now perceive. Perilous to us all are the devices of an art deeper than we possess ourselves. Yet he must bear the blame. Fool! To keep it secret, for his own profit. No word did he ever speak of it to any of the Council."[65] Using the *palantír*, Saruman was made spiritually captive once his gaze turned to the Dark Tower. Sauron probably possessed another *palantír* found in Minas Ithil/Morgul, and so he controlled Saruman from a distance. Once caught in the snare of his own deceits, Saruman raises the gamble and devises the daring and immensely foolish idea of betraying Sauron himself. Furthermore, it is Saruman who, through the black arts, breeds a more powerful breed of Orc, the Uruk-hai. "Saruman the Wise" gives them human flesh to eat.

Of Gandalf Tolkien states that he is no human being, nor that there are any modern terms that can be used for him. "I venture to say that he was an incarnate 'angel'" like the other Istari (wizards); he is an "emissary from the Lords of the West." As such, however, he knows pain and suffering and can be killed, though the angelic presence lends him unique strength and longevity. He is primarily sent to "train, advise, instruct, arouse the hearts and minds of those threatened by Sauron to a resistance with their own strengths; and not just to do the job for them."[66]

All the above do not confer upon the Istari any infallibility—as Saruman aptly proves. Gandalf has to become completely powerless and vulnerable in order to "perish" at the trial of Khazad-dûm. He has to experience that all his resistance to Sauron is seemingly in vain. It is through a supreme act of sacrifice and infinite trust that his deed is accepted, and he is returned to life with new powers. It is this

---

[65] Tolkien, *The Two Towers*, 583.
[66] Carpenter, *Letters of J. R. R. Tolkien*, 202.

supreme powerlessness at the meeting with the Higher Guardian of the Threshold that Saruman resists.

This resistance gives Saruman boundless power over his fellow human beings but renders him vulnerable to the greater power of Sauron, which he is in effect trying to rival. Gandalf's power is purified in the extreme test he undergoes, and in effect rendered selfless and made available to those around him. He never forces anyone's freedom; he only encourages and brings out the best in everyone.

In terms of spiritual science Gandalf's path is that of initiation into the macrocosm through forces larger than the individual forces. Gandalf is placed in front of objective external forces. He faces first the power of Saruman, then that of the Balrog, Sauron's emissary. He meets the four elements both above and below the surface of the earth, and is inwardly purified and cleansed, until his body is spiritualized to some degree.

On the path to the macrocosm Gandalf meets the test of the Higher Guardian of the Threshold, who asks anyone wanting to penetrate the higher spiritual world a further step of sacrifice. He asks those who want to cross to commit to the salvation of their fellow human beings: "Until now, you have worked only to free yourself, but now you are free you can help free all your fellow beings in the sense world. Up to now, you have striven as an individual. Now you must join yourself to the whole, so that you may bring with you into the supersensible realm not only yourself, but also all else that exists in the sensible world."[67] This is what Gandalf has done even before this point, and what he will continue to do until the end of the Third Age.

Gandalf represents the power of thinking at its best. He is able to see all the forces around him, and to take decisions based on full knowledge. Through him is organized all the resistance to Sauron throughout Middle-earth. He unceasingly and untiringly communicates to his allies in Middle-earth what is occurring and what needs to be done. He is the intelligence of Middle-earth personified. This is why he can openly boast, when he says before joining the fellowship: "Someone said that

---

[67] Steiner, *How to Know Higher Worlds*, 203.

intelligence shall be needed in the party. He was right. I think I shall come with you."[68]

Only Gandalf could possibly enter the court of Théoden in Edoras and apprehend the whole situation correctly. He can see that Théoden is under the spell of Sauron, via the advice of Gríma Wormtongue. He knows that Gríma covets Éowyn, and that she has been used as an exchange pawn in the designs of Sauron and Wormtongue.

Things stand in a whole other way in relation to Frodo. Whereas Saruman and Gandalf are colleagues, Frodo and Gollum are tied at the hip, so to speak. Once Frodo has experienced the heights of the spiritual world in Lórien, his path is intimately united to that of Gollum. As a device of the tale, Gollum is of course his own individual, but he is also a projection of something internal to Frodo, as we will see further.

FRODO AND GOLLUM

Frodo is a Hobbit, one of those creatures that Tolkien places below, rather than above, the human being. He who is of the lowest, is the one most bound to the fate of the Ring. Putting on the Ring and/or getting wounded characterize his various initiations. Frodo's journey takes him away from everything he holds dear to face his inner darkness. The duplicity of his "shadow" is brilliantly played out in the Sméagol/Gollum dichotomy; in the I and We that he utters at turns. Verlyn Flieger points out that Frodo goes against the light because he has to; Gollum turns against the light because he wants to. Gollum is nocturnal and hates the light of the Sun, even suffers under it.[69]

At the inn in Bree Frodo almost inadvertently puts on the Ring. He is saved by Strider/Aragorn. The other two tests that follow are those of the Old Forest and of the Barrow-wight. Frodo grows in courage, but it's nevertheless Tom Bombadil who saves him. At Weathertop Frodo realizes how strongly the Ring can work against his conscious self. He puts on the Ring and fights courageously against the Ringwraiths, receiving a lethal wound. Only Aragorn first, and Elrond later, are able

[68] Tolkien, *The Fellowship of the Ring*, 266.
[69] Flieger, *Splintered Light*, 137.

to save his life. In Moria Frodo's left side is scored and bruised when he is thrown against the wall by an Orc. On the journey down the Great River Anduin, an arrow strikes Frodo between the shoulders but rebounds against his *mithril* coat. At Amon Hen Frodo resists Boromir's coveting of the Ring and puts it on until he sits on the seat of Amon Hen. In the vision that follows, his inner ambivalence ushers in a painful and difficult struggle. He is saved by his better self just in time before Sauron's inquisitive Eye gets hold of him. He puts on the Ring once more but for a more selfless reason, wanting to face his "doom" alone before setting out on the canoe down the Anduin again.

The next trial is what we could call the "temple death" of the initiation of old times—leaving him so apparently dead, at the hand of the sting of the spider Shelob, that Sam cannot detect the difference. This is immediately followed by the beatings and tortures at the hand of the Orcs in Cirith Ungol. This is only a prelude to the veritable night of the soul. The weight of the Ring keeps growing until Frodo climbs his way to Mount Doom. And the last inner battle sees him unable to forego the Ring and throw it in the fire. This is when Gollum assaults him and bites off his finger, finding his death in the lava of the volcano. Overall Frodo suffers three major wounds:, the wound at Weathertop caused by the Morgul-blade, Shelob's sting, and Gollum's bite.

Halfway through all these very physical tests, Frodo is presented by the challenge of Gollum, an indispensable link in the accomplishment of the quest, the character that Flieger calls "the modern dragon." Ever after leaving Rivendell, Gollum will perpetually follow Frodo, except for the brief respite of Lórien. Gollum amounts to what psychology knows as the "shadow" and spiritual science calls the "Double."

Gollum is one of the Stoors, those Hobbits who have more interchange with Men. His original name is Sméagol: In an Anglo-Saxon dictionary *smeáh* stands for "creeping, penetrating"; *smeágung* for "search, inquiry, investigation where something is lost."[70] In his early days Sméagol is interested in "roots and beginnings." When he decides to retire with the Ring under the mountain, he says, "The roots of these mountains must be roots indeed; there must be great secrets buried there

---

[70] Flieger, "Frodo and Aragorn: The Concept of the Hero," *Green Suns and Faërie*, 155.

which have not been discovered since the beginning."[71] But he does not find any such secrets. In a sense he is a seeker like Frodo, though his interests and motives are far darker.

The Ring becomes the center of Gollum's life and an incessant obsession. It causes an unendurable cleft of soul. He hates the darkness in which he lives but even more so the light; he loves and hates the Ring at the same time, as he loves and hates himself. The Ring prolongs Gollum's miserable life and gives him an appearance closer to that of an animal.

Even so, Gollum is not utterly lost. As Tolkien tells us: "There was a little corner of his mind that was still his own, and light came through it, as through a chink in the dark: light out of the past."[72] Living under the mountain, Gollum does not need to wear the Ring; but even so he has become obsessed, practically possessed, by the Ring.

We will now look at length at the relationship between Gollum and Frodo. We will mostly speak of Gollum, and indicate Sméagol on occasion as that corner of the Hobbit's mind that is still connected to the light. We could call Sméagol the voice of reason.

In the Emyn Muil mountains, Sam and Frodo try at length to leave Gollum behind. When that turns out impossible, they are fortunately offered the opportunity to capture him. Frodo remembers the dialogue he had with Gandalf about Bilbo's encounter with Gollum. Lowering his sword, he decides to spare the creature, moved by compassion. And immediately he turns to Gollum to ask for help in moving through the Emyn Muil and the marshes.

Soon we witness the first dialogue between Gollum and Sméagol. When Sméagol enters the conversation, we are told that this is noticeable in a change of voice and language, a sobbing, and the fact that Gollum is not speaking to the Hobbits but to himself: "Leave me alone, *Gollum*! You hurt me. . . . I don't want to come back. I can't find it."[73] Continuing this inner dialogue, Sméagol implores Gollum to leave him and go away. With insight Frodo answers him that Gollum cannot leave him at his

---

[71] Tolkien, *The Fellowship of the Ring*, 53.
[72] Tolkien, *The Fellowship of the Ring*, 53.
[73] Tolkien, *The Two Towers*, 602.

command, and that only by helping Frodo and Sam can Sméagol free himself of Gollum.

The two Hobbits need to ensure Gollum's obedience. When Frodo ties the Elven rope around Gollum's ankle, the wretched Hobbit has a violent reaction: the rope truly hurts him. Likewise, when Frodo offers *lembas*—Elven waybread—to Gollum, he has the same reaction of loathing. It affects him physically with strong coughing. Frodo then resorts to binding Gollum to their service through a solemn promise. The only one that Gollum finds possible is a promise over "his Precious." With foresight Frodo warns him: "Would you commit your promise to that, Sméagol? It will hold you. But it is more treacherous than you are. It may twist your words. Beware!"[74] Gollum promises to be "very, very good" but also indicates something very symptomatic, that he will never let Sauron get hold of the Ring. This shows the nature of the Frodo-Gollum alliance; one wants to get rid of the Ring, the other wants to keep it for himself and away from Sauron—a dangerous proposition.

Sam witnesses the events and relates: "For a moment it appeared to Sam that his master had grown and Gollum had shrunk: a tall stern shadow, a mighty lord who hid his brightness in grey cloud, and at his feet a tiny whining dog. Yet the two were in some way akin and not alien: they could reach one another's minds."[75] While under the spell of this moment, Gollum is affected favorably; he ceases speaking to himself and addresses his companions directly, in a piteously friendly way.

When danger and fear get too close, Sméagol disappears and Gollum increases in strength. At the end of the crossing of the marshes, Gollum is terrified by the sight of the Nazgûl overhead. He is in fear that they may see everything and then report to Sauron, and he returns to his old way of speaking, addressing covetous looks in the direction of Frodo.

In the desolation between the marshes and Mordor, Gollum returns to his own inner tortured dialogue, the same he had before he made his promise to Frodo. And the narrative has this interesting comment: "A pale light and a green light alternated in his eyes as he spoke."[76] His

---

[74] Tolkien, *The Return of the King*, 604.
[75] Tolkien, *The Return of the King*, 604.
[76] Tolkien, *The Return of the King*, 618.

dialogue alternates between an "I" and a "we," between Sméagol and Gollum. Amidst other things he reminds himself that he is subjected to the Ring through his promise to Frodo. As he has vowed as well, Gollum's priority is to hold the Ring back from Sauron. But now, closer to the power of the Dark Lord, he has the dreams of grandiosity of a Ring-bearer, and to the listening Sam he reveals his desire to betray Frodo through the one who is only named as "she" (Shelob). Each time the voice of Gollum speaks, his long hand motions to reach for the Ring, only to be pulled back by Sméagol's voice.

Gollum inadvertently betrays himself by asking Frodo to give him back the Ring. Frodo warns him sternly:

> I warn you, Sméagol, you are in danger. . . . You swore a promise by what you call the Precious. Remember that! It will hold you to it; but it will seek a way to twist it to your undoing. . . . You will never get [the Ring] back. . . . In the last need, Sméagol, I should put on the Precious; and the Precious mastered you long ago. If I, wearing it, were to command you, you would obey, even if it were to leap from a precipice or to cast yourself into the fire. And such would be my command.[77]

Gollum is terrified by this very prophetic speech. Soon after, it seems that Sméagol is returning to the fore because he now remembers the tales he heard as a youth that spoke of the Men of Westernesse/ Númenor, and Frodo offers him the cautionary story of Isildur, who wrested the Ring from Sauron's finger. However, this is as far as Gollum will go in reaching towards the light.

When Frodo rescues Gollum from the Men of Gondor, he approaches Gollum at the forbidden pool and is repelled by his behavior. For a moment he wishes he had nothing to do with Gollum and realizes he could easily rid himself of his challenging presence. What holds him back is gratitude for the help received, and the ever-present voice of Gandalf who would remind him of compassion and of Gollum's role in the larger view of things. Frodo has to resort to cunning to save

---

[77] Tolkien, *The Return of the King*, 626.

Gollum from death, because such is the decree for those who bathe in the forbidden pool. To gain Gollum's trust, he reminds him of his promise on the Precious. To save himself Sméagol promises once more on the Precious that he will not return to the pool.

On Mount Orodruin, while Sam is defending himself from Gollum, Frodo arrives at the brink of the chasm and is unable to let go of the Ring. Sam, witnessing the scene in a heightened state of consciousness, sees through Gollum to the terrible enslavement that the Ring has exerted over him, and he realizes the poor wretch has lost much of his original strength.

Now Sam sees the whole thing as if from another perspective. He sees on one hand a creature completely crushed by the power of the Ring and filled with rage and lust, and on the other a figure robed in white with a wheel of fire at his breast. Frodo cries: "Begone and trouble me no more! If you touch me ever again, you shall be cast into the Fire of Doom."[78] Even though terrified, Gollum cannot resist his insatiable desire for the Ring.

Gollum is now fighting with the invisible Frodo on the brink of the chasm. In a mad frenzy he bites off Frodo's finger together with the Ring. In his crazed celebration, Gollum falls over the abyss with the Ring, wailing "Precious" for the last time, fulfilling Frodo's earlier threat.

Let us review a few of the steps of this collaboration/antagonism between Frodo and Gollum, between self and Double. After the capture of Gollum, Frodo spares him, moved by compassion. While this happens Frodo is in inner conversation with Gandalf, who is acting as his higher self. On the other hand Sméagol fights with Gollum. As Frodo was not speaking to the others but inwardly to Gandalf, so now Sméagol, the voice of reason, is not speaking to the two Hobbits but to Gollum, asking him to leave him alone. Frodo/Gandalf stands over and against Gollum/Sméagol. Here is posited the two-way deal between Frodo and Gollum; that Gollum can only leave Sméagol if the twosome places itself at Frodo's service. And that Frodo has to become familiar with his inner shadow, made objective and externalized in Gollum/Sméagol.

---

[78] Tolkien, *The Return of the King*, 922.

Something else is worth noting. When Gollum promises over the Precious, Frodo predicts that the Ring will bring him to his destruction, forewarning him of exactly what will happen on Mount Doom. When Gollum inadvertently asks Frodo to give him back the Ring, Frodo reminds him once more of the terrible consequence of coveting the Ring after he has promised to help Frodo and promised so over the Ring. There is no better and clearer reference to what effectively happens at the end. Fire is expressly mentioned as well as Frodo wearing the Ring.

On Mount Doom, close to the epilogue, once more Frodo is predicting Gollum's end, as he has already done twice previously. In Sam's "other vision," Frodo appears as the figure in white, very much reminiscent of Gandalf. And at his breast appears the Wheel of Fire. Frodo is attaining to the stature of Gandalf; he is reaching to his higher self. The epilogue is a parting of the ways. Frodo is cleansed of all attachment to the Ring, and his shadow leaves him to find regeneration through complete annihilation. In the end evil truly undoes itself. True, Frodo will still need healing from this experience and will seek it at the Grey Havens. Frodo can now fully forgive Gollum because he has seen the role that he has played in this anti-quest. Later, like Gandalf, he will also offer complete forgiveness to Saruman and be an example of compassion to his fellow Hobbits. We gain a sense that Frodo's task has come to an end and that only through the Grey Havens can he continue on his further growth.

Frodo is the one whose fate is closely associated to the Ring. Although Tolkien saw no parallels between his ring and that of the Nibelungen,[79] the mythologies of Western and Northern Europe carry many similarities, and what Rudolf Steiner says about the German Ring seems relevant to the Western Ring. In a lecture on Wagner, Steiner indicates that the gold brought over from Niflheim (Atlantis) had been a symbol of wisdom. This general, undifferentiated wisdom now becomes the domain of separate egos, a separate expression of wisdom in each individual. "Man had built a ring around himself and the Ring changed brotherhood into the struggle for existence among humankind. The element of wisdom common to all men in earlier times

---

[79] Tolkien asserts: "Both rings were round and there the resemblance ceases." (Carpenter, *Letters of J. R. R. Tolkien*, 306)

lived in water, and the last vestige of this water flowed in the Rhine. . . . The Nibelungen knew that they possessed the old universal wisdom and they now forged the Ring which thence-forward surrounded them as the "rising of egoism."[80]

It is indicative of the parallel between mythologies that Tolkien's Ring is found by Déagol in the depth of the river. It is the lowliest individual, Frodo, not the magician Gandalf, who has to undergo the test of egoism. The Ring is what amplifies the power of egoism in *The Lord of the Rings* as in the saga of the Nibelungen. Its effect on Sméagol/ Gollum is to give him power over his fellow Hobbits at the expense of separating him more and more from all of them. Its gift of invisibility is not a step towards the spiritual, rather a further isolation into the realm of the senses and the pursuit of power and the fall under the influence of adverse spiritual powers.

GANDALF AND FRODO: A CONTRAST

Frodo's path is one of sacrifice and forgiveness through a complete understanding of what lives at the "bottom" of the soul. His is the path of knowing the monsters within and all the temptations that lurk in the underworld, in the microcosm of the soul. Gandalf's path is that of the spirit to the macrocosm, the path that pierces through the veil of the senses, the path that renders understandable the mysteries of the universe. The path of Frodo is the path to the soul, to the microcosm that in the soul reflects the macrocosm. It is the path through the will into the underworld, the path that allows to pierce the veil of human destiny. The path of Gandalf reaches out through a more than human intelligence, a cosmic intelligence, into the mysteries of the universe that lie beyond the veil of the senses.

Much of what is said below has been brought by Steiner in his lectures of August 23–31, 1909.[81] The downfall of Atlantis was the result of the decadence of its Mysteries, places of instruction where the pupil came to know the reality of the spirit. The last stages of Atlantean

---

[80] Steiner, "Richard Wagner and Mysticism."
[81] Steiner, *The East in the Light of the West.*

civilization saw the confrontation of so-called white magic against black magic, something that Tolkien describes quite intuitively in his "Akallabêth"—part of *The Silmarillion*—his so-called Second Age of Atlantis/Númenor. In Atlantis there were two kinds of knowledge and paths: the path to the macrocosm (the sense world) leading beyond the maya of the senses; and the path to the microcosm (soul life) beyond the illusions veiling human destiny. The two kinds of knowledge were still simultaneously present in Atlantis.

After Atlantis the two paths separated and gave rise to various stages of post-Atlantean civilization. On one hand the path beyond the veil of the senses became the signature of old Indian and old Persian (Zarathustran) civilizations. The old Egyptian civilization turned its emphasis on the path to the underworld, the path to the microcosm. The same was true of the impulse of the Buddha in the 6th century BC.

Gautama Buddha and Zarathustra are the two initiates best representing respectively the southern path to the underworld and the northern path to the macrocosm. Gautama (Prince Siddhartha) was able to survey all his previous incarnations in the enlightenment experience under the Bodhi tree, which lasted several days. Consequently he ascended to the stage of Buddha. And Steiner concludes, "Thus man discovers the path to the former incarnations through submergence in his own being, and when his submergence is as intensive, powerful, and all-encompassing as was the case of the great Buddha, this insight into incarnations continues on and on."[82] In fact Buddha's ideas about karma and reincarnation formed the apex of his teachings. To further this path, Buddha taught compassion, love, and the Eightfold Path.

Zarathustra undertook a wholly different path of initiation; he did not progress solely through his own merits. He was actually the vehicle of a spiritual entity that cannot incarnate but can exert his influence through the carrier's personality. Due to this powerful influence, the child was perceived, culturally speaking, as a stranger by those around him.[83] The legends about Zarathustra portray a life full of dramatic events, turmoil, persecutions, and so forth. Conflicts were the natural

---

[82] Steiner, *Background to the Gospel of Saint Mark*, lecture of December 19, 1910.
[83] Steiner, *Background to the Gospel of Saint Mark*, lecture of December 19, 1910.

outcome of the novel quality of the impulses that worked through such an initiate. In comparison Buddha's life was much more serene.

When we look at Gandalf in contrast to Frodo, something of this polarity echoes. Gandalf is more than a mere human being. Gandalf is chosen; in him operates the divine. He goes through astounding biographical developments; he is called a harbinger of doom; people around him react with passion to his teachings and his very presence. Quite unlike him is Frodo who plunges into the utmost human condition to the point of being shattered by it. He learns in his body the meaning of tolerance, compassion, acceptance, and love for the human condition.

With good reason does Tolkien show us the paths to both Mysteries in his literary imaginations. Tolkien's mythology is one of the West. And the West preserved the longest the consciousness of what had been true in the Atlantis that was so present in Tolkien's consciousness, even with the Great Wave dream. The Mysteries of the West are the Mysteries of old Hibernia, a region that corresponds generally speaking to what is now Ireland.[84] They continued with the Irish Mysteries of bards and druids, which later heralded Irish Christianity. All of the above Mysteries preserved most faithfully something similar to what had held true in Atlantis: the unity of the two paths. It is for this reason that, among other things, there was a continuation of the knowledge of the battle between white and black magic that had led to the destruction of Atlantis. This is a theme that resounds through all the pages of *The Lord of the Rings*. It is no wonder that it is presented first with the black magic of Saruman (path to the macrocosm), then with the figure of Gollum (path to the microcosm), in which the mystery of the human shadow—or "Double" in Steiner's terms—is presented. To this we will turn last.

Just before our birth, besides our soul, another spiritual being enters the unconscious part of our bodies: this is the Double, animated by spirit beings who "have an extraordinarily high intelligence and a significantly developed will, but no warmth of heart at all, nothing of what we call

---

[84] Steiner, "The Mystery of the Double," lecture of November 16, 1917, *Geographic Medicine*.

the human *Gemüt.*[85] This will is much more akin to the nature-forces than to human will. And the beings of the Double occupy that part of the human bodies that the soul cannot fully inhabit.

It is the Double that gives origin to all human illnesses, those that originate from within. The illnesses that do not have an external origin come not from the human soul, but from the Double. The Double is strongly related to the forces that issue out of the earth. Before reaching the modern stage of consciousness—roughly around the beginning of the 15th century—the human being had to be protected from the forces of the Double. "Mankind had to be guarded not only from taking up anything of the theory of this Double, but from coming in contact as little as possible with anything connected with this Double."[86]

The forces of the Double are strongest in America because of the way the mountain ranges run from north to south, opening up the connection to the magnetic forces of the poles. By the 9th and especially the 12th century, there were limited but regular exchanges with America, especially from northern Europe. This allowed European initiates to study the illnesses caused by earth-magnetism in America, and allowed great progress for spiritual medicine. At that time America was only visited for the purpose of study of the effect of the Double on the Native American race.

The Irish monks continued to study the effects of the Double, and thus developed an occult medicine that would protect the human being from it. Through their influence Rome also became conscious that it would be necessary to protect Europe from what came out of the forces of the earth in America. Europe needed to be kept ignorant of what lived in America for a while.[87] Shipping to America was forbidden, and knowledge of America itself deliberately forgotten, leading to the *fable convenue* that America was only discovered by Columbus in 1492.

---

[85] Steiner, "The Mystery of the Double," lecture of November 16, 1917, *Geographic Medicine.*
[86] Steiner, "The Mystery of the Double," lecture of November 16, 1917, *Geographic Medicine.*
[87] Steiner, "The Mystery of the Double," lecture of November 16, 1917, *Geographic Medicine.*

The Double in *The Lord of the Rings* strongly binds Frodo to the place where the forces of the earth are starkest and strongest and to the very stronghold of Sauron, the epitome of the enemy of the human race. In Mordor there is no trace of life, nor any benevolence in the elements; only the forces from the depth of the earth hold sway. The Double turns strongest at Mount Doom—where the forces from the inner layers of the earth are strongest—and Frodo must muster all the energy that is possible in order to hold it to its place and ban it from his soul.

In looking at the contrast between Gandalf and Frodo, something else becomes quite apparent. Gandalf is the very intelligence of the fellowship. His consciousness surveys the whole of the world of the gods and the complex intricacies of relationships between the various inhabitants of Middle-earth. His path is a path of exalted thinking. Frodo does not possess a fraction of the knowledge of Gandalf; in fact he humbly turns to him for knowledge and guidance. Rather, Frodo's path is a path of the will. It is his perseverance against all odds that makes his path unique; his willingness to sacrifice personal comfort and acquire courage as he goes. Frodo enters Mordor without knowing whether he will have any means to return from it. In between the path of knowledge and the path of the will stands a middle path of feeling in Aragorn, which is uniquely related to the social function he performs.

If Gandalf follows the way to the macrocosm, and Frodo that to the microcosm, then Aragorn follows an intermediary way: the path of the soul placed between the macrocosm and the microcosm. It is not a path of initiation per se; it is the trial of soul that applies to Aragorn because he is the only political figure of the three, the only one who has a public function in the affairs of Middle-earth. Looking at him will offer us a reflection on political power and its ramifications. We will look at it in relation to Tolkien's political views, which were quite unique in his time, and would still be so in ours.

ARAGORN, THÉODEN, AND DENETHOR

Of the three central figures in *The Lord of the Rings*, Aragorn plays a special part. He is the only one to play a political role as the future king. He does not travel to the heights of the spirit like Gandalf, nor to the depths of the underworld like Frodo. He stays somewhere in the middle, in the more purely human realm. Even when he travels through the Paths of the Dead, he remains close to the human, getting in touch with the souls of the departed. It seems that, as he inspires the living to accept his guidance, the dead recognize in him the same power. And in healing he does the same; he follows the souls in their journey to the underworld and inspires them to take up their earthly task if their time on earth is not over. Aragorn weaves between the two worlds, but close to the boundaries of each.

Aragorn walks on a tightrope. He is able to hold a balance where others have fallen under the influence of Saruman or Sauron. His soul progress can best be understood if we look at the two tendencies which he avoids. On one hand stands Théoden who relinquishes his power; on the other Denethor who clings to it too tightly and in fact sees Aragorn and Gandalf as enemies to oppose.

It is interesting to note, as others have, that Théoden and Denethor's names are virtual anagrams of each other.[88] Their power has become decadent, without being outright evil. What the two have in common is the loss of access to the realm of wonder of the spirit due to long years of sheer resistance and societal estrangement from their Númenórean origins (indirectly for Théoden, whose race does not descend from Númenor). They are not able to regenerate their souls for the trials to come.

Théoden was born in Gondor and spoke Sindarin, thus gaining access to the Elven worldview. During his rule he was undermined from within by the cunning advice of Gríma—called Wormtongue by his detractors—who was betraying him at the service of Saruman. Gríma acted by seemingly protecting the king from outside threats but cunningly undermining his hope and his desire to stand against the will of Saruman. By the time of the story, due also to an additional weakening by illness, Théoden had practically relinquished all will and left control in the hands of Gríma.

Théoden's healing is rendered possible by Gandalf's new powers gained after his confrontation with the Balrog. In Edoras Gandalf

---

[88] Helms, *Tolkien's World*, 101.

unmasks and disempowers Gríma, before awakening the king. Théoden responds to the healing, feeling like one newly awakened.

The next test of Théoden comes from withstanding the alluring power of the voice of Saruman. When Saruman audaciously claims that he alone can help Théoden, the king can hardly find words to respond. After Gimli detects the deception in Saruman's words, Théoden finally denounces him calling him "a liar, and a corrupter of men's hearts." To this Saruman reacts with wrath, unmasking himself. Thus healed, Théoden returns with renewed energy to lead his people and to confront Sauron's legions in final battle. In the siege of Minas Tirith the king seemed like a god of old. "His golden shield . . . shone like an image of the Sun."[89] Thus redeemed, Théoden dies.

Far greater than Théoden's is Denethor's temptation. He is not confronted by Saruman, but by Sauron himself. Denethor descends from a line of regents of Minas Tirith, whose ancestry goes directly to Númenor; therefore, he carries in himself the exceptional capacities of the Men of Westernesse. Gandalf indicates that in Denethor the blood of Númenor runs truer than in most, except for his son Faramir. "He can perceive, if he bends his will thither, much of what is passing in the minds of men, even of those that dwell far off. It is difficult to deceive him, and dangerous to try."[90]

When Denethor speaks to Gandalf, Pippin sees a similarity between the two, and outwardly he perceives more royalty and power in the steward than in the magician. But his intuition tells him that Gandalf holds deeper power and fuller wisdom.

To his people Denethor has the reputation of being able to intuit the future, and even being able to read the mind of the Enemy. This appears so because Denethor is hiding that he has been looking into the *palantír*. At his death Denethor holds the *palantír*, and through his words we can understand that looking into what Sauron selectively shows him has caused the steward pride and despair. Gandalf realizes how Sauron has penetrated Minas Tirith, because one of the seeing stones was in Minas Tirith in the White Tower and the other in Mordor. Denethor resisted looking into the *palantír* until danger grew against his city. Although

---

[89] Tolkien, *The Return of the* King, 820.
[90] Tolkien, *The Return of the* King, 742–43.

he was too steadfast to fall under the direct power of the enemy, Sauron was nevertheless able to direct him towards what he wanted him to see, and thus fed despair into his heart, until madness precipitated. What Denethor knows has completely sapped him of any hope. And he believes Gandalf to be a fool trading in false hope.

There is more to Denethor's slipping into madness. Denethor does not want to bow to Aragorn; and he would rather be killed than relinquish power for himself, or his line. Thus he throws himself into the fire. When Faramir meets with his father, Denethor expresses the wish that Faramir had traded fate with Boromir "For Boromir . . . would not have squandered what fortune gave. He would have brought me a mighty gift [the Ring]."[91] The power of the Ring has not escaped Denethor's perceptive mind, but it has blinded him. Gandalf gives the regent a lesson about the Ring and its predictable effect on Boromir or his father. Denethor, in denial, naively believes he could have buried the Ring and left it out of use. Insanity is the only possible epilogue for one who has played too close with fire.

Aragorn stands between Théoden in his early dullness and Denethor and his thirst for power leading to madness. Théoden is conquered through loss of faith via a traitor (Gríma Wormtongue) and the power of Saruman. Denethor has great ambition for power and uses dubious means—looking into the *palantír* and craving the power of the Ring; Sauron acts upon him. Théoden gives up power; Denethor clings to it too strongly. Aragorn, like Denethor, has used the *palantír* and knows its power, though he used it as its lawful inheritor. However, he knows how much it took from him to just look into it once. Aragorn is able to exert power at the right moment, and wait a long time before using it, all the while standing in prolonged service to others, anonymously as a Ranger. His apprenticeship under Gandalf and long years of testing as Strider, not to mention his devoted service to the Ring-bearer, have steeled him to yield power selflessly. His love for Arwen, which is tied to the future and well-being of Middle-earth, is another major tempering factor.

Aragorn follows the path of feeling; it is human feeling that unites him with the fate of the earth to which he can relate in an almost

---

[91] Tolkien, *The Return of the* King, 795.

artistic form of perception. It is warmth of feeling that unites him to all his fellow Middle-earth inhabitants. This feeling is returned by them and becomes love. Aragorn illustrates the role that the soul takes in a balanced relationship to earth and spirit. The soul partakes of the two worlds, physical and spiritual; it mediates between the two. It lives in space and time without being bound to them. And Aragorn puts into practice these principles in the political life. As a Númenórean heir, he wants his rule on earth to be cognizant of the past and of the connection with the "true spirit of the West." Théoden and Denethor have all but forgotten why they are kings, relinquishing to or holding to the sole force dimension of power is what is left to them.

TOLKIEN, AN OLD INITIATE?

It is of interest here to see another aspect of Tolkien's worldview. He stands far and away from political utopias, though he is supremely interested in everything of a social nature. His views are, here too, deeply penetrating through the power of imagination. Below we will quote at length some of these.

Looking at World War II Tolkien comments to his son Christopher: "For we are attempting to conquer Sauron with the Ring. And we shall (it seems) succeed. But the penalty is, as you will know, to breed new Saurons, and slowly turn Men and Elves into Orcs. Not that in real life things are as clear cut as in a story."[92]

Talking about what he perceived with disgust as British or American imperialism, Tolkien said, "My sentiments are more or less those that Frodo would have had if he discovered some Hobbits learning to ride Nazgûl-birds 'for the liberation of the Shire.'" And he adds with insight, "But at least the Americo-Russian war won't break out for a year yet."[93]

Where Tolkien's words are far reaching is when they concern the fate of the present: "If anguish were visible, almost the whole of this benighted planet would be enveloped in a dense dark vapour, shrouded from the amazed vision of the heavens! And the products of it all will

[92] Carpenter, *Letters of J. R. R. Tolkien*, 78.
[93] Carpenter, *Letters of J. R. R. Tolkien*, 115.

be mainly evil—historically considered." He tempers this by explaining that what works for the good is not equally visible: "Evil labours with vast power and perpetual success—in vain: preparing always only the soil for unexpected good to sprout in."[94] In another letter to his son Christopher, he reasserts his historical views, adding, "The future is impenetrable especially to the wise; for what is really important is always hid from contemporaries, and the seeds of what is to be are quietly germinating in the dark in some forgotten corner, while everyone is looking at Stalin or Hitler."[95]

Tolkien offers us in *The Lord of the Rings* an understanding of the archetypes of the makeup of the modern human being: the triad of body, mind (soul), and spirit; the importance of what makes us modern human beings; the presence of that element that is properly speaking foreign to the soul, but an inescapable condition of the modern human being—the Double. Once again this proves the depth of the archetypal perceptions of Tolkien, and to my mind, the reason why Tolkien's mythology speaks so strongly to the modern human being.

Gandalf, Aragorn, and Frodo bring about the renewal of Middle-earth through the perfect coordination of their efforts. It is Gandalf who orchestrates it all in spirit. But it is in Frodo's hands that is placed the most important task of the ushering of the Fourth Age; the destruction of the Ring in the belly of the beast, in the heart of Sauron's kingdom. And Aragorn unites the fates of the two, and he alone will play a role in the Fourth Age. Gandalf is the mastermind, as he excels in thinking; Frodo represents the indomitable will that can be bent but not broken; Aragorn's path is that of feeling, weaving between the two. These are the three forces that weave in the human soul.

There is nothing simple or simplistic in the way the deeds of these three people keep intersecting. This is part and parcel of the enduring power of *The Lord of the Rings*. In it are reunited Tolkien's medievalistic tastes and his deeply modern outlook. The enduring power of Tolkien's masterpiece lies in positing the core questions lying at the "end of all things," at the end of times, or turning points of time. And we live at the

---

[94] Carpenter, *Letters of J. R. R. Tolkien*, 76
[95] Carpenter, *Letters of J. R. R. Tolkien*, 91.

end of times, as practically all spiritual traditions agree when referring to the present.

ABOUT THE WRITING OF *THE LORD OF THE RINGS* AND ITS POSSIBLE "HISTORICITY"

In a letter to Robert Murray, Tolkien states that "*The Lord of the Rings* is of course a fundamentally religious and Catholic work; unconsciously so at first, but consciously in the revision," adding that the "religious element is absorbed into the story and the symbolism." [96] Where do we find evidence of this?

The appendices at the end of the trilogy offer us a key insight. The Hobbits leave the Shire on December 25. This already indicates that there is a connection between the Ring-bearer and Christ. The end of the Third Age, corresponding to the throwing of the Ring into the fires of Mount Doom, is made to match March 25, the traditional Easter date in the Christian Orthodox tradition. March 25 is also the feast of the Annunciation, traditionally called Lady Day in English-speaking countries; it comes exactly nine months before Christmas. With this in mind we can start seeing the whole of the Lord of the Rings as the perspective of the Christ event seen from the "true West," which did not experience the Golgotha events but rather their reflection in the aura of the Earth. Seen under this lens, the complementarities between the three characters acquire a richer meaning.

Gandalf the spirit, Aragorn the soul, and Frodo the body are part of a whole that is meant to accomplish a larger mission for the completion of an age and the beginning of a new one. Their synergistic actions make sense because the three truly act as parts of a whole. While there is subordination of Frodo to the other two, and of Aragorn to Gandalf, each has its own essential being and role in relation to the whole being of Christ Jesus. And, on the other hand, before the climax of the end of the Third Age, Gandalf subordinates all his actions to Frodo's mission, to enable him to throw the Ring into the fire. In the larger sense, there is thus no higher Gandalf, nor lower Frodo.

---

[96] Carpenter, *Letters of J. R. R. Tolkien*, 172.

Gandalf is most clearly of all the Christlike Sun being. This is what he achieves in the transformation of Gandalf the Grey to Gandalf the White. He is explicitly portrayed as a radiant being of spirit, dazzling with light. Gandalf embodies the solar spirit who descends to earth from the cosmos. His is most clearly a planetary, cosmic initiation into the macrocosm. Gandalf is familiar with the eternal, cosmic Christ being. This is accompanied with the knowledge of cosmic history and of all cosmic necessities that embody it. Gandalf intimately knows the adversaries of humanity. It is obvious that he has to struggle to defeat Sauron; more subtly, however, he also attempts to redeem him, as is made explicit in the case of Saruman, Sauron's most important ally. He does the same with Gollum; it is thanks to Gandalf that Gollum is kept alive and plays a central role in the destruction of the Ring.

Frodo is that aspect of the Christ most intimately united with the physical body of Jesus. His is a trial of the body. He is inflicted a number of wounds and is left mutilated, like the historical figure of Jesus. His complete healing is only accomplished through his journey to the Grey Havens. Frodo has to descend to the depths of the underworld, to the knowledge of inner despair at his purely human limitations. He has to face the universal burden of humanity in the figure of the Double that Gollum exemplifies. Gandalf encounters evil made manifest as a being of the macrocosm, the Balrog. Frodo meets it as the condensed result of all the incarnational paths of the individual in the figure of the Double.

In between the two poles is Aragorn, who unites the elements of body and spirit. In the act of healing, Aragorn attains purely Christlike stature, reminding us of his role in the biblical miracles. Aragorn weaves in that area between the "highest" of Gandalf and the "lowest" of Frodo. All of this supports Tolkien's inkling of the essential Christianity of his book. It also explains why he became obsessed with deepening the accuracy of his work from a historical perspective. In my mind this could have imposed a limitation on his imaginations. The book could have been a purely imaginative perspective on the Christ event, not one that has to be sought externally in history. We will return to this after the explorations of the next chapter.

The initiation journeys of the three characters encompass the whole journey of Christ, his descent into the Underworld, and his

Resurrection. In distant Hibernia, we are told by Steiner, the initiates of the West could behold, not the historical event, but a momentous event affecting the whole of the Earth. One could say that our cosmos had been rejuvenated, and the whole aura of the Earth appeared to their eyes in a new fashion.

After the Ring has been thrown into the fire, Sam runs to Frodo and holds him, and in an altered state of consciousness he has a brief vision:

> swirling cloud . . . towers and battlements . . . upon a mountain throne above immeasurable pits; great courts and dungeons, eyeless prisons sheer as cliffs. . . . Towers fell and mountains slid; walls crumbled and melted, vast spires of smoke and spouting steams went billowing up . . . like an overwhelming wave, and its wild crest curled and came foaming down upon the land.

Here once again, and in most significant fashion, Tolkien inserts his Atlantean "Great Wave" dream.

The undoing of the Ring is the turning point of an age, just as the Atlantean Flood marked the end of another. Sam experiences in his soul the correlation between the two events, as something he has previously experienced in another incarnation. Tolkien places the ends of his ages at the time in which a certain evil has been brought to an end. Noah ushers in the new post-Atlantean Age, just as Aragorn—thanks to Gandalf and Frodo—inaugurates a new dynasty at the beginning of the Fourth Age, when Sauron has been defeated.

Let us now turn to some other of Tolkien's realizations about the writing of *The Lord of the Rings*. We will quote at length from the draft of a letter to a certain Carole Batten-Phelps, written in 1971, two years before his death. In summing up what the writing of the trilogy meant to him, Tolkien states:

> It was written slowly and with great care for detail, and finally emerged as a Frameless Picture: a searchlight, as it were, on a brief period in History, and on a small

part of our Middle-Earth, surrounded by the glimmer of limitless extensions in time and space. Very well: that may explain to some extent why it "feels" like history; why it was accepted for publication; and why it has proved readable for a large number of very different kinds of people. . . . Looking back on the wholly unexpected things that have followed its publication. . . . I feel as if an ever darkening sky over our present world had been suddenly pierced, the clouds rolled back, and an almost forgotten sunlight had poured down again. As if indeed the horns of Hope had been heard again, as Pippin heard them suddenly at the absolute *nadir* of the fortunes of the West. But *How?* And *Why?*[97]

Tolkien is describing a momentous event for the whole of earth evolution as if from an initiatory perspective. Could this be a memory echo of a moment of cosmic history?

The unpublished letter is a source of one revelation after another. Tolkien now connects the above impressions with another event: the visit of a man who spoke to him about some old pictures that seemed to fit Tolkien's narrative, but of which Tolkien had no knowledge. Hearing Tolkien's response, the man fell silent for a while, then blurted, "Of course, you don't suppose, do you, that you wrote all that book yourself?" And Tolkien answered, "No, I don't suppose so any longer. I have never since been able to suppose so. An alarming conclusion for an old philologist to draw concerning his private amusement. But not one that should puff any one up who considers the imperfections of 'chosen instruments,' and indeed what sometimes seems their lamentable unfitness for the purpose."[98]

Addressing the correspondent again, Tolkien, in reply to her letter, says:

---

[97] Carpenter, *Letters of J. R. R. Tolkien*, 413.

[98] Tolkien has something similar to say in a letter draft to Peter Szabo Szentmihalyi: "My work is not a '*novel*,' but an 'heroic romance' a much older and quite different variety of literature" (Carpenter, *Letters of J. R. R. Tolkien*, 413).

You speak of "a sanity and sanctity" in *the L. R.* "which is a power in itself." I was deeply moved. Nothing of the kind has been said to me before. But by a strange chance, just as I was beginning this letter, I had one from a man, who classified himself as "an unbeliever, or at best a man of belatedly and dimly dawning religious feeling . . . but you create a world in which some sort of faith seems to be everywhere without a visible source, like light from an invisible lamp." I can only answer, "Of his own sanity no man can securely judge. If sanctity inhabits his work or as a pervading light illuminates it then it does not come from him but through him. And neither of you would perceive these terms unless it was with you also. Otherwise you would see and feel nothing, or (if some other spirit was present) you would be filled with contempt, nausea, hatred." (413)

What has emerged in Tolkien's words, be it in his letters or in *The Lord of the Rings*, answers as many questions as it raises new ones. We can see first of all that the trilogy is the logical continuation of what preceded it in *The Silmarillion*; particularly it is thematically connected with the Second Age of Atlantis/Númenor in the "Akallabêth" story towards the end of *The Silmarillion*. To this we will turn next.

ATLANTIS/ NÚMENOR

Tolkien carried in his soul the awareness that humankind has lived in ages past—ages of a cyclical rather than linear nature. Had Tolkien entered in converse with spiritual science, his world would have been illumined as if from within. Every somehow semi-forbidden word—reincarnation, Atlantis, Lemuria—would have evoked responses from his inner world. Within his soul he carried the urgency of leaving posterity his view of the ages undergone by the West. It is not our task to vouchsafe for their correspondence with everything that we know from Anthroposophy, but rather to realize the nature of his striving and what it tells us about Tolkien himself, to which we will return in the

77

next chapter. At present we will only look at what Tolkien said about the Second Age of Atlantis/Númenor and leave aside his First Age.

Suffice to say that the First Age is an age in which humanity longs to preserve the light of the Gods and is seduced by a false light-bearer, Melkor, a clearly Luciferic figure. In the Second Age of Númenor, Sauron, a Valar and servant to Melkor, first works with his master, then ultimately wrests prominence from him. In Sauron we have an Ahrimanic figure.

To understand how Tolkien sees the evolution of Númenor, we must first add a few notes about the relationships between Elves and Men. In various places Tolkien explains that his Elves are simply exalted human beings, those who retain faculties closer to the original idea of the human being: "Of course in reality this only means that my 'elves' are only a representation or an apprehension of a part of human nature, but that is not the legendary mode of talking."[99] And further:

> [Elves] are to all intents and purposes *men*: or rather, they are Man before the Fall which deprived him of his power of achievement. . . . They are made by Man in his own image and likeness; but freed from those limitations which he feels most to press upon him. They are immortal and their will is directly effective for the achievement of imagination and desire.[100]

Thus, to all effects and purposes the Elves are those human beings who have retained qualities closest to the divine: they have converse with the gods, and through them other human beings can have closer proximity to the gods.

To understand Tolkien's Atlantis, we will turn to some general trends, then to the evolution of the lost continent, from its origins up to the Flood. At the end of the First Age, after Middle-earth has been ravaged, the exiled Elves take residence in an isle close to the realm of the Valar, Valinor. Theirs is the island of Eressëa within sight of the Blessed Realm (Valinor). Men of the Three Houses, in recognition

---

[99] Tolkien, *The Silmarillion*, footnote to p. xxi.
[100] Carpenter, *J. R. R. Tolkien: A Biography*, 100.

of their courage in withstanding the lures of Sauron and Melkor, are allowed to live further west than all other mortals in the great "Atlantis" isle of Númenor. The Númenóreans establish a great kingdom within further sight of Eressëa (but not of Valinor).

The Númenóreans are the only Men who speak an Elvish tongue; they communicate with the Elves of Eressëa or of Gil-galad, the Elven kingdom in Middle-earth. Though mortal they resemble, even in appearance, their Elven friends and therefore live a long life and pursue wisdom and art. Like the Elves they struggle to resist the temptation of seeking to live a longer life. Partly because they are aware of this, the Valar forbid the Númenóreans to sail to Eressëa, or otherwise westward. They don't want them to land on immortal land and thus long for immortality while in this world, which in fact their nature could not tolerate.

As the Second Age progresses, Sauron, an immortal who can still take on human shape, is forming a kind of theocracy in Middle-earth. He has established himself towards the East of Middle-earth, and his power grows. He can tempt the remaining Elves of Middle-earth where their weaknesses are strongest. The Elves retain qualities from humanity's early state of union with the Gods; they long for the original state of participation with the divine. They want to preserve things unchanged and prevent greater stages of separation. Sauron can still take on beautiful appearance and lure the Elves into rendering Western Middle-earth a sort of paradise on earth, as beautiful as Valinor, the land of the Valar. To this end he teaches them to forge Rings of power, in effect making recourse to inferior magic. While he wants the Elves to believe that this will be a return to the past, or a preservation of what was best in the origins, he has in mind another kind of future. The Rings, nevertheless, prevent or slow down decay and increase the natural powers of their possessor. With the help of Sauron the Elves craft three of these Rings; Men craft nine, the Dwarves seven. And Sauron builds for himself, the "One Ring to rule them all."

When the Elves realize Sauron's secret intentions, they hide their three Rings from him, and a war erupts between them and Sauron. The West of Middle-earth suffers much destruction. A few Elven enclaves survive in Middle-earth, such as the Elf-kingdom of Gil-galad to the farthest West and Elrond's Rivendell. The change ushers in the Númenórean civilization, which undergoes what can be characterized as three stages.

First Phase

During the first phase the Númenóreans submit themselves to the will of the Valar, though they don't fully understand the reasons for their ban. They form alliances with the Elves and Men of Middle-earth against Sauron, who at this time still works closely with Melkor.

The Númenóreans build their main city in Andúnië, on the Western coast looking towards Eressëa, which offers an indication of their attitudes and views. They erect a great temple to the one God Eru/Ilúvatar in the middle of the land, upon the mountain Meneltarma, the "pillar of Heaven." Their king Elros, son of Eärendil, has been appointed by the Valar.

The early kings speak Elvish, an indication of how important is their relationship to the elder brothers. The early civilization is one of peace, and the Númenóreans become great mariners, as their Elven counterparts who sail to Númenor in "oarless boats, as white birds flying from the sunset."[101] The Númenóreans, moved by pity towards the Men of Middle-earth under Melkor's dominion, bring them corn and wine, and instruct them in the science and art of agriculture and of bread baking. Men received the visitors and later remembered them in their legends as gods, whom they hope to see again.

Second Phase

Tolkien calls this stage the "Days of Pride and Glory," during which the Númenóreans start to envision disobeying the Valar. Still hungering for immortality, they now yearn for earthly goods and wealth more than wisdom. During this phase, trade expands and they start to gather tax; they also devise new weapons and machines. Men of Middle-earth no longer see the Valar as their helpers.

The wisdom of the early kings is waning, and two parties form. The majority follow the ruling king who lusts for eternal life and the

---

[101] Tolkien, *The Silmarillion*, 314.

means to attain it, defying the ban of the Valar. A small group, calling themselves Elendili, the "Faithful," retain loyalty towards the Elves to the West, though they are troubled by the problem of mortality.

The ruling class seeks now pleasure, riches, and power over their fellow human beings. And a number of Númenórean kings are seduced by Sauron, who gives them Rings of power, enslaving them to his designs. They now seek to subjugate Middle-earth by first occupying the western shores. They also persecute the Faithful, whom they uproot from the west coast and move towards the eastern sea.

On his side Sauron grows in power under the shadow of Melkor. He strengthens his stronghold of Mordor and builds the tower of Barad-dûr, wanting to subjugate Middle-earth. The antagonism between Sauron and Númenor takes root, though ultimately one could say they are not far apart from a spiritual perspective. A war is plotted against Sauron, who realizes he does not have power yet to defeat the Númenóreans. He pretends to submit to the will of the rival king and is taken hostage to Númenor, though it is already clear that he will manage to impose his will through cunning.

Third Phase

Now the Númenórean kings openly defy the Valar and their ban. They believe they can wrest immortality from the gods. The power of Sauron grows. He manages to win the trust of all the king's counselors but one. He leads them to believe that they can conquer many lands, and beyond these find the "Ancient Darkness," for "Darkness alone is worshipful, and the Lord thereof may yet make other worlds to be gifts to those that serve him, so that the increase of power shall find no end."[102] He teaches them that the lord thereof—whom he refers to as "Lord of All, Giver of Freedom"—can deliver them from the false god Eru. He is in fact directing them to Melkor. Only the councilor Amandil, one of the Faithful, resists the wiles of Sauron, who does not dare to defy his popularity yet.

Sauron starts giving new meaning to old legends and songs; he starts rewriting Númenórean cosmology and introduces new rituals,

---

[102] Tolkien, *The Silmarillion*, 325.

at first secretly, then gradually more openly. In the center of the island Sauron builds a new temple, in the middle of which stands an altar of fire. From the top of the temple smoke rises continuously for

> in that temple, with spilling of blood and torment and great wickedness, men made sacrifice to Melkor that he should release them from Death. And most often from among the Faithful they chose their victims; yet never openly on the charge that they would not worship Melkor, the Giver of Freedom, rather was cause sought against them that they hated the King, and were his rebels, or that they plotted against their kin, devising lies and poisons.[103]

Though these sacrifices are performed to forestall death, this now comes sooner and arrives accompanied with sickness and madness. Tolkien calls the new rituals "necromancy" and will later calls Sauron the "necromancer" in *The Lord of the Rings*.

To the east the Númenóreans start enslaving the people of Middle-earth. However, their major aims lie towards the West, where they are preparing a great fleet for a decisive assault, under the guidance of Sauron, who tells them that they can wrest immortality from the Valar and rule in their stead. However, the new rituals and black magic cause restlessness in the elemental world, and great clouds gather, especially from the west. When all is ready, Sauron's fleet sails towards Valinor. When they land, a great abyss opens in the waters and engulfs the invading fleet. Under the charge of the waters Númenor is engulfed and wiped out. The whole of Middle-earth suffers great upheavals; old lands and islands disappear and new ones emerge. Sauron takes refuge in Mordor "until he wrought himself a new guise, an image of malice and hatred made visible; and the Eye of Sauron the Terrible few could endure."[104]

---

[103] Tolkien, *The Silmarillion*, 328.
[104] Tolkien, *The Silmarillion*, 336.

Various themes, familiar to spiritual science, give weight and credibility to Tolkien's artistic inspiration. It was only in the Sun Mysteries, at the center of Atlantis, that there were the necessary skills for building a temple, the very temple that Plato describes. Elsewhere in the lost continent, the split occurring within the Mars Mysteries, concerned with the understanding and use of the life force, led to the misuse of the etheric, in effect becoming the practice of black magic. The confrontation of black versus white magic is central to *The Lord of the Rings*. It is most apparent in the crafting of the Rings of power or in the working of the Ringwraiths.

Atlantis and the Christ event, black magic versus white magic, the fate of the earth at the hand of this confrontation are all interwoven themes that have been part and parcel of the spiritual history of the West. Most strongly of all, this knowledge was cultivated in those that Steiner called the "last Great Mysteries" of Hibernia, which preserved the wholeness of the Mysteries known in Atlantis, carrying together the paths to the macrocosm and to the microcosm that otherwise separated in the Northern and Southern streams after the end of Atlantis, inaugurating the various post-Atlantean epochs. The West lay long in waiting for a mission that will only emerge after millennia from the end of Atlantis. We will turn to the Great Mysteries of Hibernia next, and trace their connections to the being of Tolkien and the contents of his legendarium, in particular to *The Lord of the Rings*.

Chapter 4

Tolkien and the Hibernian Mysteries

After the Flood that engulfed Atlantis, the Mysteries that had been at the foundation of the Atlantean Oracles were transmitted through the initiates who left the island towards the East. What had formed a unified stream in Atlantis found its way into Europe, Asia, and North Africa in the so-called Northern and Southern Streams.

It was known in ancient times that there are two veils occulting the full dimension of life on earth: a veil behind the perception of the senses and a veil in the soul life, one occulting the reality of the spirit at work in matter, the other hiding the reality of karma and reincarnation in the soul life. The outer path of the senses (macrocosm) was pursued through the help of those beings who have their center in the spiritual Sun, traditionally called the "upper gods," whose leader is the Christ. The path to the life of the soul (microcosm) was pursued through the help of the lower gods, beings under the guidance of Lucifer, more precisely a part of the Luciferic beings. The second path was regarded as the most dangerous.[105]

The northern stream took its departure from northern Europe, Scandinavia, and Russia, to East Asia, inaugurating the Indian epoch and later the Persian one. The southern stream traveled through Spain to Northern Africa, Egypt, and Arabia, inaugurating the Egyptian epoch.

---

[105] Steiner. *The East in the Light of the West.*

In Hibernia, the closest land to the vanished continent, the Atlantean Mysteries preserved their unity. And Steiner indicates that

> the Hibernian Mysteries really belong to those which we are entitled to call in Spiritual Science the Great Mysteries. . . . The human being learned thus to know the Microcosm, that is, to know himself, as spirit-soul-bodily Being in connection with the Macrocosm. He learned also to know the coming into being, the weaving, the arising and passing away, and the changing, metamorphosing itself of the Macrocosm.[106]

Steiner only spoke of Hibernia and its Mysteries at the end of 1923. He offered some quite startling introductions into the matter, stating that this Mystery Center "also stands in a certain sense at the starting-point of modern spiritual life, in that it has given impulses to this modern spiritual movement, and yet has taken over much from the older spiritual movements in which the primeval wisdom of man was enshrined."[107]

More than any other ancient Mysteries, it seems that those of Hibernia are highly guarded; their imaginations have a repelling power which keeps the spiritual researcher at bay. To Steiner these imaginations produced a kind of bewilderment, which he felt could only be overcome with courage in the search for truth. These were probably the Mysteries that he had to fight hardest to uncover.

Let us try to approach the question of why such repelling forces, and why these Mysteries can be said to be "at the starting-point of modern spiritual life."

HIBERNIAN MYSTERIES

All aspects of Hibernian initiation were twofold since the path to the macrocosm went hand in hand with that to the microcosm. On one hand

---

106 Steiner, *Mystery Centers*, lecture 9 of December 9, 1923.
107 Steiner, *Mystery Centers*, lecture 7 of December 7, 1923.

the pupil was led to realize the difficulties on the path of knowledge. He had to face inner doubts and disillusions to the point of doubting that something of this nature would even be possible. On the other hand he had to face how little of what is commonly called knowledge offers to human happiness.

The pupil knew that he had to strive for an inner balance that made possible for him to find joy and happiness, but it seemed far from reachable.

> Thus the pupils were driven on the one side near to one abyss, and on the other side near to another abyss, and always forced as if to doubt and to wait till a bridge had been built for them over each abyss. And they were so deeply initiated into the doubts and difficulties of knowledge that by the time they were led from this preparation actually to enter the Cosmic Mysteries they had come to the conclusion: if it must be so, then we will renounce all knowledge, we will renounce all that cannot bring happiness to man.[108]

This already gives us some inkling about the difficulty of researching into the Hibernian Mysteries: the difficulty of the path itself.

In effect a long path lay in front of the disciple of the Mysteries. All stages required a lengthy preparation, and the initiators made sure that the pupil stayed long enough at every single stage to let cosmic powers act upon him and let new soul faculties reach maturation. Through the hardship required in such soul development, it looked and felt as if the pupil would relinquish the very goals he was seeking; in a sense only by reaching this paradoxical state of mind and feelings—of tension leading to near impossibility of reaching the goal—could he go further.

Most of the experiences of the candidate for initiation were brought forth in front of two statues of very large dimensions; a "male" and a "female." The statue he met first was the male, built of completely elastic material and inwardly hollow, which could be compressed all over its surface; after being deformed it returned to its original shape. The

---

[108] Steiner, *Mystery Centers*, lecture 7 of December 7, 1923.

female was of a very soft and plastic substance that registered all imprints that were made on it. Only after each candidate had experienced it could all the indentations be smoothed out for the following candidate.

What was experienced in front of each statue was at each level intensified through the fact that the pupil became more and more conscious about what he was going through and could differentiate the successive conditions of soul and changes of consciousness he was undergoing. At each stage the polarities relating to macrocosm and microcosm were raised to a new level; and the experiences in front of the second statue brought resolution to what the first one awakened. After each step the pupil had to be able to reawaken consciously the conditions previously achieved.

The first time the candidate was brought alone to the male statue, it appeared to him that the head was something like a "soul-eye" and above it was something that stood for the Sun, giving the inner impression of representing the content of the whole macrocosm. He felt, "Here the macrocosm works through the Sun and forms the human head, which knows what are the impulses of the macrocosm and forms itself inwardly and outwardly according to these impulses of the macrocosm."[109]

The pupil felt the approach of the second statue as if it were formed by bodies of light raying inwards, and as if it stood completely under their influence. The head, rather indefinite, seemed to him to be formed out of these rays. Inwardly he could tell himself that the head was formed out of the Moon forces that worked on the organism, causing the head to grow out of it.

Each time the pupil was brought to a statue, he was left in complete silence and alone to experience the qualities of it. In front of the first, he became aware of all possible difficulties concerning the attainment of knowledge; in front of the second, he was made aware of the difficulties in the attainment of happiness. All of this together led the candidate to a yearning to find resolution to the riddles surging in his soul. "Everything in them was a question. Reason asked, the heart asked, the will asked, everything, everything asked."[110]

---

[109] Steiner, *Mystery Centers*, lecture 7 of December 7, 1923.
[110] Steiner, *Mystery Centers*, lecture 7 of December 7, 1923.

After these initial experiences, a lapse of time followed in which the first impressions were left to mature in the pupil's soul; and the questions of the pursuits of knowledge and happiness lay amplified in the tension between their ordinary meaning and the experiences just undergone. Through this tension the pupil was brought to the experience and awareness of standing "before the Power which guards the Threshold."

At this new stage the pupil was brought again in front of the two statues in the same sequence. This time, however, the hierophant remained with the pupil. And after a time the pupil saw the initiator as if he were rising above the head of the first statue, standing in front of the Sun. When the hierophant spoke, his voice sounded as if "out of a musical-harmonic," leaving a deep impression on the pupil's soul, with words that could be expressed as follows:

> *I am the Image of the World*
> *Behold, I lack Being*
> *I live in thy knowledge*
> *I become now in thee Consecration.*[111]

The pupil had expected a more immediate answer to his urge for knowledge, but now he experienced increased doubts, and a certain anxious feeling that these doubts would persist. But he felt also close to recognizing the cosmic Power that reverberated in the words just heard, and wanted to give himself to it.

Something similar to the above was repeated in front of the second statue, this time through another initiator. His voice, resounding once more out of a musical-harmonic, spoke the following words:

> *I am the Image of the World*
> *Behold, I lack Truth,*
> *If thou wilt dare to live with me*
> *I will be thy Consolation.*[112]

---

[111] Steiner, *Mystery Centers*, lecture 7 of December 7, 1923.
[112] Steiner, *Mystery Centers*, lecture 7 of December 7, 1923.

The pupil had an intimation of the possibility of inner joy and felt even closer to recognizing the cosmic Power to which he wanted to devote himself. Again the initiator left him alone, and in the pupil's soul new feelings matured. Now the realization of the distance between what the world of the senses calls knowledge or happiness and what these mean in the spiritual worlds amplified. He recognized that the idea that of a pursuit of joy through asceticism was a complete illusion, because the second statue warned him that she "lacked Truth." Moving a step further from his first encounter with the two statues, he now felt that knowledge and happiness took a whole new form in the spiritual worlds.

New experiences emerged in the pupil's soul as well. It was as if he could hear the Inner Word speaking from the statues. From the first statue spread a sense of fear that ideas have no being, and that the pursuit of knowledge leads to illusion. And the second statue warned him that on the path to happiness, he would find no truth. In the overpowering strength of these feelings, the pupil's outer senses were as if suspended. The feelings matured to the point that after a time the pupil could see, as if written in letters of fire, the word "Science" above the head of the first statue, and the word "Art" on top of the second statue.

Having attained these new revelations, the pupil was led back to the temple, though not to the statues, by the two initiators. One of them directed him towards the other initiator, who showed him the "Form of Christ." The first priest said to him, "Receive the Word and the Power of this Being into thy heart," while the other added, "And receive from Him what the two images wished to give thee—Science and Art."[113]

The experiences from the two statues continued to act on the soul of the pupils, each in its own way. The first statue caused a feeling of soul numbness or soul freezing, that went so deep as to become a body numbness; altogether these feelings and impressions caused an altered state of consciousness. Although at first it felt like a state of unproductive vacuum, it gradually led way to the feeling of being taken up by the cosmos. After a long time something new entered the field of consciousness, leading the pupil to inwardly say to himself something like "The rays of the Sun, the rays of the stars are drawing me, they are drawing me out into the whole Cosmos, yet I remain actually

---

[113] Steiner, *Mystery Centers*, lecture 7 of December 7, 1923.

together with myself."[114] And this was accompanied with the rising of the most varied impressions of inner winter landscapes, impressions that corresponded in many ways to what he had experienced of winter in his own life. Now he felt as if he were moving in time through a series of winter landscapes while out of his body, but nevertheless experiencing them through his senses. This awareness was multiplied for each of his twelve senses.[115] It evoked a sense of having become all in all like the elastic and hollow male statue.

The experiences of the senses were felt each separate from the other, so that the pupil felt his ego split into each of the senses.

> From this arose a living longing for union with a Being out of the hierarchy of the Angels, in order that from this union with the Being out of the hierarchy of the Angels, he should receive ability and power to control the splitting-up of the ego into the individual sense-experiences. And out of all this there arose in his ego the experience: "Why have I my senses?"[116]

Together with this experience surged the insight that what is connected to the senses and the nervous system is related to the whole periphery of the earth, and that the senses unite the human being with the winter. Out of this realization the pupil could regain a unified condition of soul and surmise that he had experienced forces that come out of the cosmic past and that have a destructive impulse. He understood why this experience had to be preceded and announced by a state of soul numbness.

The experience out of the female statue stood in stark contrast to the first one. The pupil fell into a condition of inner heat that Steiner calls a "fever condition of the soul," which manifested in physical symptoms

---

[114] Steiner, *Mystery Centers*, lecture 8 of December 8, 1923.

[115] In addition to our most obvious five senses, Steiner speaks about another seven, more inner senses. Modern science intuits some of these, as in the instance of the sense of balance; in another instance it lumps some of them together, such as touch and warmth. For more about this matter, see Steiner, *Study of Man*, lecture 7 of August 28, 1919.

[116] Steiner, *Mystery Centers*, lecture 8 of December 8, 1923.

of oppression, heavy breathing, and pulsing of the blood. This was accompanied with anxiety and heaviness that led the pupil to express to himself something like "I have something in me which in my ordinary earth-life is claimed by my corporality. This must be conquered, my earth-ego must be conquered."[117] The second state of being had to be experienced once more for quite a length of time before the pupil came to the realization that this was a familiar state of consciousness, that of the dream, unlike the previous state of soul-numbness that he had not previously known in daily life.

The state of dream evoked in the consciousness marvelous summer landscapes, and the accompanying feelings would range from great joy to intense pain, according to the corresponding expression of the being of summer. He was aware that this dream of summer—not the summer itself—was related to the soul-physical experiences that led to it. And he came to the conclusion "In that which the dream of Summer gives, which I inwardly experience in my human being, in that lies the future."[118]

Not only did the pupil realize what was present in each of the conditions resulting from the two statues; he also realized that the two conditions followed each other in a meaningful way, because he could go from one experience to the other, with a sort of empty stage coming in between them. He knew that the dream of summer offered him a glimpse of the future, and that past and future had met in his soul-life.

The candidate to initiation now started to see the interweaving of past and future, one of the key signatures of the Hibernian Mysteries. He saw in the physical world all that dies in matter, as what appeared to him in the winter imaginations. And he saw how out of this dying surged something like nature dreams that contain the germs of the future. In between this dying and becoming, he perceived the central place of the human being. If the human being were not there, then no dream would come out of the dying; there would be no future following the past. There would be no future Venus, Jupiter, and Vulcan ages of evolution after the Saturn, Sun, and Moon previous Earth conditions.

---

[117] Steiner, *Mystery Centers*, lecture 8 of December 8, 1923.
[118] Steiner, *Mystery Centers*, lecture 8 of December 8, 1923.

Now he could perceive his previous experiences in front of the statues under a new light. This could be summed up in relation to the first statue in the following terms:

In spaces far and wide shalt thou learn
How in Blue of Ether-distance
World-Being first vanishes
And finds itself again in thee.[119]

And in relation to the second statue the experience now echoed in the following words:

In the depths shalt thou solve
The riddle of fever-heated evil
How Truth is enkindled
And through thee finds foundation in Being.[120]

The above were further revelations following the identification of the first statue with Science and of the second with Art. Now it was clear that knowledge acquired by earthly means would always lack Being. True knowledge could be acquired with the words echoing from the first statue by losing oneself in cosmic spaces. Out of the annihilation experienced through the destructive impulses behind the winter landscapes, the pupil would learn to conserve his identity in the vast cosmic distances.

And out of the second statue came what completed this inner process that countered the tendency of fantasy to disregard Truth. He knew that Imaginations could now grow out of his inner being, like the imaginations of plants, animals, or human beings; something that is presently deeply connected with the reality of these plants, animals, or human beings. This was no longer an illusion deprived of Truth, but a deeper penetration of Truth.

The movement from the winter landscape to the dream of summer can be summarized in the ability to encompass spiritually the vast

---

[119] Steiner, *Mystery Centers*, lecture 8 of December 8, 1923.
[120] Steiner, *Mystery Centers*, lecture 8 of December 8, 1923.

cosmic distances, and then return and plunge into the depths of inner being:

> The pupil learned to bring this whole intensity of inner impulse into union with the whole intensity of outer impulse. Out of the relation to the winter landscape and the relation to the summer landscape he has struggled through to explanations concerning external nature and concerning himself; he has become closely related to external nature and to himself.[121]

Thus he unites effectively the paths to the macrocosm and to the microcosm.

What had been achieved up to this point needed now to be recapitulated at a greater stage of consciousness, when the pupil was able to control, recognize, and differentiate each step of the processes that have been described so far. For example, in the experience in front of the first statue, he needed to be able to control and recognize the initial condition of numbness, his moving out towards the cosmic expanses, and his ego feeling multiplied in all the twelve sense-experiences.

When the above was reached in relation to the first statue, the pupil could call back to memory what he had experienced in descending from the spiritual world before birth in relation to his condition of numbness. In moving out into the cosmic distances, a feeling would be evoked of what lay further back into his pre-earthly life, when he was surrounded by all the spiritual hierarchies. And when he evoked the experience of feeling split into twelve, he reached the middle-point of his journey between death and birth.

The other part of the journey was experienced when the pupil could consciously retrace the conditions created by the experience of the second statue. Thus, the initial condition of anxiety and soul distress would lead him to fathoming what immediately follows death. When he passed through the experience of the dream of summer landscapes, he would see the further stages of the journey after death. And when he could render conscious the feelings of oppression in his heart and

---

[121] Steiner, *Mystery Centers*, lecture 8 of December 8, 1923.

breathing, he reached an imagination of the middle point between death and a new birth.

When the pupil had reached maturity for these inner experiences, the initiator would summarize them for the pupil thus:

> *Learn in spirit to see Winter-being*
> *To thee will come the vision of the pre-earthly*

> *Learn in spirit to dream Summer-being*
> *To thee will come experience of the post-earthly.*[122]

Notice here the difference between seeing on one hand and dreaming on the other, which offers a clear differentiation between the two experiences.

Through his insights into the death and continuous regeneration of nature, the candidate to initiation had attained vision into the pre-birth and after-death realms of existence. Other final results could be obtained through consciously revisiting and amplifying the effects of contemplating the statues in the three successive stages.

By entering again the condition of soul numbness generated by the first statue, feeling his body as something foreign to him, and his soul somehow separating from it, the pupil could enter into a conscious beholding of the Moon condition of existence that preceded our present Earth. This was a participatory beholding from within. He felt himself part of a fluid, gelatinous condition, unlike the present liquid state. "And the pupil felt himself within it; he felt himself organized in this half-soft mass, and he felt the organization of the whole planet streaming out from his own organization."[123] He lived in a state of consciousness in which nothing in the environment was anything else than a natural product, not having yet reached a solid state; a place where nothing manmade existed. His own existence felt like part and parcel of the whole planet-Moon existence.

At a second stage, when he overcame the state of numbness and felt his being streaming towards the vast expanses of space and to its

---

[122] Steiner, *Mystery Centers*, lecture 8 of December 8, 1923.
[123] Steiner, *Mystery Centers*, lecture 9 of December 9, 1923.

boundaries, he felt something coming towards him, pressing on him and filling him, which is what we know of as the astral principle. The pupil let himself be filled by the enlivening, refreshing Sun light and heat to the point of feeling inwardly aware of his own bodily organization, to the point of feeling the impressions of and differences between each organ.

The pupil was now living in this element of enlivening, instreaming astral light, which fashioned him and which he could feel as pure, creative Nature-goodness. He knew that these were the powers that gave him form and sustenance. These were impressions of a natural-moral character. The above characterized the pupil's experience of the Sun-existence of the Earth.

When the pupil progressed further to experiencing himself in each of his sense experiences, and felt his ego split up in as many of his senses, he moved back to the beginnings of planetary evolution to the Saturn-existence in which the primal beginnings of humanity found their being and experience in the heat element and its variations. All of the above formed one side of the experience pertaining to the past of Earth evolution.

On the other side, relating to the second statue, he could have a glimpse of the future stages of earth evolution. At the level of this experience lay the feeling of pressure on his breath, of feeling as if he could not breathe out, as if he had to reawaken. This is how he regained access to the summer-dream condition. In this state of being, physical heat was felt at the same time as soul-heat. He had awakened in imagination of what will be the Jupiter condition: "For we shall only become Jupiter-men if we unite physical heat with soul-heat. As Jupiter men we shall come to this, if we caress in love a human being, or it may be a child, we shall be to that child at the same time an actual pourer-forth of heat."[124]

At a next level the pupil had to relive the condition of soul in which he experienced the necessity of overcoming the tendencies towards evil in his own ego. At this stage, light, which was also soul-light, emanated from the heat in the pupil's inner experience, and he had an inner inkling of what would be the reality of future Venus-existence.

---

[124] Steiner, *Mystery Centers*, lecture 9 of December 9, 1923.

At the final stage light became thought, a thought that is engendered by the Word, and he felt himself transported into an imagination of future Vulcan-existence, for "In the Vulcan-planet the Word spreads itself out. Everything in the Vulcan-planet is speaking living Being. Word sounds to Word. Word explains itself by Word. Word speaks to Word. Word learns to understand Word. Man feels himself as the World-understanding Word, as the Word-world understanding Word."[125]

The grandeur of the experiences and vistas opened to the pupil of the Hibernian Mysteries, the breadth of the cosmology embraced in inner experience, explains why Steiner calls these the last Great Mysteries. And in these Mysteries, which spanned in knowledge past, present, and future, the Christ was spoken of as the one to come, in the same way as after Golgotha the Christ would be spoken of as the one who had come in the past. These were truly Saturn Mysteries, the Mysteries of cosmic time, the Mysteries of death and immortality.

In the experience in which the pupil was shown the Christ by the two hierophants, the initiation process showed the candidate that all of earth evolution tended towards the Golgotha event, leading Steiner to conclude:

> There was in fact upon this island, which was later to go through so many trials, a Center of the Great Mysteries, a Center of Christian Mysteries before the Mystery of Golgotha, in which in the right way, the spiritual gaze of a man living before the Mystery of Golgotha was directed towards the Mystery of Golgotha.

At the time of the actual events of Golgotha, in Hibernia great festivals were celebrated that portrayed what was to come in great imaginations; however, these pictures were presented as if they were memories of the past. In fact, "These pictures existed on the island of Hibernia before they could be produced from historic memory of the past, but as they only could be produced out of the Spirit itself."[126]

---

[125] Steiner, *Mystery Centers*, lecture 9 of December 9, 1923.
[126] Steiner, *Mystery Centers*, lecture 9 of December 9, 1923.

Our exploration so far has revealed not only why the Hibernian Mysteries can rightly be called "Great Mysteries" but also why Hibernia "also stands in a certain sense at the starting-point of modern spiritual life, in that it has given impulses to this modern spiritual movement, and yet has taken over much from the older spiritual movements in which the primeval wisdom of man was enshrined."[127] Here Steiner wants to point to both continuity and discontinuity.

As they corresponded to an older type of consciousness, preserved through special conditions in Ireland, the consciousness of the West that Steiner calls "a last echo of the ancient instinctive earth-wisdom"[128] was bound to be overwhelmed by what came from the East as historical consciousness of the events of Golgotha. In Ireland those Mysteries could be preserved because the people of Hibernia were protected from the Luciferic influences and the impulse towards egohood was lessened. Over time modern ordinary consciousness supplanted the ancient wisdom treasures of humanity. It was in effect a time of darkness drawing over the spiritual life of the West.

All of the above indicates as well why the Mysteries of Hibernia were spiritually protected, and why they would repel any but the most serious spiritual researcher, why none but Steiner could reach them in his time, and why even he could only do so only towards the very end of his life. The Hibernian Mysteries could only be disclosed to the one who approached them with deep, inner spiritual activity and with courage. They are as much Mysteries of the past as they are apocalyptic Mysteries of times to come. Spiritual science has rendered them newly accessible.

The relevance of the Hibernian Mysteries for the present comes from the link they formed with the Mysteries of Atlantis. Central to those was the confrontation between black and white magic, which ultimately led to the continent's destruction. Knowledge of the Mysteries revealed the whole dimension of the Earth's apocalypse, the grand vision of earth's evolution as it is tied to the central role of the human being.

The Hibernian Mysteries entailed knowledge of the soul's journey through the underworld. They were Mysteries of death and resurrection,

---

[127] Steiner, *Mystery Centers*, lecture 7 of December 7, 1923.
[128] Steiner, *Mystery Centers*, lecture 9 of December 9, 1923.

Saturn Mysteries, and Steiner encountered their representatives in those individuals whose life after death had received a strong formative impulse in the Saturn sphere. We will therefore turn to the nature of the Saturn beings and to examples of those individuals they influenced most, who had a previous-life experience in the Mysteries of Hibernia.

INDIVIDUALITIES HAVING UNDERGONE HIBERNIAN INITIATION

In *Karmic Relationships*, volume 7, Steiner reveals that the Saturn sphere can only be penetrated, even by the initiate, when he can oversee the span of years going from age fifty-six to sixty-three, the Saturn seven-year phase of life. Saturn beings live in an intense consciousness of the past, and carry little awareness of the present. These are beings who do not gain awareness in the moment; only after the fact can they know with great exactness what they have brought about, and how they have interacted, felt, and thought. It is as if they could perceive imprints of everything that has preceded the present moment; the imprints have become records preserved for eternity. The Saturn beings can behold this immense wealth of records not only of themselves, but of all other cosmic beings throughout planetary evolution. "Saturn Beings may therefore be characterized by saying that they gaze back upon memory, if I may express it, of all the beings of the whole planetary system. Everything is inscribed in this faculty of cosmic remembrance, cosmic memory of the Saturn Beings."[129]

Steiner indicates that not only is this realization shattering; so is the revelation of the karma of those individuals who stand most strongly under their influence. Among these are the French literary giant, Victor Hugo, and the one who has been called the "Italian liberator" or "the hero of two worlds," Giuseppe Garibaldi.

Of Victor Hugo we hear from Steiner that, in the Saturn-sphere,

> He beheld his experiences in the Hibernian Mysteries
> in the light cast by the Saturn Beings over the far,

---

[129] Steiner, *Karmic Relationships*, volume 7, lecture 4.

far distant past, and majestic pictures of pre-earthly times, of Moon periods and Sun periods came alive in him. When he was born again, *all that before his earthly incarnation had been bathed in the past,* colored by the past, *transformed itself into mighty pictures, albeit visionary pictures which cast their light into the future* and came to expression in transcendental romanticism.[130] (emphasis added)

In experiencing these revelations while in the Saturn-sphere, Hugo "forgot the Earth altogether." The Hibernian initiation of Victor Hugo brought to fruition and shed majestic light upon his previous earth lives. In his Hugo incarnation the personality had a firm foothold in the present and carried strong impulses and ideas for the future.

Contrary to Hugo, Garibaldi was a man of action. Still, he carried the Saturn impulses of the Hibernian Mysteries in a way similar to Hugo. And here a contrast is visible in the fact that Garibaldi is eminently fit to stand with both feet planted firmly on the earth—witness his enormous political achievements—and still seems to hover somehow above the earth, living strongly in his own imaginative world.[131]

Garibaldi thought in immediate and seemingly simple ways, baffling his contemporaries to whom he appeared extravagant or illogical. This was because he acted out of deep inner impulses. Most historians are puzzled that after his astounding and successful effort to liberate Italy, he offered the territory as a "gift" to the king of Savoy, Victor Emmanuel, who had little part in its liberation. There is in effect no way to understand his behavior from a purely historical-political logic. Garibaldi acted out of his inner sense of duty towards Victor Emmanuel, who had been a pupil of his in the Hibernian Mysteries. The same can be said in relation to the other two central figures at the beginning of Italian nationhood, Giuseppe Mazzini and the Count of Cavour.

---

[130] Steiner, *Karmic Relationships*, volume 2, lecture 12.
[131] See Steiner, *Karmic Relationships*, volume 7, lecture 5 of June 11, 1924, and *Karmic Relationships*, volume 1, lecture of March 23, 1924.

HOW DOES THE ABOVE RELATE TO TOLKIEN?

Can we not see much of what has been said above in relation to Tolkien? We can, at least on two levels: in relation to his opus and in relation to character and temperament. The opus is the most immediate layer. The personality can best be approached through Tolkien's letters and through the insights of those who observed him most closely, particularly his biographer, Carpenter.

In his opus Tolkien has expressed a view of the infancy of humanity, of pre-history and history, which is startling, to say the least, to those who do not see the deeper wellsprings that shape culture. Why is Tolkien referring to Atlantis and his Great Wave dream over and over again? Why does he bring back the memory of the end of Atlantis at the beginning of the Fourth Age, when Frodo has finally thrown the Ring into the fire of Orodruin? Why does the past echo in the moment that is to announce a future full of possibilities?

Through one of his characters in the unfinished *The Notion Club Papers*, Tolkien tells us that the mythic Númenor (his name for Atlantis) was the dividing line between myth and history. Furthermore, the title of his other unpublished book, *The Lost Road*, points to the "Straight road to the Ancient West" which is no longer possible after the Flood of Atlantis, when the world is "bent."[132] By this Tolkien means that human consciousness is radically changed after the end of Atlantis and that it is no longer possible to sail West to Atlantis or further West to the primeval paradisiacal lands of Eressëa and Valinor.

The constant interweaving of past, present, and future is one of the key signatures of the Hibernian Mysteries that we see present in Tolkien's soul. And in between the two weaves the central event of Golgotha, whose importance is instinctively felt by Tolkien from a historical/mythical perspective. We may remember that this event was presented in Hibernia before the fact as a memory of something that had already happened.

There are a few more threads worth emphasizing that are present in the Hibernian Mysteries as they are in Tolkien's opus. The Saturn Mysteries are the Mysteries of time, of death and immortality, and

---

[132] Carpenter, *J. R. R. Tolkien: A Biography*, 173.

Tolkien refers to the centrality of these themes quite explicitly in his letters when he surveys his work.

In addition Hibernia predicates the continuity with Atlantis in more than one way. Whereas the post-Atlantean Mysteries separate the paths to macrocosm and microcosm, we have seen that these continuously interweave at each step of Hibernian initiation. So do they in the narrative of *The Lord of the Rings*. Gandalf and Frodo represent the two aspects of ascent to the macrocosm and descent into the microcosm that were accomplished side by side in the Hibernian Mysteries. They really act as a higher unity-individuality. The two paths to the microcosm and macrocosm could in effect be imaginations of the historical event that altered all of earth's evolution.

Closely associated to these is the theme of the Double, and the impulses of white and black magic that differentiate in the late stages of Atlantean civilization. These are present in the confrontation between Gandalf and Saruman, or Frodo and Gollum.

Paths to the microcosm and to the macrocosm are also reflected in Tolkien the person. On one hand lies his capacity to participate more fully than his contemporaries in the life of nature. And this is mirrored inwardly in how fully Tolkien relates to the imaginations of myths and legends, to which his contemporaries have little access. The calls to Science and Art of the hierophants of Hibernia seem deeply rooted in his soul. They reappear as an echo rather than what we expect as the fully modern impulses.

It is very tempting, almost logical, to see Tolkien as someone who has little immediate interest in the present or even in what lies in front of him. This is how one could interpret some observations of his biographer, Carpenter:

> It occurs to me that in all externals [Tolkien] resembles the archetypal Oxford don, at times even the stage *caricature* of a don. But that is exactly what he is not. It is rather as if some strange spirit had taken on the guise of an elderly professor. The body may be pacing this

shabby suburban little room, but the mind is far away,
roaming the plains and mountains of Middle-earth.[133]

And Carpenter fathoms much the same when he tunes into Tolkien's
voice, which he qualifies as strange, deep, but without resonance and
"with some quality in it that I cannot define, as if he had come from
another age or civilisation."[134] This elusive quality seems to reflect
Tolkien's feeling that not only himself but the other Inklings were born
out of time.

Owen Barfield observed likewise that Tolkien seemed to have little
interest in social and political events of his time. Barfield is seemingly
right, but only to a certain extent, when he confirms Carpenter.
However, this is not what the record bears, when we dig deeper under
the surface.

Tolkien has actually an intense and deeply anguished interest in the
events of his time. One can in effect realize that his *The Lord of the Rings*
matured through the critical events of World War II, that he needed to
penetrate to the archetype of the confrontation with evil in his time in
order to bring his trilogy to fruition.

In his letters it is not lack of interest in the present that one can
detect, but rather two overlapping streaks: a deeply imaginative way of
relating to modern events, and a rather pessimistic view of the present.
Tolkien, deeply anchored in the past, does not manage to bring his
artistic eschatological panorama fully into his conscious soul. The same
hope that Tolkien offers his readers is the one that eludes him when he
surveys the world around him consciously. Let us hear him on some of
the accounts relating to politics.

Writing in relation to his son Christopher joining the Royal Air
Force, Tolkien calls war an "animal horror,"[135] and further, "The utter
stupid waste of war, not only material but moral and spiritual, is so
staggering to those who have to endure it."[136] Looking at the larger
picture of World War II, his views are summarized in an imagination:

---

[133] Carpenter, *J. R. R. Tolkien: A Biography*, 14.
[134] Carpenter, *J. R. R. Tolkien: A Biography*, 13.
[135] Carpenter, *Letters of J. R. R. Tolkien*, 72.
[136] Carpenter, *Letters of J. R. R. Tolkien*, 75.

"For we are attempting to conquer Sauron with the Ring. And we shall (it seems) succeed. But the penalty is, as you will know, to breed new Saurons, and slowly turn Men and Elves into Orcs. Not that in real life things are as clear cut as in a story."[137] From all of the above we can recognize a deeply original way of looking at the world, "odd" in a similar way as what people may have felt of Garibaldi in his time.

We already saw Tolkien's comments in his letters in relation to British or American imperialism. Tolkien is all but blind or oblivious. His imaginative consciousness points the way to a deeper, rather than shallower understanding of reality, an understanding that isn't easy to communicate to his contemporaries.

One cannot fail to detect with what an anguished heart Tolkien contemplates modern history. His burden is that of having a deeper, not lesser, understanding of the undercurrents of history. It works more efficiently backwards in time than in the future. When he refers to the future, we can see that there are hesitating inklings that he cannot fully affirm, only divine.

In a letter to his son Christopher, Tolkien reasserts as elsewhere his historical pessimism, but adds, "And at the same time one knows that there is always good: much more hidden, much less clearly discerned, seldom breaking out into recognizable, visible beauties of word and deed or face—not even when in fact sanctity, far greater than the visible advertised wickedness, is really there."[138] However, Tolkien cannot fully articulate what this good is, at least not as well as he does from an artistic perspective.

The content of Tolkien's literary legacy with the constant movement from past and present to future and back, the interpenetration of the Mysteries of macrocosm and microcosm in *The Lord of the Rings*, the pervasive tone of his personality, Tolkien's urge to give England a mythology of the West—all consistently point to the legacy of Hibernia.

The above explains something that S. Caldecott detected in relation to Tolkien's effort to locate historical English places in relation to his mythology: "[Tolkien's] mythology was in part an attempt to explain the "Elvishness" of England." Tolkien had originally envisioned the city

---

[137] Carpenter, *Letters of J. R. R. Tolkien*, 78.
[138] Carpenter, *Letters of J. R. R. Tolkien*, 80.

of Avallónë on the coast of the Lonely Isle (Tol Eressëa), as "England itself, before it was invaded and disfigured by Men. The Elvish city of Kortirion was none other than Warwick [close to Birmingham]. . . . But as time went by, In Tolkien's imagination England moved eastward . . . while the Lonely Isle floated westward."[139] Could this be an attempt to recapture memory of the Elvish Hibernia? Tolkien's youthful impulse to write an English mythology may finally more precisely be his soul's attempt to recapture the legacy of the West that came from Hibernia and marked the depth of the English folk soul.

When we look at Tolkien through the lens of spiritual science, we can detect in him the representative of the "true West" that he wanted to be. We can see it in the continuation of the Mysteries of the West that lived in Hibernia, to whose spirit Tolkien seems to be united to the very core. Tolkien is at home with the Saturn impulses of the West. He contemplates the apocalyptic nature of evolution as a matter of fact in his artistic pursuits and carries much of it in his daily consciousness. His artistic output strikes a deep chord in anyone who has at some conscious or preconscious level the fate of the earth at heart. And this brings us to a last aspect of his Saturnian inspiration.

In the archetypal images of the "true West" lies the power of *The Lord of the Rings* over the modern mind. Much of the path of inner devotion and sacrifice that external, materialistic culture abhors is presented with compelling appeal in a book that millions of people have read, people who would not consciously subscribe to Tolkien's message or who would abhor hearing it told from traditional, dogmatic Christian sources. Therefore I cannot but concord with fantasy writer Stephen R. Lawhead when he intuits, "What an extraordinary thing I thought: though Tolkien makes never so much as a glancing reference to Jesus Christ in a single paragraph of all *The Lord of the Rings'* thick volumes, His face is glimpsed on virtually every page."[140] Nothing could have made Tolkien happier.

---

[139] *The Book of Lost Tales*, quoted in Caldecott, *The Power of the Ring*, 142.
[140] Quoted in Pearce, *Tolkien, Man and Myth*, 82.

PART II

Owen Barfield

Chapter 5

Owen Barfield: Evolution of Consciousness and Imagination

Owen Barfield was part of the celebrated circle of the Inklings, much as Tolkien was. The two had little understanding for each other, feeling no doubt that they had little common ground. It was much through C. S. Lewis that bridges could be created and that the two Inklings could find themselves in the same circle.

Owen Barfield, the most future-oriented of the group, had a function that C. S. Lewis dimly intuited, though he could not quite grasp it, seeing Barfield as "Second Friend . . . The man who disagrees with you about everything. He is not so much the *alter ego* as the anti-self." To this G. B. Tennyson counters, "Barfield is not so much our antiself as our better self."[141] What is he meaning with this? The answer lies in Barfield's ability to grasp the realm of ideas as it presents itself in the culture at large—of which Barfield has an extensive knowledge—and to converse with them in order to lead them forward.

Owen Barfield's biography stands in stark contrast to Tolkien's from the fact that Barfield has everything he needs in terms of affluence and material possessions to start with; his biographical challenges lie elsewhere.

---

[141] Barfield, *History, Guilt and Habit*, ix.

CHILDHOOD AND YOUTH

Owen Barfield was born in 1898, the youngest of four. The parents were thinking of calling him Humphrey, so the story goes, before changing their minds on the way to registering his birth and opting for Owen. The family moved from London's suburb of Muswell Hill, where the child was born, to Whetstone, further out from the capital, when he was twelve. Both parents came from large families. His father had not received a formal school education; he exerted as a solicitor. The mother was an ardent feminist, but decided not to be too involved in order not to tarnish her husband's reputation. At age seven or eight Barfield started going to Highgate School, a public [private] school for upper-middle-class children. It had quite a reputation, having being founded in 1585. As soon as he could, Barfield started enthusiastically reading Latin and Greek.

In Barfield's background there was nothing like the influence of Mabel's Catholicism on Tolkien; quite the contrary. In later years Barfield described his family as "predominantly critical and skeptical. Individual enthusiasm was likely to be interpreted as 'a bit humbugging and affectation'"; and himself thus: "I suspected anything in the nature of what seemed like powerful emotional experience, in terms of such things as poetry, as being a kind of self-deception."[142] He distrusted what could come through emotions to the point that he could not immediately trust his own at all, or even be sure of having them.

All in all he grew up in a family without any religious feeling, actually rather anticlerical. In relation to Christianity he grew up in the understanding that it was something like a well-meaning story but with little historical grounding. However, he could detect that his father had a hidden deeper inner reverence for "the moral teachings in the gospels—especially through Tolstoy,"[143] or in such a matter of not allowing his sons to play on their family tennis court on Sunday morning, though it was accepted in the afternoon.

Two experiences of a different nature revealed to the power of the Word in Barfield's early formative years. He first discovered the power

---

[142] Sugerman, *Evolution of Consciousness*, 5.
[143] Sugerman, *Evolution of Consciousness*, 4.

of words after writing on the chalkboard "Mr Kelly [teacher] is a fool" from the reaction that this generated, and the feelings that arose in him in response. Around age twelve, Cecil Harwood, his schoolmate and life-long friend, commenting with keen interest on the beauty of the Latin expression "Cato, eighty years of age, walked out of life." The adult Barfield recollected this was "the actual moment when [I] was first made aware that it was possible to enjoy language *as such*—the very nature of language."[144] He had seen the power of a metaphor. Although he knew about metaphors before, he now realized they could be enjoyed.

From here on, all major developments in Barfield's youth were related for good of for ill with language. It was first of all an inner hindrance that revealed to him the power of the word. Barfield developed a serious stuttering as "he passed from the Shell (the form after Fourth and Remove) to the Fifth Form"[145] to such a point that he could not say anything. This started in 1914, and Barfield himself indicates that the stammering may have had something to do with the beginning of World War I. It was "a great shadow in my life" he commented later. In fact vestiges of this affliction accompanied Barfield all his life long.[146] Facing the failures of therapy, he came close to considering suicide. And in response to this great challenge, the Word responded with poetry.

Barfield discovered what others have perceived in relation to stuttering. In singing or reading poetry, it was considerably relieved. But something more happened through poetry. It was introduced to him by his classics master, who also opened the doors to English literature to the youth. This foundation in classics, both in language and literature, became a cornerstone in Barfield's education and foundational experiences.

Through poetry Barfield grew into the appreciation that the medium offered him more than a relief from stuttering. In it he saw the gift of hope and the possibility of being lifted a little beyond the

---

[144] Blaxland-de Lange, *Owen Barfield*, 28.

[145] Blaxland-de Lange, *Owen Barfield*, 13.

[146] James Wetmore describes Barfield at age ninety-eight as a "man of exceeding literary and spiritual stature but hampered in speech with an ever-invasive stammer." Barfield relates this to "often [feeling] assailed by unbidden childhood memories." James R. Wetmore, "On the Edge of the Unthinkable," 52.

ordinary self. Poetry could alter one's consciousness, even so little. And Barfield pushed here against the limits of family conditioning. Around age twenty, being impacted by the power of poetry, he tried to write some himself. "I tried to convict myself of believing it because I wanted to believe it, I mean of believing that it meant more than just my subjective feelings, and that there was something behind it, more to it."[147] This was also the origin of *Poetic Diction*, which he qualifies as "a theory of poetry as a form of knowledge."

Soon, he was reaching beyond the family's blind spots to society's blind spots. In his adolescence he lived the contrast between the naive optimism in progress of the times, in which he had scarce trust, and the realizations of the growing dead-ends that Western civilization faced. In this pessimistic outlook, poetry, especially lyric poetry, formed a counterweight; he realized here was an oasis in the desert of materialistic culture. He saw that the world acquired a deeper depth and meaning when seen through the eyes of certain poets. "Poetry had the power to change one's consciousness a little."[148] And this he could also approach from the perspective of the development of language, in effect philology. The power of poetry, experienced as a life-saver and giver of hope, awakened new questions in the young soul, and the desire to understand this power of poetry, residing in the Word, led him to work counterculturally.

Barfield later commented that "the way in which a particular word, in a particular passage, in a particular context, produces a kind of magic which alters the meaning of the word, gives the word an entirely new meaning." Restating this, "The poet has given new meaning to the word by the particular context and the way he uses it."[149] The other aspect that struck Barfield was the revelatory quality of poetry. After reading Wordsworth: "It isn't just the poetry you enjoy. When you go back to the mountains or the woods afterwards they are something different." The above leads him to see "that poetry is a form of knowledge, because you felt you knew more about the things you see, about what you were looking at." And more precisely (in the Introduction to *Romanticism*

---

[147] Sugerman, *Evolution of Consciousness*, 6.
[148] Blaxland-de Lange, *Owen Barfield*, 101.
[149] Sugerman, *Evolution of Consciousness*, 6.

Comes of Age), "I had had two things strongly impressed on me, firstly that the poetic or imaginative use of words enhances their meanings and secondly that those enhanced meanings may reveal hitherto unapprehended parts or aspects of reality."[150]

At the same time that he was turning to the word, Barfield deepened his appreciation for music and rhythm. From his childhood he had acquired love for music, which he could hear from his parents who both played the piano. In later years he characterized his deep interest in music in a way that may have been something of an overstatement: "Supposing (a wildly hypothetical question) you were offered the choice of doing without any poetry for the rest of your life or doing without any music, well—I would give up the poetry."[151]

In high school through his interest in gymnastics he had become Highgate's senior gymnast. Combining this with music was something natural, and this led him to dancing, which was to occupy his further years and offer him important karmic connections. In Morris dancing, the intense physical exertion and the music brought him into a realm of quasi-mystical inner experience. Language and literature on one hand, music and dance on the other were to form two overlapping themes in Barfield's twenties, before reaching the first literary turning points. The formative friendships in and around the Inklings added another dimension to the whole. This was itself interwoven with another theme; his meeting with Anthroposophy.

When he entered Wadham College in Oxford (1919 to 1923) Barfield turned away from Latin and Greek, deciding to dedicate himself to English literature. And philology became a central focus, particularly the evolution of words in relation to human consciousness. At the time he published some articles in magazines, among them "The Reader's Eye" in the *Cornhill Magazine*, all about what effect can have some good poetry on the reader; and "Form in Poetry" in *The New Statesman*, of which more will be said below. These were Barfield's first attempts to consider how poetry works on human consciousness.

While in Oxford, Barfield started going to Cornwall in the summer with a troupe of musicians. Part of this travel was organized by the three

---

[150] Sugerman, *Evolution of Consciousness*, 7.
[151] Sugerman, *Evolution of Consciousness*, 4.

Radford sisters who wanted to take the music to the Cornish villages. One summer Barfield became infatuated with a young woman, a cousin of the Radfords, who did not return his interest, an episode that led to a time of depression and despair. In retrospective Barfield saw this as part of "being caged in the materialism of the age."[152]

The way he characterized the episode at the time, to his friend Leo Baker in August 1920, is quite expressive of the larger backdrop of the crisis.

> I am being forced in on myself like an ingrowing toenail. It has come to such a pass that I seem to be living in a land of dream. My self is the only thing that exists, and I wear the external world about me like a suit of clothes—my own body included. . . . When I am alone at night, I sometimes feel frightened of the silence ringing in my ears. Something inside me seems to be so intensely and burningly alive, and everything round me so starkly dead."[153]

Here Barfield seems to be describing quite accurately the universal condition of the human being standing at the abyss. However, a part of him can observe things with detachment.

The heavy, dark cloud did not dissolve for years of what he later called "acute depression." This lasted until a trip to Switzerland when, at the very end of his stay, "suddenly one evening, one fine evening . . . the clouds sort of lifted—I know this sounds very dramatic, but it is rather essential—all the misery that I had felt, all this lifted with it."[154] At that time he wrote nine sonnets, which were published in the *London Mercury*.

In retrospect Barfield assessed *Poetic Diction* as "a way of looking back to that time, a kind of development from this—what I call— Sophia experience."[155] Barfield also commented about the episode that

---

[152] Blaxland-de Lange, *Owen Barfield*, 20.
[153] Blaxland-de Lange, *Owen Barfield*, 104.
[154] Blaxland-de Lange, *Owen Barfield*, 104.
[155] Blaxland-de Lange, *Owen Barfield*, 21.

he knew he "would be able to find all the beauty I had fallen for in this woman in the whole world of nature." And so it was since he now felt able to experience in life what art had brought him through the poetry of Keats, Shelley, Shakespeare, and the Georgian poets. He was now firmly grounded in what would be his cardinal impulse: understanding the evolution of human consciousness.

It was also at this time that Barfield strengthened his relationship with Maud Douie, who would soon become his wife. Maud had a great love for music, singing, and dancing. At that time Barfield was very much involved with the musical projects of Maud; he also produced a little show with her, which they called a "children's theater." After marrying Maud, Barfield wasn't earning a living, while she had some little savings. About this period in his life he said, "For six or seven years I was a gentleman of leisure, much of which I spent writing *History in English Words* and *Poetic Diction*."[156]

Barfield endeavored to find a home within the literary tastes of the age. His major biographical struggle lay in finding that cultural ground in which his questions could find an answer, but there was very little that could truly help him. Looking backwards he could see most of all the beacon of the Romantics; forward only Anthroposophy could satisfy his deeper yearnings. And this is summed up in his wanting "Romanticism to come of age."

In 1929 Barfield went to Bonn for three months and worked at his unpublished novel "English People." The manuscript was rejected by various publishers, and at this time he realized he would need to earn his living in some other way. Maud's distancing from Anthroposophy ruled out getting more deeply involved with it, such as becoming a teacher in a Steiner School. This led him to joining his father's legal firm around 1929. Here we can sense another theme in the inner tug of war that leads him to Anthroposophy and that which pulls him away from it. This tension paradoxically opened the doors to new possibilities. What Maud played in a seemingly negative way, the Inklings played in a positive fashion. Here was a natural platform of expression for the budding writer and scholar.

---

[156] Sugerman, *Evolution of Consciousness*, 11.

In Barfield's youth, some themes were deeply interwoven. His interests led him to the oasis of Romantic poetry, which led him beyond what he perceived as the cultural desert of the present. Anthroposophy lay in waiting, so to speak, since it figured so prominently in his friendships, particularly with Leo Baker and Cecil and Marguerite Harwood. One could say it was just a matter of time before Barfield would understand the stature of Rudolf Steiner and his teachings, and the place they could occupy in the modern cultural desert. On the other hand, his friendships and the timing of his studies led him in the direction of one of the most active and lively places of cultural interchange of the times: the circle of the Inklings in which his friendship with C. S. Lewis, established in 1919, played a central role.

APPROACHING ANTHROPOSOPHY AND EVOLVING HIS OWN WORK

Barfield appreciated the creative power of the poet, "the way in which a particular word, in a particular passage, in a particular context, produces a kind of magic which alters the meaning of the word, gives the word an entirely new meaning."[157] The other aspect that struck Barfield was the revelatory quality of poetry. After reading some of the most insightful poetry, Barfield felt that the object he had enjoyed in a poem, be it a creek, a mountain, or the woods, became a fuller life experience afterwards, leading him to recognize poetry as a form of knowledge.

Barfield wrote a first essay, "Form and Poetry," on the above question in the *New Statesman*. It was a response to a critic's sole concern with poetry's external form at the detriment of its content. Among other things, he commented that every word of the poem was "the final record for each person of the whole series of thoughts or sense-impressions received by him every time he has spoken or heard that word."[158] Here he is pointing out that words are rich repositories of meaning, especially when used in poetry.

---

[157] Sugerman, *Evolution of Consciousness*, 6.
[158] Blaxland-de Lange, *Owen Barfield*, 106.

A second article was a piece of original philological research on the origin and evolution of the word *ruin*. Part of this was included in the later *Poetic Diction*. Here he looked at how the word evolved from its first meaning, imbued with movement, into the fixed result of that movement. He explored all the nuances of meaning that had been added to it by the work of Chaucer, Gower, Spenser, and Shakespeare.

We can see that from this original love for the experience of poetry naturally emerged his love for the word and philology, which indicated that word meaning evolved in time. This is what launched him into the matter of evolution of consciousness. It was only natural that these original inclinations be amplified in the meeting with Anthroposophy.

Thanks to Astrid Diener's research, it is possible to place Barfield's first commitment to Anthroposophy being kindled by at least early July 1923, date at which Lewis recorded it in his diary.[159] Barfield's encounter with Anthroposophy is best described in his "Owen Barfield and the Origin of Language" 1977 lecture. Barfield first heard of Rudolf Steiner by the end of 1921 or beginning of 1922 and began to read some of his lectures; the aura of Theosophy that still lingered around Steiner's circles put him off somehow. At that time, he later realized, he was still under the spell of Darwin's theory of evolution. Barfield stated that Steiner's *Philosophy of Spiritual Activity* allowed him to overcome his own "residue of undigested positivism" and to see that Coleridge had done the same.[160]

His first positive response to Anthroposophy echoed and magnified his reaction to the power of poetry. He realized that three experiences were somehow equivalent:

5. "The discovery that the forms of language created by poets produced a certain change of consciousness"
6. "Older forms of language . . . could produce a similar change, as it were of their own accord"
7. "The often surprising things that Rudolf Steiner reported with such confidence as the findings of his spiritual research, acted on him in the same way as did poetic or figurative language."

---

[159] Diener, *The Role of Imagination in Culture and Society*, 92.
[160] Sugerman, *Evolution of Consciousness*, 16.

This for him was an objective change regardless of belief or disbelief.[161]

Barfield had been prepared for the encounter with Steiner by a series of close karmic connections. His friends Leo Baker (priest in the Christian Community), and Cecil Harwood and his wife Marguerite, had already been interested before him. With them he started going to some weekly lecture readings at the house of George Kaufman (later Adams).

Barfield did not become a blind adherent, nor did he accept everything at once. He continued his process of studying language side by side with Anthroposophy. Thus for example he discovered only after some time that what he was calling "original participation" was equivalent to Steiner's "atavistic consciousness." He further realized that "Anthroposophy included and transcended not only my own poor stammering theory of poetry as knowledge, but the whole Romantic philosophy. It was nothing less than Romanticism grown up."[162]

Barfield joined the Anthroposophical Society most likely in 1923. In meeting Anthroposophy Barfield immediately realized the importance of the *Philosophy of Spiritual Activity* and launched into a deep study of it. He finally attended a lecture on August 24, 1924, in which Steiner spoke of Laurence Oliphant and his previous incarnation as Ovid, and regretted declining an interview with Steiner, offered to him by George Adams.

By this time, nevertheless, he had fully realized the weight that spiritual science could add to all his personal research, particularly in relation to the evolution of consciousness:

> The essence of Steiner's teachings . . . is the evolution of human consciousness. . . . I, in a way, came to the same conclusion on my own before I heard of Steiner. He began where I left off. *All I had done was to establish, in a hostile intellectual atmosphere,* that there *was* such a thing as the evolution of consciousness from a more

---

[161] Barfield, *Romanticism Comes of Age*, 199.
[162] Barfield, *Romanticism Comes of Age*, 201.

pictorial, more living, if you like, form or quality to our own. He assumes that, to start with, and builds on that this terrific edifice.[163] (emphasis added)

Here a theme emerges that will appear in our later explorations. Barfield's soul journey led him from the experience of the death of culture in modern times as his own soul death, to what could carry him to the other side, and what he could offer to his contemporaries.

Summarizing his path into Anthroposophy, Barfield reminds us of how he pursues his path into Anthroposophy with an alternation of resistance and acceptance, until coming to a firm conviction. And along this path came the "very welcome (and for this reason very suspect)" discovery of the central place of Christ. In this he had to struggle through the culture of his upbringing that meant in him "almost a conviction that *any* theory implying that the world as a whole has any meaning, let alone a spiritual source, *must* be due to subjective wish-fulfillment." Here Barfield is saved from this inner tug of war by "how precisely it fit with his own halting notion of the development of meaning in language."[164]

At this early stage of his life Barfield launched into great literary activity, publishing books, poems, and essays. And these would spell out very rigorous ideas about the evolution of consciousness.

POETRY AND THE EVOLUTION OF CONSCIOUSNESS

Barfield left us both books of essays and others of pure fiction. In between stand his semi-autobiographical books to which we will turn in the next chapter. Much of Barfield's literary activity stood in service to the English-speaking world (though not only) in countering the positivistic materialistic trends of the time, with a thinking that offers insight into the primacy of the spirit in all things material.

Barfield reached a certain level of success beyond Anthroposophical circles. His short residence in the United States served to spread his

---

[163] Blaxland-de Lange, *Owen Barfield*, 109.
[164] Barfield, *Owen Barfield and the Origin of Language*.

message to the wider world. In time the references to the legacy of Rudolf Steiner became more and more explicit in his writings, though he always respected the individual's freedom in pursuing truth up to its sources.

Barfield's works are a powerful ladder for the seeker. For many it may be a first and unsuccessful attempt that may ripen in the future. For others Barfield opens whole new vistas that effectively challenge the death of culture in present time and offer viable alternatives. For a smaller, but still very significant portion, Barfield is not only the inspiration to stand in the world in a new manner; he is also the door to the whole new world of spiritual science. As we will assert at the end of the next chapter Barfield is a herald of Anthroposophy for the time and the people of the consciousness soul. He is the one who can bring them to the door, encourage them to knock and enter.

We will therefore look at Barfield's cardinal ideas in this chapter before turning to Barfield's deeper being in the next. The next step will be possible through Barfield's own autobiography, and the books that carry much of his own journey, particularly *This Ever Diverse Pair* (1950), *Unancestral Voice* (1965), and to some degree *Worlds Apart* (1963).

Barfield primarily dealt with the art that was most conducive to his inquiry into consciousness and its evolution. In his own words, poetry is unique among the arts in as much as "consciousness is also the actual *material* in which she works. Consciousness is to her what their various mediums (marble, pigments, etc.) are to the other arts; for words themselves are but . . . symbols of consciousness."[165]

Poetic Dictin reflects in its genesis the rise of Barfield's early burning questions and their interaction in the meeting with Anthroposophy, in the following stages:

- At first reading poetry without having a formed opinion or set expectations about it.
- Later realizing that poetry changes and enhances the meanings of the words it uses.
- Envisioning the book as what he called an "academic exercise."

---

[165] Barfield, *Poetic Diction*, Appendix 1: Note on Chapter 1, 182.

- Leaving the book aside for a time until he came across Steiner's work, which offered him the missing perspective he needed to further his initial effort.

Barfield recognizes as the debt owed to Steiner a kind of thinking imbued with the "utmost intensity of feeling," but a feeling that is no longer personal exactly because it has reached this level of intensity. This is reflected in the professed methodology of his approach.

In the preface to the first edition, Barfield tells us that the book unfolds from phenomena to general principles and from those back again to phenomena. In speaking about poetry Barfield purports to start from his inner experiences, including what for him is poetry and what is not. However, he adds that he will start from personal experience but not finish with it. In fact the book goes beyond a theory about poetry; it points the way at the same time to a theory of knowledge.

The element of imagination, proper to poetry, is present throughout the book, as in all other books, inasmuch as "the 'general principles' take the form rather of pictures and metaphors than of propositions."[166] In fact the imaginative element in the writing is rife with the imaginative content of fresh metaphors.

Barfield has rendered accessible a number of ideas that cannot be easily separated, since they build upon and reinforce each other. For the sake of clarity we will look at the evolution of consciousness as related to language, the essence and role of imagination, and the central concept of polarity.

Barfield has us realize that the further back we move in history, the more the meanings of common words tend to the concrete. The Greek word *pneuma* can be translated as "wind," "breath," or "spirit." But originally the word had an encompassing meaning, which only later split into three or more. The same that happens in phylogenesis is recapitulated in ontogenesis. The child who says "dad" refers the same word and meaning to a variety of objects. He will only learn to separate and differentiate later on.

Most modern philologists see the rise of metaphor twice. And since metaphor in our time is preceded by individualized thinking, they

---

[166] Barfield, *Poetic Diction*, 4.

assume that the same was true of early metaphor; hence the theory of root sounds from which arose the early metaphors. They fail to see that individualized, conscious metaphor was preceded by unconscious, or preconscious, and preindividualized metaphor.

Barfield characterizes the early stage as "the 'metaphorical period' of humanity, a wonderful age when a race of anonymous and mighty poets took hold of a bald inventory and saturated it with poetic values."[167] If we look more closely we can separate various periods in the evolving relationship between language and consciousness:

- The first poetic diction developed in the concrete language of mythologies. Here primary meanings arose out of nature. Since they are given, they cannot be apprehended consciously; they could not be understood, only experienced. The human being could not create yet; only the Gods could.
- At this stage literature and poetry were rhythmical, just as nature is rhythmic. This was expressed in the metrical form, which arose "when men were conscious, not merely of their heads, but in the beating of their hearts and the pulsing of their blood—when thinking was not merely of Nature, but was Nature herself."[168]
- After a long interval arose the written records of the Vedas, the Odyssey, the Iliad, in which we find meaning emerging from myth, and nature imbuing human thinking. At this stage the poet was seen as "'possessed' by some foreign being, a god or angel, who gave utterance through his mouth, and gave it only as and when it chose."[169]
- The balance was destroyed in the transition from Plato to Aristotle, whose logic and Categories were refinements of pure thought, though a thought that could still apprehend spiritual reality. Now the individual poets entered the stage of history.
- Gradually the purely rational gained ascendancy, and language gradually lost its intrinsic life. The grammatical structure of

---

[167] Barfield, *Poetic Diction*, 76.
[168] Barfield, *Poetic Diction*, 144.
[169] Barfield, *Poetic Diction*, 103.

language hardened. This evolution was accompanied by new antitheses such as truth and myth, poetry and prose (rational), objective and subjective. At the point of balance between the two principles (rational and poetic) often appeared the great poets of a culture (e.g., Dante, Shakespeare). It is shortly before Shakespeare that prose was used experimentally as an imaginative medium.

It is interesting to note that Shakespeare coined more new words than any other English writer; this means he unearthed new meaning. He fathered such words as *pedant*, *critic*, and *majestic*. He was also the first to use the words *create*, *religion*, and *magic* in a context and in reference to other than supernatural objects. The same is true for transferring the words *anguish*, *bounty*, *mercy*, *comfort*, *compassion*, and *devotion* from a religious to a secular context. He was also the first to use the word *inherit* for the passing down of moral and physical qualities.

– Summarizing all of the above and announcing future themes, Barfield concludes: "The progress is from Meaning [here meaning is given and of transcendental origin], through inspiration to imagination, and from imagination, through metaphor, to meaning; inspiration grasping the hitherto unapprehended, and imagination relating it to the already known."[170]

In turning to Coleridge, Barfield agrees that "Poetry is the best words in the best order," and comments, "in other words it's the best language." This reality of poetry, or of the best poetry, brings about "a 'felt change of consciousness,' where 'consciousness' embraces all my awareness of my surroundings at any given moment, and 'surroundings' includes my own feelings."[171] This felt change of consciousness is the key element in appreciation of poetry. The moment of change gives rise to artistic pleasure. Barfield likens this change of consciousness to what we retrieve from dreams when we return to waking consciousness. The feeling of pleasure is tied to the experience of change.

---

[170] Barfield, *Poetic Diction*, 148.
[171] Barfield, *Poetic Diction*, 40.

In the highest examples of poetry we can achieve an "expansion of consciousness." Referring to such an example from Shelley's poetry, Barfield says that "the image contains so much truth and beauty that henceforth the eyes with which I behold real boats and waves and swans, the ears with which in the right mood I listen to a song, are actually somehow different."[172] The act of internalizing the metaphors of such a poem not only enables us to perceive something new; it also contributes to the emergence of new soul faculties that render such new perceptions possible. The appreciation of poetry and the awakening of new faculties is a ladder taking us from knowledge to wisdom,

In examples like the above, poetry becomes the gateway for a consciousness able to perceive and think the world with both intellect and "utmost intensity of feeling." Neither conscious understanding nor intensity of feeling take an exclusive role; rather, they reinforce each other. We are talking here of what Barfield at times characterizes, in borrowing Coleridge's terminology, as "secondary imagination."

IMAGINATION

In line with Coleridge, Barfield distinguishes the everyday primary imagination, through which all human beings naturally make sense of their world, from the secondary imagination, which needs to be cultivated and developed. It was Coleridge who introduced the term *imagination* with a fresh new meaning, particularly in its exact differentiation of the term from *fancy*. The first denotes an exact soul faculty leading to lawful images and an enhancement of thinking; the second an arbitrary use of images.

The world around us cannot be perceived by pure perception; perception has to be complemented by the presence of imagination to bring forth from within what allows us to comprehend the pure sense phenomena and understand the world. It is our primary imagination of "cat," "door," or "table" that allows us to separate from the jumble of perceptions what belongs to cat, door, or table. In a world without the sediments of the previous collective efforts of imagination, we would be

---

[172] Barfield, *Poetic Diction*, 47.

assaulted by a perpetual stream of undifferentiated perceptions devoid of meaning. It is imagination that allows us to restore the sense of unity that perception alone cannot give us. What differentiates primary imagination from secondary is the fact that the first one proceeds unconsciously.

In poetry and the arts, though by no means automatic, imagination can be cultivated consciously. In the specific case of poetic activity, the primary imagination makes things, whereas secondary imagination produces meaning.

When this activity of secondary imagination is more consciously turned to the act of perception, as in Goethe's phenomenological science, nature is grasped in an act of participation rather than detached observation. If secondary imagination is not used in poetry, then the poetry of the times mirrors the habits of mind of an age. In the contrary case, as Shelley asserts, the poet is actively creating the taste by which they can be appreciated; this explains why they are often appreciated posthumously.

POLARITY

Through imagination we can reconcile what in nature and in human consciousness we would otherwise perceive as unreconcilable opposites; life and death, wakefulness and sleep, light and darkness, expansion and contraction, lightness and heaviness, etc.

In nature these opposites work in and through each other. They are like parts of a continuum, where one of the two, though predominant, always works with the other. Our dualistic understanding bound to the senses cannot reconcile the interpenetration of polar opposites. It is only through what has been called secondary imagination that we can behold both sides of a polarity and reach a fuller, conscious participation with the phenomena of nature.

What was unconscious in earlier stages of humanity can now be gained through an imaginative and participatory consciousness. The early Indians, Egyptians, or Greeks, or indigenous people still relatively untouched by modern civilization, who lived in the perceived reality of myth could experience a fuller dimension of reality but could not reflect back and articulate it to a self that lived separately from it. Modern human beings have the possibility and challenge to gain a new sense of communion, in conjunction with an awareness of self.

For Barfield the attainment of imagination has far-reaching evolutionary implications.

> The function of imagination is to materialize spirit, using imagination in the sense that has mostly being given to the word since the Romantic movement or a little earlier. But if you look at it in terms of evolution of consciousness, you would more accurately say that only the first stage, the first half if I may put it so crudely, of evolution can be characterized as the materialization of spirit; but the second part—that is, the progress in the direction of final participation—is really the opposite. It's the spiritualization of matter.[173]

The human being's participation through consciousness—final participation—does not affect only the human being itself; it affects our objective world through the spiritualization of matter.

In being able to produce imaginations, we increase the element of will in our thinking, and this also increases our capacity to seek for the truth. In final participation a "cosmic consciousness" holds sway that does not do away with individual consciousness.

Participation in the world, consciousness of self, form the terms of a polarity. This could be expressed as outer and inner worlds. To the awakened consciousness, polarity is the stuff and substance of both outer and inner worlds; and the world is alive with and animated by polarity after polarity.

We can now look back at what we have been describing up until now. In looking at the evolution of language and consciousness, Barfield has introduced us to two opposing principles—the rational/prosaic and the poetic, another example of polarity. Through the rational principle,

---

[173] Sugerman, *Evolution of Consciousness*, 26.

single meanings split up into a number of separate, different concepts. This is therefore the principle that differentiates.

The poetic is the principle of "living unity." It looks at the commonalities and similarities between objects. We could say that the poetic principle is interested in what things are, in the deeper essence of things; the rational principle can only tell us what they are not. The rational/prosaic gradually overtook the poetic in the history of humankind.

The individual poet of more recent times is the one who can intuit relationships that others do not see, that the culture has forgotten, and bring them forth through metaphors. "In Platonic terms we should say that the rational principle can increase *understanding*, and it can increase *true opinion*, but it can never increase *knowledge*."[174]

In the timeless dimension polarity corresponds to what Coleridge calls "two forces of one Power." The higher unity outside of time becomes opposition at the level of time. Seen from the perspective of eternity, union and opposition are present simultaneously and all the time. "Conceived as a process in time . . . unity comes before the separation of tension and opposition is restored afterwards."[175] In fact the higher the opposition, the greater is the unity.

It is through polarity that we can as human beings become truly individualized and truly universal; in fact the more individual, the more universal one becomes. This is a primeval, existential kind of polarity. At the intellectual level, polarity is a paradox; at the level of experience it is lived as a mystery. Only through imagination can it be both understood and experienced.

Contemporary science limits itself to observing nature in its quantitative aspects. The qualitative aspect does not enter scientific consideration unless it can be turned into a quantitative analysis, but then we are back to square one, so to speak. Science relies exclusively on passive sense experience. Qualities per se are "occult," cannot be seen without an active sense experience. Reconciling the terms of polarity that are present in the world of qualities can be done by bringing together the analytical element of thought with the feeling element in art.

---

[174] Barfield, *Poetic Diction*, 141.
[175] Sugerman, *Evolution of Consciousness*, 20.

Bringing together the rigorous scientific analysis and the feeling/artistic perception, Goethe brought science to a new level. He transformed passive thinking into active, living thinking. He achieved imagination, and went beyond to a sense-free perception of the archetypal level of reality.

Barfield lived in the world of imagination and polarity. This made him an accomplished poet, in essence and in fact. He was a poet in the art of poetry itself, and a poet in the expression of ideas. And what Barfield says about the modern poet, he could have said about himself.

The two principles, poetic and rational/prosaic, correspond to two forms of consciousness, but they alternate with each other much more readily and quickly in the mind of the modern poet. The modern poet can write poetry, but he can only appreciate it when he looks back to it; when he steps out of the poetic mood into the rational mood. The rational principle cannot create, but it allows appreciation. Writing a poem about love means being immersed in the mood of love, but being able to look at it objectively and appreciate it implies stepping out of that mood.

The modern poet has to fight against a language that has become more and more fragmented and codified. The language has increased in structure and fixity because it has become more and more rational and specific. And the modern poet can thus only find the poetic principle in himself. In the sense that the poet "fights *against* language, making up the poetic deficit out of his private balance—in this kind it is perfectly true to call the poet the creator, or re-creator of meaning itself." Here creation means "the bringing farther into consciousness of something which already exists as unconscious life."[176]

At present the poet must be strong in the rational principle as well as in the poetic. And since consciousness is the building material of poetry, a great poet must be a great mind, and be at home in abstract thinking. As examples of these Barfield brings forth Keats, Shelley, Milton, Dante, and naturally Shakespeare.

Commenting that some poets, of a seer/prophet kind, may have little rational principle in themselves, and therefore need an interpreter, Barfield points to the other possibility. The more balanced the two

---

[176] Owen Barfield, *Poetic Diction*, 106.

principles, the more the poet has control over the source of his inspiration, and no interpreter is needed. This means that the great poet is also a great critic.

Looking towards the future, Barfield concludes, "There is nothing to prevent us looking forward to a time . . . by the personal endeavor of poets themselves towards increased self-knowledge and self-control—at which point at last the poet shall be creating out of full self-consciousness."[177]

---

[177] Ibid, 104.

Chapter 6

Karmic Themes: The Paths Outward and Inward

―――――――――――――――――

Barfield strives to show his contemporaries the way to imagination, which offers a new relationship to knowledge and a new place in the world. He can be considered a herald of the redemption of the Consciousness Soul in the English-speaking countries, and more broadly of the human being of the Consciousness Soul of the present. He serves that purpose to all who struggle with the separation and emptiness of the Consciousness Soul and therefore the need to strive beyond what is given through it.

Barfield not only illuminates the way to the attainment of imagination. He also shows us how this imagination has been reached in a single individual, in Barfield himself, through those that are his most autobiographical books. Through some of his most striking works of fantasy, two of which will be explored in the next chapter, he also shows us examples of artistic imaginations.

We will look at various aspects of Barfield's life in order to get to the deeper Barfield as an archetype of the striving human being of the time of the Consciousness Soul, who wants to reach genuine spiritual insight and alter his relationship to environment and self. Two themes closely intertwine in the author's life. We have looked at the importance of his meeting with Anthroposophy. We will now explore his relationship to C. S. Lewis, which was central to his literary pursuits.

Along the way to achievement of imagination Barfield meets the one he calls "Burden," who is more than a literary device; a force in Barfield's life, both personal and universal. The attainment of imagination places Barfield in relationship to Michael, the being of Anthroposophia, and the Christ. This is once more a universal journey that Barfield illustrates in his own particular instance.

In this personal/universal journey Barfield offers us a blueprint of human development towards the spirit at the time of the Consciousness Soul. He completes this movement in turning to Anthroposophy, and therefore looking towards the spirit of Central Europe, from which spiritual science takes its origin. Once more he offers us a deeply archetypal image, of what is needed in the West in modern times.

KARMIC CONNECTIONS: EXTERNAL CULTURE (C. S. LEWIS AND TOLKIEN)

Barfield tells us he discovered Anthroposophy "almost the same year I was married [1923]; and she reacted very strongly against anthroposophy. . . . It was a kind of sword through the marriage knot, right through, almost right through; though we had enough in common to get on pretty well together."[178] This influenced Barfield's career path to a great degree.

When the manuscript of *English People* was rejected by various publishers, Barfield realized he would need to earn his living in some other way. Maud's distancing from Anthroposophy ruled out working directly within it. These circumstances led him to joining his father's legal firm, very likely in 1929. We will turn to what this meant for Barfield shortly.

One door closed in one direction, while another door opened up that led to the influential group the Inklings, starting with one of Barfield's most important karmic connections. C. S. Lewis and Barfield met in the fall of 1919 in Oxford, while studying as undergraduates. Their love for literature, philosophy, and the classics formed a rich common ground. Soon after, the circle enlarged to Leo Baker, Cecil Harwood, and W. Eric Beckett. They gathered to explore and debate

---

[178] Blaxland-de Lange, *Owen Barfield*, 31.

literature, philosophy, religion, mythology, art, etc. This offered a taste of what the later Inklings would be, and strengthened the friendship between Lewis and Barfield.

Much of the famous "Great War" of ideas between Lewis and Barfield was fought in "walking tours" of Barfield's inspiration, philosophical disputes that would go from woods and fields to pubs and last from one afternoon to various days. For Barfield, no doubt, the Great War sharpened his intellect and offered an informed firsthand audience for presenting his ideas in the most efficient way. At bottom the debates were seemingly unsuccessful for their first objective, since Lewis was unable to accept or understand the concept of polarity or the reality of imagination. However, they led to so much more in Barfield's life.

Barfield was keenly aware of the continuity of the thread that ran through his whole life, commenting that though there was an early and a later Lewis, there was in a sense only one Barfield. One Barfield, two Lewises is a universal formula of the choices that are possible at the time of the Consciousness Soul. We live in the time of detachment, separation, alienation. Barfield was aware of this dilemma since his early days. He was offered the possible horizon of inner unity from the meeting with Anthroposophy.

The culture that he met around himself, Lewis no more nor less than others, knew this inner split of soul. Barfield met it in his friend and conversed with it deeply. Lewis felt this split in a different way; it was projected outwardly. In his *Surprised by Joy*, Lewis called Barfield his "Second Friend" and his "anti-self."[179] G. B. Tennyson in the introduction to *History, Guilt and Habit* argues that this anti-self could be called the "better self." In fact there was nobody Lewis admired more than his friend, as in his testimony that "Barfield towers above us all." And this ambivalent admiration continued in later years. At the end of 1954, when leaving Magdalen College Oxford, Lewis wanted Barfield to succeed him. Everything was set for this to happen. Nevertheless Barfield was turned down on the basis, spurious or real, that he was too old.

---

[179] Zaleski and Zaleski, *The Fellowship*, 110.

This split of soul that he detected among others in one of his closest friends occupied Barfield's mind over a long period of time. *Orpheus* was written around 1950; conceived as the fusion of two Greek myths; it is difficult for an audience to immerse into it without a previous knowledge of Greek mythology. At the origin of the poetic drama were Barfield's observations about Lewis. There was something that mystified him about his friend after the year 1935. He wrote in his letters that Lewis was somehow "no longer fully present in what he said" and that what he said sounded hollow, especially in comparison to the earlier Lewis. Barfield explains in relation to the writing of the drama:

> From about 1935 onward . . . I had the impression of living with, not one but two Lewises; and this was so as well when I was enjoying his company, as when I was absent from him. . . . This experience gradually became something like an obsession with me, and it must have been somewhere about 1950 . . . that I made it part of the emotional base for a long narrative poem [*Riders on Pegasus*, unpublished].[180]

Barfield, knowing his friend's analytical bent and his work with fiction, hoped he could offer a way to reconcile and unite the passions in his breast. But the door to phenomenological science or to Anthroposophy remained closed to Lewis, who admitted "the works of Dr. Steiner are extremely difficult reading: unassisted popular opinion of them is likely to be no more reliable than the same opinion on Kant or Whitehead."[181] Lewis could hope that a smaller step would be possible for his friend: the apprehension of the nature of imagination, which had been central to the themes of the Great War.

In the same letter quoted above, Lewis shows another tension that compounds the intellectual tension in his soul. If spiritual science is an infatuation he should free his friend from, why can he not detect the signs of imbalance that it should produce, not just in Barfield, but in his other Anthroposophical friends? In another letter Lewis faces the

---

[180] Blaxland-de Lange, *Owen Barfield*, 266.
[181] Blaxland-de Lange, *Owen Barfield*, 174.

dilemma that it isn't easy to write off Barfield as a madman infatuated with Steiner:

> Being frequently in controversy with my anthroposophical friends on this subject [the rightness of Steiner's ideas], I believe I should have been very quick to notice any evidence that adherence to the system was producing either intellectual or moral deterioration. Of such evidence I have found not a shred. The friends of whom I speak are all highly educated people and I have not found anything to diminish my respect either for their characters or capacities.[182]

And yet Barfield recognized that something simmered deep in Lewis's soul that would offer him fuel for growth, if not in this lifetime then in a future one. In *Worlds Apart*, written in 1963, Simon Blaxland de Lange sees the contrast between the characters of Hunter and Upwater as those of the two groups that Barfield characterizes as Maccabeans and Nicodemians. For the Maccabeans (pre-Christian, and concerned with the welfare of humanity, such as H. G. Wells, Middleton Murray, and Toynbee) the human being is very much the same today as he was yesterday. Barfield links these most with the spirit of the Jewish people as it is expressed in the psalms. Interestingly, the character of Hunter is said to be built primarily upon Lewis's personality. Even Hunter's concluding initiation dream is at least partly based on one of Lewis's dreams of "great heavy doors shutting slowly."[183]

Nothing is simple or black and white in this historical and famous relationship between the two authors. We can detect an important aspect in the impact that the two had on each other's minds. Lewis meets his anti-self with antipathy; he is continuously challenged out of his comfort zone and, to his merit, endures the tension. The philosophical debates of the Great War rage in his own mind even when Barfield is absent: "I am often surprised at the extent to which your views occupy

[182] Blaxland-de Lange, *Owen Barfield*, 174.
[183] Blaxland-de Lange, *Owen Barfield*, 251; the excerpts are taken from two letters of Barfield to Philip Maret: one of May 31, 1964; the other of April 9, 1971.

my mind when I am not with you and at the animosity I feel towards them."[184] And Barfield shows something similar going on in his mind, when, after Lewis's death he muses that on occasion he still continues "mentally arguing epistemology" with his old friend.[185]

Barfield met a major "obstacle" in his wife Maud and in his profession as a solicitor. To preserve his marriage he had to learn to navigate his being different as an Anthroposophist, and preserve his integrity while speaking to the best in her sensitivities. In working as a solicitor he had to meet contemporary culture at its most mundane level. He had to make a livelihood in what appeared for him, certainly at the beginning, as the driest of all possible pursuits for one enamored of the Word at its highest. And yet, this was part and parcel of meeting himself, knowing himself, and being able to speak to the world at large.

On a more immediately positive note, Barfield's membership in the Inklings, and most of all his friendship with Lewis, offered him a way to sharpen his intellect in countering the most frequent objections, in forming and "packaging" his message,

Barfield challenged Lewis in what looks like a merciless shaking to the core of all his assumptions. In this sense he was truly Lewis's anti-self, and ultimately the better self. Barfield did not state unequivocally what he owed to Lewis and his willingness to stand in relation with what others perceived as Barfield's argumentative nature. Where others simply left, Lewis offered an inkling to his friend of where modern culture stood in one of its best representatives, and how he could speak to it. The friendship and all it entailed honed the needed skills for someone to write *Saving the Appearances* or *Worlds Apart.*

We see above a theme that is to dominate all of Barfield's life. What appears at first as a limitation—his not being able to work within Anthroposophical movements—actually exposes him to the wide world. Barfield's personal connection through Lewis to one of the most important literary circles of the English-speaking culture places him at the center of cultural renewal in his time. It offers him a place of constant dialogue and interaction with some of the liveliest representatives of culture. He can endlessly test the formulation of his

---

[184] Blaxland-de Lange, *Owen Barfield*, 164.
[185] Blaxland-de Lange, *Owen Barfield*, 176.

ideas and adapt it to what the culture of the time can accept and absorb. If this sounds like a lucky stroke of destiny, it did come nevertheless at a price, even what appeared at first a very heavy price: turning his back on his vocation to become a solicitor, turning away from the poetic principle to the rational and prosaic aspect of the Word, which is the domain of a solicitor.

Barfield invites us to turn our ideas into lived ideals; to reach an experience of knowledge that changes us to the very core. The first, already immense, stride in this direction is the attainment of imagination. May it be by design that Barfield mapped the path to imagination that would speak to the people of the Consciousness Soul, and also showed in himself an example of how to reach that goal?

THE PERSONAL BARFIELD

What follows comes from Barfield's most personal books: primarily *This Ever Diverse Pair* (1950) and *Unancestral Voice* (1965). Some additional themes emerge from *Worlds Apart* (1963).

This Ever Diverse Pair was written when Barfield experienced both an intense struggle within his profession as a solicitor and also a very difficult period in his marriage. To Shirley Sugerman Barfield describes the polarity between Burgeon and Burden—central to the book—as a kind of polarity as tension, very much as tension. And the tension at one stage became so violent that, together with other pressures, it very nearly resulted in a nervous breakdown; and I think I've always thought, looking back, that I avoided a nervous breakdown, largely by writing that little book *This Ever Diverse Pair* and really in a way I did it out of that impulse, out of desperation, rather than having any hope of ever publishing it as a book. The characters Burden and Burgeon are embodiments or symbols, or whatever, of a very real experience of polarity and tension in my own life.[186]

Ironically, Barfield talks about the writing of *This Ever Diverse Pair* in the later book, *Unancestral Voice*, in which the confrontation between Burgeon and Burden reappears on a minor scale. Barfield

---

[186] Sugerman, *Evolution of Consciousness*, xviii.

offers us some key insights about the inner character Burden. He calls this part of himself that comes to confront him "almost a separate and rather hostile entity, this matter-of-fact *persona* that bore his name and conducted the affairs of practical life—particularly his professional life—without much reference to him." Referring to the writing of his previous book, he adds:

> By doing so [acknowledging and even exaggerating the split personality]—and by writing a book about it—he had detached himself just in time, from the *persona*, which he seemed to be in danger of actually becoming. The acknowledgment had consisted in his bestowing on the *persona* a name like enough to, yet different enough from, his own—christening him "Burden" in fact.[187]

The names of the pair are aptly chosen. *Burgeon* as a verb stands for "to put forth, as buds," as a noun, for "bud, sprout." *Burden* is defined as "that which is borne with difficulty, obligation, onus." The first element of the pair points to that which is of promise to the future; the second to that which comes from the past and which we carry in ourselves as a hindrance. He represents what spiritual science calls the Double.

Blaxland de Lalange asserts of Barfield's arrival in America in 1964, and of his writing of *Worlds Apart*, that this was "the point where he was no longer forming his own conception of man and the world but seeking ways in which his particular message might be communicated to a wider audience than the select few who could appreciate, say, *Poetic Diction* and *Saving the Appearances*." He was seeking to refine the message and place it in a context where it could better be appreciated, addressing first and foremost the academic world.[188] In this book, intended for a more academic purpose, Burgeon resurfaces as the moderator of a dialogue between eight characters who represent all facets of modern disciplines of knowledge. Burden only appears indirectly for the role he has played in Burgeon's past, as we will point out. Through what is said about

---

[187] Barfield, *Unancestral Voice*, 18–19.
[188] Blaxland-de Lange, *Owen Barfield*, 67.

Burgeon we can shed light on the positive role that Burden has played for his inseparable twin.

Finally, in *Unancestral Voice* Barfield details his journey into the attainment of imaginative consciousness. In the crossing of the threshold the Double only plays a marginal role. He is confined to an early chapter of the book, in which Burden is easily subdued by Burgeon. The rest of the book is a sort of journey into the territory of imagination.

Let us now look more closely at how the inner forces battle in Barfield until he can cross the threshold and attain imaginative consciousness.

Meeting the Double

Relating to Sugerman about the prelude to his inner confrontation in *This Ever Diverse Pair*, Barfield offers us the nature of the contrast he lived in entering the legal profession:

> It does come out, I think, very strongly in the fact that I went into the law, law being almost by definition the very opposite of the poetic. It's abstract, and so forth, and the poetic is living and organic, or however you like to put it. And my being instinctively in the one, and being compelled to live with my mind and activity very much in the other did lead, over a great part of my life, I suppose, to a kind of polarity as tension, very much as tension.[189]

It is quite significant that Burgeon/Barfield's awareness of the inner tension is preceded by a dream in which Burden meets with the Burgeon persona in a concert hall. Burden is going in the direction of Burgeon, looking for a place to sit. "It was a moment before I established the identity of that intelligent, anxious, tolerably ugly face under the bowler hat, though I know it well enough, and the moment I had done so, I woke up—feeling a little frightened. It hasn't happened again."[190]

Burden is tied in part to Barfield's professional persona, which exacts attention from him whenever his mind pursues something of

---

[189] Sugerman, *Evolution of Consciousness*, 21.
[190] Barfield, *This Ever Diverse Pair*, 9.

larger interest, a shadow that leaves little time to Barfield the writer and knower. Barfield writes in exasperation: "But the only thing on which I am allowed, and indeed expected, to fix my attention, is Burden. So I'm writing about him." And with keen insight he adds, "I am responsible for the professional existence, almost for the existence at all, of Burden." And further, "The original idea was, that [Burden] was to earn the bread and butter, and I was to support him as a sleeping partner."[191] This arrangement of convenience turns sour when Burgeon realizes that Burden is turning into a sort of Frankenstein's monster.

The tension that Barfield posits at the beginning is restated in the fact that the book brings him against an initial resolve to "abandon all writing on personal subject-matter."[192] This is restated in bringing us back to what Barfield held as his original life's intention:

> I wanted, above all, to be objective, to write about Nature and events and quite other people, using my own feelings solely as instruments of perception and fountains of diction, sacrificing them like the glass in the window, to let the light and the warmth of the outside world. And now here I am, at it again![193]

In a more humorous dialogue between self and Double, the above tension appears in one of Barfield's poems titled *Sonnet*:

> *I am much inclined towards a life of ease*
> *And should not scorn to spend my dwindling years*
> *In places where my sort of fancy stirs;*
> *Perched up on ladders in old libraries*
> *With several quartos pouring off my knees.*[194]

---

[191] Barfield, *This Ever Diverse Pair*, 4–5.
[192] Barfield, *This Ever Diverse Pair*, 6.
[193] Barfield, *This Ever Diverse Pair*, 7.
[194] Clayton Hunter and Kranidas, *A Barfield Sampler*, 33. In *Unancestral Voice*, talking about his retirement Burgeon indicates that "it would, he decided, be the best way of doing what he had always hoped to do after his retirement, namely reading" (89).

Day after day Burden exposes Burgeon to a caricature of the Word, and to a consequent fear of how he will experience it, empty of its true being, in his profession. He realizes that because of what feels like a soul-deadening activity, he finds himself avoiding the company of children and has little to say to his friends when he has occasion to relax with them. He calls this new soul condition "rhematophobia": "There is a close connection between rhematophobia [fear of the word] and that other complaint (a mild or incipient form, presumably, of schizophrenia) by which this diary was first begotten, and which it is seeking to remedy."[195]

Part of Barfield's profession is to deal with the written word, and the need to chisel with precision its use. This is when Burden overwhelms Burgeon, when all ingenuity that could go towards more creative uses has to flow into the profession of the law. "Then I bite his head off again for expecting to lend my vast creative powers to the task of helping him run his horrid little squabbles."[196]

On the way to the culmination of the crisis, Barfield has to confront various layers of his persona, such as the one created or reflected by the family environment, and the one present in his professional milieu. His family culture and upbringing affected him to the point that he distrusted emotional experience such as enthusiasm or anything else he could experience in the realm of feelings, including what could be generated by poetry.

In the book Barfield sees a similarity between Burden and his father. He sees gestures, attitudes, or expressions, and notices that he sees them and feels them coming in a way, and leaves them unchecked. "The instant after, *I see the effect from the outside*, and it is in these instants that I do occasionally feel something approaching to affection for that animated rag-bag of doubts and worries, my partner Burden."[197] Here the writer takes a first step of acceptance for his inner shadow.

The confrontation with the professional Double is one of lesser relevance; one that Barfield more easily tackles with humor. It takes place in the Law Society's Hall. Here in a sense Burgeon apprehends

---

[195] Barfield, *This Ever Diverse Pair*, 40.
[196] Barfield, *This Ever Diverse Pair*, 66–67.
[197] Barfield, *This Ever Diverse Pair*, 60.

some of the possible futures of his persona in the three archetypal characters of Lynx, Glossy, and Applejohn. Without going into details, these are the equivalent of the Doubles of the profession, each tinged by a particular temperament or combination thereof.

In between ups and downs, there is practically no doubt throughout the book that a major crisis is coming. Burgeon starts observing the coming effects of the crisis over his Burden persona and wonders how he himself will deal with them. The crisis is precipitated through the agency of great pressure and the perfectly antipathetic client. Burden threatens to kill Burgeon gradually: "I've begun already, as you know very well." And Burgeon realizes that his words are true. Burden threatens to turn into the perfect "Applejohn," whom Barfield characterizes as "the one craftsman of our profession [who] likes documents as such."[198] When Burgeon threatens his partner with the coming retirement, Burden answers that he will settle and pick up a hobby. But when reference is made to death, Burden has no answer.

After the storm Burgeon reflects, "I had won one of the hardest battles of my life, and for a long time I lay quietly and peacefully in bed." And he adds: "For it is the Burdens of this world who keep traditions alive, it is the Burgeons who create them. The Burdens cannot make anything; they can only collect and preserve."[199] The realization of the above leads Burgeon to wonder at how he has left himself become a "sleeping partner" rather than becoming creative even in the practice of the law.

The epilogue comes quite appropriately through a "legal dream" in which restorative justice ("Equitable Jurisdiction" in the book) is applied to both Burden and Burgeon. This is set in a fictitious future of 1990, some fourteen years after the law supposedly changed.

In the court of law where the resolutions are taken, it is said of Burden that he is a "normally steady character without either great ambition or great ideals."[200] He is enamored of daily life's comforts: food, ease, security. Through his intellectual rigor he is suited to the profession of the law. He is condemned to be of assistance to a household

---

[198] Barfield, *This Ever Diverse Pair*, 96.
[199] Barfield, *This Ever Diverse Pair*, 93.
[200] Barfield, *This Ever Diverse Pair*, 113.

of parents in poor health, by helping them with menial tasks and helping with the three children.

Of Burgeon we hear that he is neither an egoist nor one too attached to habits, and that his intellect has a capacity to move beyond purely earthbound concerns, unlike Burden. But Burgeon's mind can actually soar in an ungrounded manner; therefore he needs to find a firmer footing. Burgeon can enter into a conflict of wits, but shirks from a conflict of will. The study of and work with the law is actually felt by the judge to be a good antidote to his tendencies. Burgeon feels he could have faced any decision with equanimity but this resolution is an anticlimax.

Burgeon apologizes to Burden for the crisis episode, and Burden is now confined to his limits. The book finishes with Burden wearing his bowler hat, as in the opening dream, and disappearing from sight. And Barfield concludes: "As for myself, I turned my face grimly towards the Office. And the effort of doing so awoke me with a jerk."[201]

It is remarkable how Barfield has touched at diverse aspects of the personal hindrances, and understandable therefore how the book played the therapeutic role that Barfield attributed to it, if nothing else because of Barfield's ability to look at Burgeon and Burden with detachment and humor. In a move forward in relation to the Double, what had been Barfield's inability to speak in his stuttering becomes now rhematophobia, the fear of the spoken word. The encounter with his father—the family Double—and the recognition of their similarities is coupled with an affectionate acceptance. The professional persona appears in the responses that diverse individuals offer to inveterate habit and loss of passion or basic interest for their profession, in Burgeon's case that of the so-called "Applejohn," the one who is enamored of the documents themselves, not of what they mean for their case or for their clients. And finally Barfield touches on the purely personal dimension of his hindrances when he recognizes that his thinking needs more grounding.

Something more appears on second reading. It is by meeting the Double face to face that we can dissipate its strength and hold on the core of the personality. Barfield indicates that after the dream in which

---

[201] Barfield, *This Ever Diverse Pair*, 120.

he comes face to face with his Double, no such dreams follow. And he shows us that an individual who can suffer from the afflictions of the Double, while also detachedly observing them, will learn to converse with it, and eventually transform it.

The movement of inner integration that is announced in *This Ever Diverse Pair* is continued in *Worlds Apart*. It appears clearly only when we look at Barfield's professional and personal evolution in relation to the character of Burgeon, the one of the eight that is obviously Barfield himself, or most like him.

In the book Burgeon is concerned about the silos forming between scientific disciplines. He devises a way to invite eight academics of the most diverse disciplines over a three-day dialogue. Burgeon introduces the proceedings by noticing how much each specialist at present avoids talking shop with another specialist. He invites an atmosphere of utmost sincerity and frankness, pointing out that "few, if any, people are capable—at all events in our time—of conversing in the manner which has become traditional in philosophical dialogues from Plato to Brewster and Lowes Dickinson."[202]

The characters Burgeon invites are a physicist (Brodie), a biologist (Upwater), a psychiatrist (Burrows), a lawyer-philologist (Burgeon), a linguistic analyst or analytical philosopher (Dunn), a theologian (Hunter), a retired Waldorf school teacher (Sanderson), and a young man employed at a rocket research station (Ranger, twenty years younger than the rest). The characters do not receive much of an introduction or characterization. Thus, for example, when Burrows is first mentioned, we are simply told that he is not concerned about thinking, except on how it affects his emotions.

The dialogues touch on every possible field of knowledge, and only every now and then are we offered some glimpses about the characters themselves. We will turn here to what is said about Burgeon himself. At the end of the first part of the second day, Brodie proposes that Burgeon lead the projected Socratic dialogue since he is used to cross-examination. And in effect Burgeon will gather evidence and cross-examine very much in the style of an attorney or solicitor. The conversation will be held between Brodie and Burgeon, with Burgeon acting like the eager

---

[202] Barfield, *Worlds Apart*, 13.

but supposedly naïve layman who tries to understand what the scientists of his time are saying but is halted by what he perceives as contradictions or thinking that denies its very own premises. Here the author ironically illustrates how Burgeon's—Barfield's—profession has allowed him to follow intently a line of reasoning with empathic interest and also with accuracy and capacity to detect inner contradictions, to then point to them clearly and humorously.

At the end of the Socratic dialogue, Brodie, who has thus been cornered, takes refuge in numbers, in excuses like "everybody thinks" and "all the studies show" or on calls to a "common sense" that cannot confront the contradictions or dissolve perplexities, a common sense that does not appear to hold water and that Burgeon has no difficulty in unmasking. Burgeon/Barfield has fully integrated the lawyer's mind that fate and Burden have apparently thrown in his way. He has debated from the best perspective that a lawyer could approach.

The meeting with the Double is the prelude for reaching the threshold of the spiritual world, and its first step, the acquisition of imaginative knowledge for which Barfield strove lifelong. It is articulated fifteen years after *This Ever Diverse Pair* in *Unancestral Voice*. It is still Burgeon who speaks in this book, though Burden makes a short appearance.

Attaining Imagination

In the first chapter of *Unancestral Voice*, the characters Burgeon, Rodney, and Middleton have been discussing intensely D. H. Lawrence's *Lady Chatterley's Lover* in the wake of the scandal that the book's publication has raised in the press when Lawrence is brought to trial. The next morning, a turning point takes place. It owes its genesis to the fact that Burgeon spends the time upon awakening deliberately recollecting the content of the previous night's conversation. He starts to recognize patterns that were present in the conversation. Later, while he is shaving, no less, the turning point occurs:

> He did not hear any voice. And yet a train of thought began presenting itself to him in the same mode in which thoughts present themselves when we hear them from the lips of another. They included thoughts that

he himself was not aware of having ever previously entertained. For the most part the thoughts were "given" in this way were naked of words. He himself had to find the words before he forgot the thoughts—and in order that he may not forget them. Occasionally, however, an actual phrase or sentence came with the thought, without an effort being required on his part.

And further, "If all this was surprising enough, it startled him a good deal more (but only when he came to reflect on it afterwards) that most of what reached him in this way purported to be neither speculation nor judgment but actual information on matters of fact."[203] After the fact Burgeon notices that he has never felt "more fully conscious and clear-headed."

The imagination that he receives allows Burgeon to better understand the opinions of the parties in Lawrence's trial. He acquires a higher perspective, one that is to a great extent devoid of judgment. He can now attribute the various opinions to a shift that is happening in man's being in his time. This is a change in the constitution of Western man "gradually developing and informing some sort of delicate structure or complex of forces in the front part of the brain and at the same time in the organs of reproduction."[204]

After this first visit from a higher realm of thought, Burgeon is left with the results but not the presence. The experience leaves him when he has to reimmerse himself in the duties of the day-to-day. It does not come back for a time. Meanwhile Burgeon is left with the question, "How was I able to think these thoughts at all?" Moreover he questions the information received in terms of its reliability and about how it could be tested.

What helps Burgeon is a book that fate places in front of him in a bookshop, titled "Joseph Karo: Lawyer and Mystic." This is a reference to a real book and a real mystic, moreover a mystic who is also a lawyer. Joseph Karo called "Maggid" that "something like a voice that spoke

---

[203] Barfield, *Unancestral Voice*, 11.
[204] Barfield, *Unancestral Voice*, 13.

within the mind 'in silence and solitude. But not an audible voice.'"[205] In those terms, the experience of Joseph Karo does in effect resemble those of Burgeon.

The awakening of the experience of imagination brings up in Barfield that inner confrontation that was present through family "inheritance" of suspicion about anything involving enthusiasm and strong feelings, all of which in his family was seen as "affectation." This was part and parcel of the confrontation between Burgeon and Burden that had been a prelude to a situation that evolved towards a nervous breakdown in *This Ever Diverse Pair.* Now this confrontation reemerges, though on a minor tone. Burden downplays Burgeon's experience as "simply the old Neo-platonism turning up again."

Burden doubts of the reality of the experience Burgeon has had; Burgeon doubts there could ever be anything more real than the experience itself. He names his experience, and the source of it, "Meggid," borrowing from Joseph Karo, and decides that he will wait to see if the experience will return in order to also learn about the nature of its source.

In Chapter 3 Burgeon returns to his understanding of the debates around *Lady Chatterley's Lover,* calling to mind the conversation with Rodney and Middleton; associating his thoughts with the content of the book itself and certain of its passages, particularly the contrasts between the pleasures of the mind and the role of sensuality. All along, however, Burgeon resists the temptation of spiritual pride that indicates that his thoughts are superior to those of his intellectual opponents.

Once more Burgeon feels the approach of the Meggid speaking in him, asking him to go back in his reasoning before proceeding further. Burgeon realizes the potency of man's drives descending from the head to the lower organism. He sees this in relation to man's historical development. He now understands the intermediate stage of medieval literature as a descent into the heart. One of the statements of the Meggid becomes strikingly provocative: at the time of Ovid, sex was "not yet aware of itself as physical."

The Meggid proceeds to inform Burgeon that "the potency which made the sexual act possible and be recognized in it—but which also

---

205 Barfield, *Unancestral Voice,* 16.

made so much else possible—had found its way down from the head to the heart." Because the potency had not yet completely descended but only reached the heart, the individual did not become aware of the potency of physical sex. Rather "it was the potency of feeling, of feeling in all its subtlest and gentlest overtones."[206] At present the potency has fully descended into the lower organism. This indicates to Burgeon that Lawrence was right in what he was perceiving, though not right in the conclusions he drew from it. This potency is for modern man, as Lawrence had somehow perceived, a surviving link with the cosmos. In line with the above, for Lawrence, the Logos "meant the insipidity of intellect, because intellect had no potency."

At last Burgeon understands clearly where his position differs from that of Lawrence. The potency has become the domain of the human being, and his only, so that now he can give it back to the Logos. And it could take two opposite directions: down into the loins, or liberated creatively in the mind. He sees both how Lawrence and his supporters are in a sense completely right in having a certain understanding of the mood of modern time, but at a deeper level completely wrong. He sees that ultimately the remedy for a world at loss, "the desperate cry, going up from a world more out of joint than ever before in its long history, for creative mind and for the treasury of knowledge which that alone can unlock from the strong-room wither it has been withdrawn, to set us free." Either that or "enthusiastic copulation."[207]

Later in the book when the voice of the Meggid becomes more familiar, Barfield adds:

> And it was at this point that he first realized that the Meggid himself was now *speaking in him* [after hearing himself say "The Jewel in the Lotus," an expression that appeared new to him even as he proffered it]. How long that had been going on he could not say, for it was *definitely "in" and not "through"*; there was no question of his being used as a microphone; and yet it was *almost as much as hearing someone else speak as it was like speaking*;

---

[206] Barfield, *Unancestral Voice*, 31.
[207] Barfield, *Unancestral Voice*, 35.

and this because his lips were uttering, and with the confidence of personal experience, *things he must indeed have thought,* but *could not possibly say he knew them from experience,* since he had not lived them, or had never lived up to them—had never taken them seriously, as he took, for instance, eating and drinking seriously.[208] (emphasis added)

I quote this passage at length because, in reconciling his experience with his understanding of it, Barfield makes us aware of polarities and seeming contradictions. The Meggid speaks in him, not through him. It is like speaking, though it is revelation at the same time. Barfield consciously understands the thoughts, though they lead him beyond the realm of immediate experience.

Finally, Barfield will lead us from the realm of personal experience into the universal dimension of it. The Meggid indicates to him that his brain, like any other brain, usually reflects as a mirror. And the mirror is a boundary beyond which lay concealed forces of destruction, but also a place that is a center of rebirth and creation:

> You are one of those who have at least peeped behind the mirror. And what you have found there so far is thought [not beings]. But these thoughts are other than your memory-thoughts, of which they are none the less the source and origin. For these are the creative thoughts themselves . . . they are nothing remembered, because they are one with the life itself that supports and enables the act of memory. Therefore it is that, when you experience them at all, you cannot experience them—as you do the memory-thoughts—as being "your own" because spun from your brain. They own an objectivity which in terms of everyday life you can better compare with perceiving than with thinking. And yet they are indeed your own in the deepest sense of all, because, unlike the memory-thoughts, they are

---

[208] Barfield, *Unancestral Voice,* 111.

also your substance and your life; so that to perceive them is verily to perceive the spirit within you in the act of creating.[209]

The great value of *Unancestral Voice* as a book lies in showing us one individual experience as an example of a possible universal experience: the transformation of dead thinking of a mirror-like quality into a living thinking in which thought becomes in effect a perceiving of the idea. And all of this is reported in the most precise of possible ways at the end when Barfield indicates that perceiving the ideas means to participate as well in the act of the creation of the spirit. Everything that Barfield has been writing in his books is now illustrated from biography in a concrete example, namely, Barfield's own. The author shows us how he himself has attained what he offers as a hope to others in writing, articulating the truth of the time of the Consciousness Soul, that it is no longer sufficient to point to an abstract truth; what is needed is showing the way through personal example.

Burgeon has completely crossed the threshold and nullified the residual objections of Burden. He is walking the first steps of imaginative consciousness. Burgeon/Barfield has no longer reason to doubt the validity of the Meggid and of its revelations. And he now has a more appropriate name for the Meggid.

In effect, the Meggid reveals:

> I am indeed a servant of Michael; but *because I am spirit without body I may also truly say that I am all those wherein I am contained*, I am all that speaks through me. . . . Men have called me by many names. . . . Men have called me also *Sophia*. . . . But at the turning point of time, by that central death and rebirth which was the transformation of transformations, by the open mystery of Golgotha, I was myself transformed. I am that *anthroposophia* who, by whatsoever communications howsoever imparted she

---

[209] Barfield, *Unancestral Voice*, 220.

shall first have been evoked, is the voice of each one's mind speaking from the depths within himself.[210]

From the above it is clear, even if veiled, that the Christ is present behind everything that is said in connection to the revelation of the Meggid' Elsewhere Barfield makes this step more overtly in relation to his upbringing and to the transformation of the Double in his life. In *Owen Barfield and the Origin of Language* the lecturer reminds us of how he pursued his path into Anthroposophy with an alternation of resistance and acceptance, until coming to a firm conviction. And along this path came the "very welcome (and for this reason very suspect)" discovery of the central place of Christ. In this he had to struggle through the culture of his secular upbringing. Here Barfield is saved from this inner tug of war by "how precisely it fit with his own halting notion of the development of meaning in language."[211]

In one of his most successful books—*Saving the Appearances*—Barfield links all of the threads of his exploration to the central place of the event of Golgotha:

> I believe that the blind-spot which posterity will find most startling in the last hundred years or so of Western civilization is, that it had, on the one hand, a religion which differed from all others in its acceptance of time, and of a particular point of time, as a cardinal element in its faith; that it had, on the other hand, a picture in its mind of the history of the earth and man as an evolutionary process; and that it neither saw nor supposed any connection whatever between the two.[212]

Concluding the same book, Barfield can link the transition from original, unconscious participation to final and conscious participation to the Christ event via imagination: "Original participation fires the heart from a source outside itself; the images enliven the heart. But

---

[210] Barfield, *Unancestral Voice*, 221.
[211] Barfield, *Owen Barfield and the Origin of Language*, lecture of June 21, 1977, 8.
[212] Barfield, *Saving the Appearances*, 167.

in final participation—since the death and resurrection—the heart is fired from within by the Christ; and it is for the heart to enliven the images."[213]

Barfield has been achieving more than meets the eye in his inner journey to imagination. He has achieved a great deal of integration of the forces of the soul, and not surprisingly this has led him to a clear understanding of the Christ being.

INTEGRATING PATH OF THE SENSES (MACROCOSM) AND PATH OF THE SOUL (MICROCOSM)

We have already pointed out that Barfield would not have been the author we know if he had not overcome the soul abyss that threatened his mental sanity at the time of writing *This Ever Diverse Pair.* Indeed, Barfield himself indicates it.

We can therefore recognize two gestures and two paths that Barfield approaches differently. The path to nature observation and to overcoming the fallacy of superficial sense observation that does not incorporate qualitative elements, as in modern science, is the path that Barfield can outline cognitively. This is what Steiner calls "Spirit Beholding" in his Foundation Stone Meditation. Before that he used the term "Saturn Path," or path to the macrocosm.

On the other hand Barfield comes very close to that other path of exploration of the soul life, which has occupied us in this chapter. This is what Steiner calls "Spirit Recollection," or Moon Path since it is the path to the microcosm that we cross through the threshold of the Moon sphere. Barfield explores this second path artistically, and he also comes very close to characterizing the methodology in terms that mirror those of Steiner. Even in the midst of the deepest crisis, Barfield can maintain an observatory stance. In his words:

> If over a fairly long period you dislike and shrink from nearly everything you have to do, *you are also conscious of positively willing everything you do.* Then, when you do

---

[213] Barfield, *Saving the Appearances*, 172.

get a chance to relax completely, this *purely volitional self,* reacting from the normal condition of strained exertion, makes itself felt in surprising ways. You find *it is still there, though it does not do anything*—this mysterious unknown whose whole function is, precisely—doing. . . . I am not saying that *your will* necessarily becomes stronger, only that *at such times you become very conscious of it.* It upholds you; you seem to float on it as on a sort of buoyant, hyaline sea.[214]

Barfield is indicating that even while the will is immersed in the events that surface the deepest movements of antipathy in the soul, it can still observe with detachment. Let us compare the above with what Steiner has to say about the Moon Path. This is a path in which "one can advance on the opposite side [microcosm] by entering deeply into the will, to the extent of becoming wholly quiescent, by becoming a pole of stillness in the motion one otherwise engenders in the will." Instead of becoming an unconscious part of world movement, one can consciously come to a standstill. Through this, "one succeeds in keeping the soul still while the body moves through space; succeeds in being active in the world while the soul remains quiet; carries activity, and at the same time quietly observes it; then thinking suffuses the will, just as the will previously suffused thinking."[215] Barfield comes close to the realization that this volitional self can take the stance of a complete observer, and the will is thus transformed.

Ultimately, walking the Moon path, or path of Spirit Recollection, means awakening to the reality of karma and reincarnation in our own biography. And Barfield's striving confirms that this was awakened in his artistic perception, witness two if not more of his artistic works of fiction: his play *Angels at Bay* and his novella *Eager Spring.*

The trilogy of *Angels at Bay* is composed of 'The Wall,' 'The Human Dynamo' and 'The Paranoia' Wing. The three are intimately intertwined, through the continuation of the theme of human estrangement from the spirit and the reconnection to it through the commitment of those

---

[214] Barfield, *This Ever Diverse* Pair, 90.
[215] Steiner, *Awakening to Community,* lecture of February 6, 1923.

who develop new spiritual faculties and a dedication to spiritual science. Barfield invites the spectator to witness how initiatives that human beings take on earth are inspired and supported by different kind of beings. Among these are some who want to advance human beings' freedom and connection to the spirit, and others—in the play especially one by the name of Semjaya—work to enslave him and estrange him from the fountainhead of the spirit. The Wall stands for that apparent dead-end of human consciousness which denies the spirit, and sets the tone for the first two plays. In the third, the movement of reversal is announced by the Archangel Remiel: "In this region the tall Wall crushes, between the living and the dead. Across our threshold passings to and from grow common."[216] The play is no doubt inspired by Steiner's *Mystery Dramas*, though no plagiarism is apparent.

In *Eager Spring* one and the same scenario is explored from the perspective of the evolution of consciousness in a span of some five centuries, and with the veiled reference to reincarnation. This "ecological novella" is structured along two stories. The first is that of a modern couple, a scientist husband and a literary wife. The story is revisited by Virginia herself in her own supposed novel, placed at the birth of the machine age in England (the 15th century) when the understanding of surviving alchemy vies to compete with the new materialism.

The modern story revolves around the couple; Leonard is the typical modern scientist, confined to his field of inquiry. Virginia is interested in English literature, especially from the Middle Ages. Not unlike Tolkien and Barfield, she is interested in exploring how people thought and felt in earlier times. Her destiny crosses paths with Harry Coppard (a sort of parallel of Jean Giono's *The Man who Planted Trees*) who acts from his will and with Herapath, an Anthroposophist. Leonard's ideas are pretty much set and formed. Virginia's mind is much more flexible; she wants to write a fiction book and is still open as to what direction it would take.

Gradually Virginia becomes deeply concerned about the fate of the earth, in conjunction with her soul and spirit's awakening. Naturally, she deepens her interest in Anthroposophy, via Herapath, and this precipitates a deep crisis, prelude to a rebirth.

---

[216] Barfield, *Angels at Bay.*

Virginia accepts to be "used" as a tool in finding out more about the hidden truth of the pollution around the so-called eager spring. The epilogue leads to her exposure to the pollutant that completely threatens her life. She goes through the complete powerlessness of knowing that even a little success like hers is but a drop in the fight against an all-too-powerful enemy. But this deepest of inner crisis leads her to the realization of her deeper, enduring being beyond the confines of time, and leads her to accept her fate with equanimity. It also leads her to revisit the story from the perspective of a time in history when a deeper view of reality was more common.

In her writing Virginia sets her characters in 15th-century England at the beginnings of the Industrial Revolution. Virginia of present life shines through the character of Maria. In that incarnation she meets with Paolo, a "trovatore" who has worked all his life to perceive the hidden dimensions of reality, the beings that actually stand behind sense perceptible events. It's as if Coppard and Herapath take new characters: Herapath is the doctor; Frank Coppard is Paolo, the trovatore. The story subtly repeats the themes of modern life, but offers them from the perspective of Paolo and the awakening Maria. They confront the foreman Godfrey, an impersonation of an evil being.

In the unfolding of events Paolo recognizes the countenance of Ahriman, both over the forge and over Godfrey. The epilogue makes use of a sword forged of meteoric iron to kill Godfrey through Paolo. He is helped by Maria, who plays a role similar to that played by Virginia in real life. Maria dies like Virginia eventually will, not killed by the biocide, but by Godfrey/Ahriman. When Godfrey is killed, no blood flows from his veins, but a dragon's countenance is seen floating in the clouds by the miners. The forge collapses under water and fire. Virginia can clearly illustrate through her story that hers, like that of Maria, is a spiritual battle for the soul of the human being in our time, a battle in which each human soul plays a role. Leonard, who reads Virginia's story at the end of the novella, "did not know that he had indeed started for the first time to think."[217]

---

[217] Barfield, *Eager Spring*, 143.

The paths of Spirit Recollection and Spirit Beholding form the first and third panels of the Foundation Stone meditation. Most interestingly, in between them lies that of "Spirit Mindfulness" or "Spirit Awareness," the one in which the Christ being is explicitly mentioned. In Him the polarity of macrocosm and microcosm is harmonized. The Christ is at work in creation under His cosmic aspect; he was present historically in Palestine in the world's most encompassing Mystery Drama.

It is not surprising therefore that Barfield turned his attention to that set of meditations which explicitly link macrocosm and microcosm: the Calendar of the Soul. In fifty-two verses each week of the year links the spiritual happenings of nature in the cycle of the year with corresponding soul gestures. In his autobiographical lecture *Owen Barfield and the Origin of Language*, Barfield speaks of his "long, long love affair with the little book." And logically he tried his hand at a translation, unique among the many English ones, in being a freer paraphrasing of the verses, rather than a closer, sentence by sentence, word by word translation.

It is not surprising that Barfield strives to integrate the paths that are characterized in the Foundation Stone Meditation as Spirit Beholding, Spirit Recollection, and Spirit Awareness. He strives so naturally to render Steiner's spiritual science accessible to his fellow human beings that the forces of the soul express the yearning for unity that is part and parcel of spiritual science; the striving to "truly think," "truly feel," and "truly live," which conclude each of the first three stanzas of the Foundation Stone Meditation.

Because of how he walks the path that he intellectually maps out, Barfield has been able to play a central role for the time and the people whose soul constitution is most intimately linked to the Consciousness Soul.

THE NATURE OF TRUE KNOWLEDGE AT THE TIME OF THE CONSCIOUSNESS SOUL

With the attainment of full Imagination, Barfield has fulfilled what he longed for knowledge to be. This is the knowledge that he differentiated from the notion of "intellect alone." In the latter we are kept separate and confined within the limits of the physical body. True knowledge takes us to a new level of participation, one that is conscious and therefore different from original participation or atavistic knowledge. This new kind of knowledge is one that changes us inwardly, ever so slightly, makes of us a different person. Knowledge is therefore an experience.

The new kind of knowing is one that requires passing through a stage of inner death, which awakens fear in the soul. It starts with a feeling of estrangement from the external world and from other human beings. What is the inescapable reality of the time of the Consciousness Soul can be lived in a numb state of consciousness, or amplified consciously before true knowledge is attained.

The ultimate goal of true knowledge is to completely modify our relationship to the world. Barfield speaks of having to overcome in himself "the tremendous deep incision made by Darwinism in contemporary thought."[218] More broadly he challenges to overcome positivism as "the philosophical statement of the position that there is an unbridgeable gulf between mental experience of the world on the one hand and the objective world of nature on the other."[219]

While we struggle to rebuild a truer world of thought, we run the risk of carrying new thinking in some field of knowledge, while carrying alongside "residues of unresolved positivism" (RUP). An example is that of C. G. Jung, who comes close to overcoming RUP in his expression of the archetypes, which go in the direction of transcending body-bound reality. However, he formulates the collective unconscious as the aggregate of what is left behind by civilization as a whole, the aggregate of what has been produced in physical bodies, rather than something that has its independent existence in the world of spirit, from where it plays an influence on human beings on earth.

Barfield shows us clearly, in thought and through reflection on his own experience, what it means to live at the time of the Consciousness Soul, and what it means for the English and English-speaking people, of whom he is an apt representative, to be the people who most fully carry in themselves the impulse of the Consciousness Soul.

---

[218] Sugerman, *Evolution of Consciousness*, 14.
[219] Sugerman, *Evolution of Consciousness*, 13.

Barfield argues that in the complete hypothetical possibility of stopping an individual at the stage of Consciousness Soul, he could only be characterized negatively by what he is not, because he is at his most separate, most cut off. The English people, who carry the Consciousness Soul par excellence, are themselves part of an island. They carry this further in the realization, as Novalis said, that "Every Englishman is an island."

In this condition of being isolated, cut off, it is not surprising that the Englishman embodies the modern scientific spirit to the utmost. Modern science applies foremost to man in his physical body. English people excel in the sciences of our time; on the other hand, continues Barfield, England has produced very little in terms of philosophy or pure mathematics.

The English outlook is so materialistic that it pushes this view of the world to its limits, up to the point at which it is no longer tenable. How could it explain that, if everything is constantly due to random conditions and events, it maintains its order and its being? What the English spirit and science do is draw the clearest of boundaries between matter and spirit. "[English philosophy] sought for matter everywhere—*in order not to confuse it with Spirit.*"[220] This means the complete severance of microcosm from macrocosm, another way to characterize the state of modern human being at the time of the Consciousness Soul.

In the Consciousness Soul the individual is so cut off from the macrocosm that he doubts of his own existence. It is out of this nothingness that must first arise the feeling, then the growing awareness, and finally certainty of her own beingness. In English Romanticism the revolt against the confinement of being to the senses and the refusal to move beyond it led someone like Keats to say "I am certain of nothing, but the holiness of the heart's affections and the truth of imagination." Attaining imaginative consciousness, or some degree of it, was for the English Romantics the means to reclaim the purely human and build a bridge to the spirit at the point of complete severance that the Consciousness Soul imposes as a necessity, though not as a final condition. In fact the Consciousness Soul, concludes Barfield, places

---

[220] Barfield, *Romanticism Comes of Age*, 110.

us at the choice between death by nonbeing or the possibility to expand towards the macrocosm.

The step that our time requires is to move from some individual's personal certainty of the truth of imagination—which the Romantics had reached—to knowing why imagination is true, and thus being able to understand the reality of imagination (when one cannot apprehend it) in order to direct our efforts towards it. The Consciousness Soul can only recognize it knows when it can add that it has experienced. This means that ultimately we must move from a theory of knowledge as it is first formulated in Goethe—where it still did not fully know itself—to what comes into expression and possible experience in spiritual science through Steiner's legacy.

The last quoted statement may encapsulate much of what Barfield's work has been about. Through experiencing in himself, and sharing the results of his experiences, he has shown the people of the Consciousness Soul that there is another possibility at the fork on the road. At the place in which the Consciousness Soul can signify the complete severance of macrocosm and microcosm, he has shown the way into fully conscious participation in the macrocosm.

More can be said in relation to Barfield's being and work. We will return to it when we will contrast his opus—particularly the nature of his literary imaginations—with that of Tolkien.

Chapter 7

Barfield's Artistic Imaginations

Whereas Barfield's imagination went mostly into his edifice of thought, the two most complete artistic imaginations came at the early stage of his literary career. At the time of *The Silver Trumpet* imagination, Barfield had begun to integrate Steiner's ideas into his own. By the time of *The Rose on the Ash-Heap*, Anthroposophy was already a familiar territory.

The Silver Trumpet has been recognized as the first work of fantasy of the Inklings. It is a work that is accessible to and appreciated by the wider general public. It is appreciated by some of those critics who have otherwise little access to Barfield's edifice of thought.[221] We will retell the story in four stages, stressing here and there some of the elements before attempting to let the story reveal itself.

THE SILVER TRUMPET[222]

While the events take place in an imaginary Mountainy Castle, none of the setting appears in the first chapters of the narrative; only the birth

---

[221] An example is that of Philip Zaleski and Carol Zaleski, whose assessment of Barfield's work, apart from a great appreciation for *The Silver Trumpet*, discusses "unremarkable short stories and plays and a realistic, unpublishable novel [not specified]. He opened the vein of mythopoeic gold for his fellow Inklings but failed to mine it successfully himself; the loss is palpable." (*The Fellowship*, 112)
[222] Barfield, *The Silver Trumpet*.

and childhood of the twins, the Princesses Violetta and Gambetta, are explored at length. The king and queen are of little account throughout the first parts of the narrative and beyond. Another three characters play important roles: Miss Thomson, the Lord High Teller (of the Other from Which) and Little Fat Podger.

Violetta and Gambetta are twins to all appearances identical; Gambetta is the first by one minute, as she reminds as on several occasions. Miss Thomson, a "kind-hearted old lady" of which we hear that she is also "growing a witchery sort of woman in old age," casts two spells at the birth of the twins.

The first is for them to "Always be as like as one to another pea," which she calls "a gift." The second prophesies: "As long as you both live, you shall love each other more than all else in the world," and most importantly, "As long as one of you is living, both shall *be*." When the mother thanks her for granting her daughters' happiness, Miss Thomson answers "Don't be too sure about that."[223]

Violet would naturally tend to be beautiful, whereas, left to herself, Gamboy would turn ugly. Together, however, they even out, turning neither quite as beautiful nor quite as ugly. Every change in one, whether a wrinkle or a dimple, is reflected in the other. And thus it is nearly impossible to tell one from the other. Added to this is the fact that as princesses in Mountainy Castle, they are dictated to wear the same dresses and do everything alike until they reach age twenty-one.

Violet lives fully in the feelings. When she sees a ragged boy crying, her own eyes fill with tears. She gives him an apple and listens to him. Then she cannot help but crying for all the other ragged boys. Gambetta sees the boy's behavior as a manipulation for pity and for inciting the gift. She is the skeptic, turning to cynical. And the narrator voice adds that the two princesses "were as different inside as a Church from a Booking Office."[224] Violet is fond of singing and dancing. She loved hundreds of things, but Gamboy remains the one she loves most, at least until the future arrival of Prince Courtesy. And Gamboy keeps to herself and loves only one, and that is Violet. And further, they represent

223 Barfield, *The Silver Trumpet*, 2.
224 Barfield, *The Silver Trumpet*, 3.

158

two ways of loving people: Violet loves them "to like seeing them well and happy," Gamboy "to like them to do what you tell them."[225]

In spite of these differences, nobody is able to tell their differences in the castle, except Lord High Teller of the Other from Which, a "very wise man." Not only he could tell of their differences, but he also knows of the magic of names, and gives them the new names of Violet and Gamboy.

Another character plays an important part in immediate succeeding events and is introduced in the beginning: Little Fat Podger, the "Curator of the Royal Dump" a jester figure who "cure[s] the King's megrims."[226] His head "seemed far too large for that crooked little body."[227] He acts like a jester, with sudden movements, gestures, all between the comic and the awkward; interrupts his sentences with seemingly odd remarks. While this causes amusement in others, he himself does not like to be laughed at. While he lifts the spirits, he is also the one capable of listening and offering advice.

And finally, let's underline the role of the practical Miss Thomson, whom we will see from the very beginning to the very end. She is both wise and kind-hearted. She plays a role through magic at the very beginning of the tale in relation to the twins. She will play a key role at the very end.

The Arrival of Prince Courtesy with the Silver Trumpet

One morning, Prince Courtesy, son of the King of the neighboring kingdom of Dravidia, comes to the court. He has been sent by his father "to seek adventures and to choose a maiden."[228] His arrival is preceded by a sound heard in the distance. "Princess Violet knew it must be a silver one, because the noise it made was like a bell." To which Princess Gamboy replies "Nonsense. I don't believe you can tell what it is made of."[229]

---

[225] Barfield, *The Silver Trumpet*, 14.
[226] Barfield, *The Silver Trumpet*, 21.
[227] Barfield, *The Silver Trumpet*, 36.
[228] Barfield, *The Silver Trumpet*, 7.
[229] Barfield, *The Silver Trumpet*, 4.

Upon hearing it a second time, Violet feels very happy "because it seemed as though there must be a piece of silver somewhere inside her which was still vibrating on and on to the trumpet, till she fell in a dream in which she was listening to church bells across the water on a summer evening."[230]

When the trumpet sounds again, Violet dreams of hearing the booming sound of a bell while laying at the bottom of the sea.

Gamboy always reads a book [the black book]; when trumpet sounds, she loses her place in the book and her memory takes her back at a time she was an infant, and she wonders if she really is wiser than her sister. Everybody who hears the bell is awakened in wonder. But a moment later they turn away "as though they were ashamed of something."[231]

The Prince, dressed in silver armor of chain-mail, first consults with the King, who consents to Prince Courtesy trying to win the heart of either daughter. It is the Little Fat Podger, whom he meets next, who informs of how different the sisters are. Prince Courtesy is amused by the little fellow, but also a bit confused by what he perceives as too fast a way of speaking. But he knew he could trust him, because "HE FELT IT IN HIS BONES" (emphasis in the text).[232]

The Prince is first led to Gamboy, to whom he says awkwardly "Pardon my intrusion. . . . you must believe that it is your beauty that has stolen my manners."[233] Gamboy has no time or interest for him and dispatches him off with an offhand remark.

Upon seeing him from a distance, arriving to the castle, Violet first sang "Create a sensation of glory, all in the land of Judea. . . . She always sang it when she was excited."[234]

When Violetta approaches Prince Courtesy soon after Gamboy, he does not notice the difference and says he would rather be left alone. After she talks to him, he then realizes that they must be different though they look alike. Courtesy becomes immediately very fond of Violet from the beginning; although he still mistakes one for the

[230] Barfield, *The Silver Trumpet*, 4.
[231] Barfield, *The Silver Trumpet*, 6.
[232] Barfield, *The Silver Trumpet*, 8.
[233] Barfield, *The Silver Trumpet*, 9.
[234] Barfield, *The Silver Trumpet*, 5.

other, "very soon he knew quite well which was which."[235] In fact he becomes the one who can recognize them when others, except Lord High Teller, cannot. Violet still loves Gamboy above all else; Courtesy doesn't love her at all. But Gamboy is always in between them, full of envy, managing to tarnish their happiness.

One evening five musicians playing strings come to the court and playing a fugue, each musician in turn echoing the other. It touches the two sisters in the same way at first. Violet thinks it's even better than dancing. Gamboy does not form any thought about it. However, it has a calming effect on her, and she remains silent for the rest of the evening. "And the Prince put his arm through Violet's and Violet put her arm through Gamboy's and they were the three of them so quiet and happy that they never forgot that evening all the rest of their lives."[236] What the five musicians achieve has more lasting effects than the Silver Trumpet, but they will only reappear at the very end of the story. The effect of their music gives us a foretaste of the epilogue of the story.

Apart from that magic moment, Gamboy has not changed. From that time onward Prince Courtesy resorts to blowing the Silver Trumpet in order to stop Gamboy's evil intentions, moods, comments, etc. When the trumpet blows, Gamboy becomes dreamy and is silent. But she is not inwardly subdued, and Courtesy has to resort to using the trumpet continuously. In fact in between times she seems nastier and more determined than ever. Thus the two start to quarrel more openly, and Courtesy feels terrible after each quarrel, knowing that he is also hurting Violet's feelings.

Soon the prince asks Violet to marry, and she immediately agrees, dancing and singing "Create a sensation of glory / All in the land of Judea."[237] Naturally, her first thought is to inform her sister. Gamboy threatens not to see her anymore if she marries the prince and puts her in the place of having to choose between the two. Violet speaks about love, and Gamboy replies cynically that Prince Courtesy only loves himself. And that she is no fool.

---

[235] Barfield, *The Silver Trumpet*, 10.
[236] Barfield, *The Silver Trumpet*, 11.
[237] Barfield, *The Silver Trumpet*, 13.

"But inside Princess Violet's head something seemed to snap suddenly. . . It was the spell cast on her by old Miss Thomson at the christening, for there was one thing in the world strong enough to break it, and that was her love for Prince Courtesy."[238] And from that moment, it is him whom she loves above all things, though her love for her sister goes unchanged.

After their engagement Gamboy does not speak to the couple, but she doesn't leave them alone either. As a result Violet feels unhappy and Courtesy uncomfortable. Gamboy now actively starts her deception, telling Violet that what she does is such because she is only concerned about her sister's happiness. Courtesy knows that all Gamboy says are lies; Violet does not.

Wanting to get married, Prince Courtesy fears that he might have to marry Gamboy instead of Violet. Under the advice of Little Fat Podger, he opts to wait until the sisters turn twenty-one, at which point they are allowed to dress and behave as they please, rather than be the same in all things.

When the time comes, Gamboy is pleased about the freedom this change gives her for the first time. Gamboy decides not to groom her hair and to dress all in black, while Violet looks very beautiful in her white dress. Now their faces also looked different, in spite of still being the same.

At the wedding the Prince's herald blows on the trumpet. Gamboy finds herself kissing Violet, but then feeling ashamed of herself. The old king names Prince Courtesy and Violet King and Queen. Gamboy grows all the more envious and spiteful, but now starts taking a more active role in the lives of the new sovereigns and in the affairs of the kingdom, through the knowledge she has been acquiring in the black book.

The Growing Power of Gamboy

In the year following the wedding, Gamboy's tantrums grew "more frequent and more violent."[239] The King keeps great distance from her, and this is all the more painful for Violet.

---

[238] Barfield, *The Silver Trumpet*, 14.
[239] Barfield, *The Silver Trumpet*, 17.

Prince Courtesy's father had asked insistently that his son protect the trumpet by never letting it off his sight. Violet insistence in having the trumpet for a day tests his limits until the king relents, even though inwardly he feels troubled by the decision. Violet does not care to keep it under lock, and that very night it disappears. It Is Gamboy who has found it and hidden it in the hayloft above the stables. The princess hated and feared that strange instrument and the power it had over her, for "she was too proud, you see, to surrender to anything except her own self-will."[240] Even her love for Violet turns now into a kind of hatred.

For the first time the attention of the story moves from the castle to beyond its walls, through Gamboy's agency. It is as if inner and outer joined forces to challenge the status quo in the castle. We are told that there had been a poor harvest and the peasants were impoverished. The treasury was depleted, and the king had to curtail his own expenses and dismiss the musicians, who had such an emblematic role in bringing peace between Gamboy and the royal couple.

Famine is now threatening, and the people's discontent grows. Gamboy walks the land in disguise, fomenting discontent. The people put all blame on the shoulders of the king, for they still love Violet. And the king is overcome with anguish, devising all possible ways to face the situation.

At the height of the crisis, the pregnant Queen Violet falls ill and the doctor prescribes rest, further requiring that she avoid any possible shock. The king is further depressed by the series of events.

Observing his master's chagrin, the Little Fat Podger studies how to amuse and distract him, but with little success, until one day he observes the king laughing at a clumsy, large green toad crossing his path. Having a little workshop where he could devise various contraptions with wood and mechanical devices, he decides to build a large wooden mechanical toad that he could animate from within. He gives himself no pause until he completes a large mechanical toad "ten times larger than life" that he can animate from within. This happens just as Gamboy was about to go to stir the townsfolk and Violet has given birth to a daughter, Lily. Seeing the Podger's creation before her ill sister or her brother-in-law, Gamboy decides to play a fatal turn on her sister, giving the jester an

---

[240] Barfield, *The Silver Trumpet*, 18.

envelope for him to deliver to the queen. In his deep preoccupation with the building of his machine, Little Fat Podger has not heard about the doctor's order relating to Violet, and from inside his contraption he cannot hear, having forgotten to build ear-holes. Thus, when he entered the queen's chamber, Violet receives a great shock at the sight and this becomes fatal, because the jester did not hear her scream and did not realize the danger. This was exactly what Gamboy had intended. But the king sees only Podger's responsibility and orders him arrested.

Anonymously stirred by Gamboy's accusations against the king, the townsfolk march to the castle. King Courtesy sees the angry crowd and speaks to them with his "funny polite voice"[241] and offers himself without defense and willingly against their animosity, adding that the queen has died. Suddenly the crowd's mood turns from anger to sorrow, and they leave the palace. Even though momentarily successful, the king retreats more and more into himself, deeply affected by Violet's death.

The king loses interest in the affairs of the kingdom, and at first does not even want to see his daughter because she reminds him of Violet. Fortunately for the kingdom, Lord High Teller has become the king's lord chancellor. The king wants to put Little Fat Podger to death, since he cannot see the hand of Gamboy in all the unfortunate events that plague him. The lord chancellor pretexts that the jester has died, and sends him in disguise to a nearby town.

After six months the king starts returning to a closer to normal life. The next harvest has been plentiful, and his reputation is growing among his subjects. Now he returns to see Lily, who in the meantime grows to be as beautiful, or even more beautiful than her mother, as we are told that "as her heart was like Violet's and like Gamboy's, her face blossomed into what Violet's face would have been but for Gamboy's wrinkles and old Miss Thomson's queer spell."[242] As the king wants her to learn to dance, he realizes with surprise that Lily could do so even without being taught. The king seeks his daughter's presence, feeling rejuvenated by his presence. But there is a part of his soul that remains untouched. The king's sadness and sense of loneliness after his loss do not abate.

241 Barfield, *The Silver Trumpet*, 24.
242 Barfield, *The Silver Trumpet*, 25.

After Violet's death the king loses heart in antagonizing Gamboy, knowing how much his wife loved her. But Gamboy, using the arts of the black book, will now consolidate her hold over King Courtesy and his daughter Lily.

Gamboy's cunning evolves. Naturally she still does many of the nasty things she is known for. She would still study from her black book and meet with the "Amalgamated Princesses" (princesses who had disobeyed regulations and had been banished from their countries, and were no longer princesses) and be their recognized leader. But, whereas before she had been completely predictable in her behavior, now she starts acting contrary to what she was known for, at least in some parts of her life.

She starts giving more attention to her looks and to entreat the king with her attentions; she pays attention to the tone of her voice, to the gestures that make her appear kind to the eyes of the king, having noticed his state of despondency, verging on despair. And the king responds ever more favorably to her advances. Lily, however, has completely different feelings toward Gamboy than the king was starting to have.

On one occasion, when walking with the king, Lily had been frightened by a toad and fainted. The king did not realize where the fear stemmed from, for "although not very clever, he was very wise."[243] The king talks to Lily about how to develop strength to be able to face the toad, and then presents him to her a second time. Though she does not faint this time, Lily is still terrified. The king himself had been quite amused at the sight of a toad, and he thus cannot understand the great difference of reaction between himself and his daughter.

Soon after this event, the king meets with Gamboy, who now looks more and more like Violet. In his delusion the king starts to see her more and more like his beloved late wife. And, letting his guard down, he confides the accident that happened to Lily. Gamboy reassures the king, but she actually knows a lot about toads from her black book, for "there was a good deal of magic in that book. And, of course, as it was a black book, it was Black Magic."[244]

---

243 Barfield, *The Silver Trumpet*, 27.
244 Barfield, *The Silver Trumpet*, 29.

Having gained the king's confidence, Gamboy now works at weakening Violet's defenses, the matter being easier with a child. At first she calls her "my dear," which was what the ladies of the Amalgamated Princesses called each other. She makes her feel like a trusted adult, at her hour of greatest need. Gamboy thus manages putting her at ease and letting her lower her guard. She then stages a "fortuitous" event, in which it looks like Gamboy herself is terrified of toads. Lily is startled at the discovery and now even more terrified. She falls unconscious to the pleasure of Gamboy, who now sees how easily she can subdue the girl to her plans. Gamboy now alternates feigning compassion for her niece, but without answering whether she can protect her from the fear of toads, Gamboy leads Lily to believe that she is as helpless as herself.

When Lily wants to go talk to the king, Gamboy plays on the child's feelings by asking her not to trouble the already perturbed father with further issues: "If you love him, you will say nothing about it."[245] Utterly confused in her innocent feelings, Lily asks now for Gamboy's protection, and sleeps in the room next to hers. Gamboy, however, doesn't guarantee that she can protect her: Left alone in the room, Lily is truly terrified and helpless. Soon after Lily has a dream in which is "revealed" the truth about Gamboy, but too late now for any other course of action. After that she wakes up with a high fever and in a delirious state, mistaking Gamboy for her mother, Violet. Gamboy completes her work by taking over the power of the king in the council and by confining Lily to a specially built tower in which the child is supposedly safer from her fears.

Gamboy completes her deception by telling the king that she has talked to Lily and helped her as much as she could. She advises him not to talk to the child, in order not to stir feelings needlessly. The king interprets this as kindness and is further enamored of Gamboy, who continuously plays on the likeness to her sister to further deceive him. She imitates virtues in gestures and evokes the king's memories. The identification is total, to the point that the king now echoes what he said to Gamboy at their very first meeting: "pardon my intrusion . . . you must believe that it is your beauty that has stolen my manners." And

---

[245] Barfield, *The Silver Trumpet*, 32.

Gamboy thinks to herself: "What a fool he is! But he is rich, and a King, and I would like a Prince to my son or a Princess to my daughter."[246] Only an external force can now change the dire conditions inside the castle. It comes under the form of another prince from another kingdom: Prince Peerio.

The Arrival of Prince Peerio and the Sounding of the Silver Trumpet

Prince Peerio is the son of King Strein of the kingdom of Strenvaig. He has fallen in love with Princess Lily after seeing a painting bought by a rich merchant. The narrative specifies he "had fallen in love, not with the picture, but with the Princess,"[247] which denotes an early maturity in the prince.

His father banishes him because he wants him to marry the daughter of a neighboring monarch. Upon leaving in autumn, the dejected prince is worried about his father feeling alone without his presence. He travels with a minimum of belongings, from town to town to reach Mountainy Castle, stopping from time to time to work in order to purchase what he needs. The journey is not a linear one, and at one point he finds himself in the same town he thought he had left behind. After walking for two months, he is told he is only three miles away from the castle. Here he comes to the inn of Mine Host, who turns him away for lack of room. Prince Peerio, "who had come to understand a good deal about faces . . . saw at once that the man was not really unkind but only very troubled."[248] So he offers to help him with the washing of the dishes.

Good fate has brought him to the inn where the concealed Little Fat Podger works as a cook. The cook expresses himself with many little, funny movements, sudden gestures, impromptu sayings, interrupted sentences, all of which make him look funny. But Peerio realizes immediately that the cook doesn't think this is funny and worth laughing at. Rather he realizes that "the head, which seemed so very much too large for that crooked little body, was crammed full of some trouble of its own which couldn't get out."[249]

---

246 Barfield, *The Silver Trumpet*, 32.
247 Barfield, *The Silver Trumpet*, 34.
248 Barfield, *The Silver Trumpet*, 35.
249 Barfield, *The Silver Trumpet*, 36.

Peerio at first a little taken aback by his manners. He tells him of his travels, starts to disclose his own story to the cook, and then mentions the princess, whose painting he has carried in his travels. When asking to see the picture, the cook is shaken by the resemblance of Lily to Violet and confesses that he once knew the mother. He offers to help Peerio by introducing him to Miss Thomson, and warns him of the cunning of Gamboy.

Peerio doesn't want to give away that he is a prince, so he approaches the castle in disguise. He meets an idle stable-boy, who informs him about the machinations of Gamboy and of the Amalgamated Princesses, of how the king is completely under her spell. Peerio is wise and advised not to show his feelings when the stable-boy mentions Lily.

Absentmindedly taking the stranger into the castle, the stable-boy informs him that it has been ten years since the king married Gamboy, whom he now calls Violet; that it is known that Gamboy stirred revolt against the king, and that the stable-boy's own father was as beguiled by her as is now the king. He tells him about the Amalgamated Princesses and their machinations, adding that that Gamboy deals with magic, and that she "is a mumblin' and a mutterin' to 'erself or the Devil"[250] while she reads from the black book. The stable-boy also reveals that for a while Lily was entrenched in a high tower. All along Gamboy has been listening to them under her window, and is now aware of the intentions of Prince Peerio.

After her recovery from her illness, Lily is weakened and changed. She is silent and absent, answering questions with only yes or no. She has lost interest in people and in her surroundings, so much so that her servants avoid her. She has grown terrified of darkness and is practically scared of her own shadow. She is completely dependent on her aunt for a false sense of security. She hardly sees her father, who is even more completely dependent on the queen. She has lost interest in books, in animals or stars, and she is forgetting everything she previously has known, wondering at what possible use knowledge would have. Nothing brings her pleasure and, alone in her tower, she is still terrified of toads.

The king thinks of little, not even of Violet, and considers himself happy in the most empty meaning of the word. The queen keeps him

[250] Barfield, *The Silver Trumpet*, 39–40.

sedated through magic potions she pours in his tea. And she takes the affairs of the kingdom in her own hands.

The stable-boy adds that the above state of absence from self is also the case for all other castle dwellers: there is a spell over the castle, and only Queen Gamboy seems alive. "She too was silent, but not with the silence of death. She was silent rather as ants and spiders are silent."[251]

Nothing that the stable-boy tells him changes Peerio's feelings for Lily, and he wonders what he could devise. But now Queen Gamboy put a spell on Peerio, turning him into a "great grey-green lolloping toad."[252] Because he has been clutching to the letter of introduction to Miss Thomson—believing he is holding on to Lily's portrait—this remained unchanged. With this little thread of hope remaining, he takes the letter in his mouth and steers his course towards the town, hardly knowing how he will ask for Miss Thomson.

Meanwhile the stable-boy chances upon the Silver Trumpet in the hay loft where Gamboy hid it. Delighted by its sound, he plays on it over and over again. Everybody stands as if awakened, at least for as long as the echo of the sound carries. Gamboy dreams back to the time when she was a child and had a sister Violet, and starts questioning what she is doing at present. King Courtesy calls to Violet. Once more the first awakening and joy is followed by shame.

Gamboy's facial expression has changed for a moment, but then everything resumes as before.

> And some say that, this time, Violet herself, deep down in her grave, heard the Silver Trumpet, and that she stirred and trembled there, and that her face too began to change, taking new wrinkles to its white brow, and that a look of cunning began to creep into her eyes underneath their coverlet of darkness.[253]

Princess Lily first scolds her maidens-in-waiting for letting music be played close to the tower. After another sound from the trumpet,

---

[251] Barfield, *The Silver Trumpet*, 41.
[252] Barfield, *The Silver Trumpet*, 43.
[253] Barfield, *The Silver Trumpet*, 45.

Lily awakens to the realization of her deep unhappiness. She sends a messenger to Miss Thomson to summon her to the palace.

King Courtesy is awakened, though made sad at the thought of his beloved. The king summons the stable-boy, who brings him the Silver Trumpet, and he decides to lock it up. The stable-boy returns to town to tell the citizens all that has just happened. And the townsfolk decide to march to the castle and ask an audience of the king.

Prince Peerio's Triumph

Princess Lily's messenger reaches Miss Thomson who sends back her reply, "Tell your mistress that Miss T. always helps those who have the courage to ask her."[254] Meanwhile Peerio is proceeding to town, always with the letter in his mouth. Miss Thomson, proceeding in the opposite direction to Peerio, sees the strange toad with a letter in his mouth and recognizes her name on the envelope. After realizing it is Peerio, she tells him that in order to recover his shape, he must be met by somebody who loves him just the way he is at present. She spends a quarter of an hour telling him what he needs to do.

Continuing on her way, Miss Thomson arrives at Lily's tower when the latter has almost returned to her habitual state. The two meet, and Lily explains her fear of toads. Then, as she has done with Peerio, Miss Thomson speaks to Lily for a quarter of an hour, telling her what she has to do to overcome her fear of toads.

Contrary to her habit of years, Lily goes to sleep in complete darkness and leaves the windows open. She is assailed by terror but reminds herself to be strong and keep trusting, telling herself, "Death is better for me than another eight years like the last."[255] When she hears a noise by the window sill, she knows this must be a toad, and facing her fears goes towards it, sees it, and kisses it.

Under the light of the moon she sees the creature transform into a beautiful prince wearing the silver chain-mail he has left behind at his father's castle. This puts an end to her fear.

---

[254] Barfield, *The Silver Trumpet*, 45.
[255] Barfield, *The Silver Trumpet*, 48.

Princess Lily recognizes Peerio as her own prince. She confides her story and cries out all her past misery. After clearing her grief, she immediately turns her thoughts to her father.

Peerio now knows what to do. He first sends out for the little cook. And while Gamboy holds council with the Amalgamated Princesses, vainly promising them that they would all be queens in the future, Prince Peerio walks straight up to her "and he bounced her up and down the floor . . . until he had fairly shaken the breath out of her. Then he did that again."[256]

Thus subjugated, Gamboy is taken under the custody of the Head Gaoler. From there Peerio goes to the king's chambers, announcing to the king that he will marry his daughter the next day.

On the morrow, a Sunday, the couple gets married, she in her mother's white dress, he in his silver chain-mail suit. Queen Gamboy is allowed to assist the wedding ceremony.

After being pronounced wedded, the prince takes the Silver Trumpet to draw sound from it, four times in a row. What follows are incredible changes in Gamboy's face; she first loses her wrinkles and the air of cunning that dominated her face. As the trumpet keeps on sounding, more changes follow:

> Her features went on changing and sliding into one another, like clouds over the sky, moving and clearing until there, beside her husband, white-robed and laughing in the sunlight, stood none other than Queen Violet herself! . . . And some say that deep down in the grave other features upon another face had been changing too and sliding—that to this day a body, which is Aunt Gamboy's, lies buried in the churchyard.[257]

Restored to herself, Violet calls for the Silver Trumpet and offers it to the king, entreating him to guard it safely. "Whereat the stooping King straightened his old back as by a miracle."[258]

---

[256] Barfield, *The Silver Trumpet*, 49.
[257] Barfield, *The Silver Trumpet*, 50–51.
[258] Barfield, *The Silver Trumpet*, 51.

The king names Peerio and Lily the new king and queen of Mountainy Castle. The people of the town arrive marching to the palace, and from another direction arrives Miss Thomson and the five musicians who had played at the castle before. So too arrives Little Fat Podger.

A Second Look at the Story

What is most remarkable about this story is that it preceded everything that Barfield was to say in the following years, even his first two books, *Poetic Diction* and *History in English Words*. It was even the first work of fantasy of the Inklings, preceding the *Chronicles of Narnia* and *The Hobbit*. And yet, everything of relevance that Barfield will popularize in the following years is already expressed elegantly and with power in this tale. *The Silver Trumpet* chronicles the human historical journey from original participation to conscious participation. It moves from the tableau of the precarious equilibrium between Violet and Gamboy with Prince Courtesy in between, to the higher stage of consciousness brought about through King Peerio and Queen Lily.

The tale starts with a perfect example of an eternal polarity of the soul. Nothing in the relationship between Violet and Gamboy is static, nor is it in a perfect equilibrium. We know things are bound to progress and progress fast.

Violet likes hundreds of things and loves to dance and sing; Gamboy loves little beyond Violet and herself. Violet is moved to excess within her feeling life; she loses herself in the ragged boy and in those who are in need. She can look with wonder and listen with empathy. Gamboy reminds us of the other extreme of cynicism: that we can separate ourselves completely, and interpret what others do as means for an end or manipulation of our feelings. The narrator reminds us that there are two ways of loving people: Violet tends "to like seeing [people] well and happy," whereas Gamboy "to like [people] to do what you tell them." Violet can recognize the qualities of objects, as she shows in the instance of the Silver Trumpet. Gamboy flatly denies it is possible. Violet yearns for something eternal that her words only vaguely fathom: "Create a sensation of glory/All in the land of Judea." Gamboy, at the other extreme, likes to discriminate and understand; she seeks knowledge but in the wrong place, in the black book.

Gamboy is that part of the soul that cannot live without Violet, and vice versa. It is said in the words of Miss Thomson that "as long as one of you is living, both shall *be*." And these words come true at the end of the story after Violet has supposedly died.

In between the sisters comes the wedge of Prince Courtesy; the already precarious equilibrium is altered. All the more so because the sisters reach the turning point of the birth of the ego at age twenty-one. Now they are clearly recognizable in the way they present themselves to the world; and though they still look alike, their faces betray different, clearly recognizable expressions. Soon after hearing the Silver Trumpet and seeing Prince Courtesy, Violet sings "Create a sensation of glory/All in the land of Judea." Though Violet still is as fond of Gamboy as she was before, she now loves the prince above her. And Gamboy, who has never really loved Violet in the full meaning of the word, starts to swing between love and hate. Her primary love turns into its opposite. And in between the two, Prince Courtesy introduces the Silver Trumpet.

Prince Courtesy has an easy path; he comes from nobility to meet with other nobility. He does not have to seek hard Mountainy Castle. Once there, he finds his way through his "intuition." He cannot fully understand Little Fat Podger but—and Barfield overemphasizes it— "HE FELT IT IN HIS BONES" that he could trust him. He cannot at first recognize Violet from Gamboy in the opening scenes, nor can he immediately after, but soon enough he becomes one of the few who can always tell them apart. He does not seek a relationship with Gamboy because he doesn't trust her; he knows she lies but cannot understand of what she is really capable. He will not understand her later when her cunning and capacity for evil grows through the inspiration of the black book. And the narrative epitomizes prince Courtesy in the assessment that "although not very clever, he was very wise."

Prince Courtesy is wiser than clever; Violet is completely lost in a world of sympathy that includes her own sister but cannot see through who she is. In between them and above them hover the tones of the Silver Trumpet, which has a different effect on the sisters. The innocent sister is transported into one grandiose dream after another. The cynical one alternates between wonder and shame. Over time Gamboy can no longer stand the call of conscience that comes from her higher self. But neither can Prince Courtesy and Violet reach that world, or reach it permanently. With the help of the Silver Trumpet they can contain Violet's outbursts, but after these her evil streak comes out reinforced. And the Silver Trumpet can only work if it is kept hidden from Gamboy.

Around these three figures stand three emblematic but central characters. One is the wise Lord High Teller, who knows the "meaning of names." The second is Little Fat Podger, who raises people's spirits, listen and advises, and is as wise as Lord High Teller, but in another way. The last is Miss Thomson, whose wisdom and kind heart are the doorways to magic.

Change comes when Gamboy can "mature" her innate tendencies at age twenty-one, when the ego can illuminate latent predispositions. Gamboy changes, or evolves through the wisdom she finds in the black book. Whereas she did not please in doing the good, now she deliberately pursues evil. She no longer leaves her intentions run to the light of day for all to see. Now she wants to seem good in order to better cultivate evil intentions. She masters the art of deception on her sister—leading her to her death—on King Courtesy, and on his daughter Lily.

Gamboy knows how to confuse the feelings of Violet, the king, and their daughter, and it is clear that the couple cannot see through Gamboy's machinations. Lily can for a while, but her age does not help. We know that Lily brings the capacities of Violet to a next stage. Whereas the mother had to learn to dance, Lily already knows how to do it and needs no instruction in the matter. She can also recognize more clearly Gamboy's schemes, though she does not yet have the ego presence that would enable her to stand up to her aunt. Her latent capacities, announcing the future stage of the play, are deliberately squashed by Gamboy.

The second stage of the tale is that of the complete fall and estrangement from any divine source. Violet dies, squelched by the excessive strength of Gamboy. She will go on living a life of the spirit separate from earth, as we see at the end of the play. Gamboy's evil magic drives her out. When conscious evil is pursued systematically, Violet is driven out of the soul. The instrument that calls the best in each sister and everybody else, is lost just after the sisters have reached maturity. Prince Courtesy's intuition is no match for the attacks of Gamboy, who is bent on imposing her will upon every last person, Amalgamated Princesses included. We are told by the stable-boy that it was as if there was a spell over the whole castle and that only Gamboy "seemed" alive. In a sense at first sympathy and participation prevail through Violet having the upper hand among the sisters. Then complete antipathy and separation through the evil designs of Gamboy rise to the surface, and black magic drives out the last of Violet from the soul.

Gamboy reigns not only over the castle but also over the minds of the townsfolk. Help can only come from outside. This is where Prince Peerio enters the story. And from the beginning we know we have moved to a next stage. Prince Courtesy is sent out in the world to do his father's will. He foregoes adventures as soon as he sees Violet. It is otherwise with Prince Peerio, who has to leave behind the support of his father when he decides to pursue a Lily he has never met. He is cast out and wanders from town to town. But we are told that "he was a very wise young Prince (wise in his schooldays and wise when he started out from home),"[259] and moreover that he "had come to understand a good deal about faces."[260] He would not confuse Gamboy for Violet even at first sight. In fact his discrimination is so high that when he sees Lily's painting, he falls in love "not with the picture, but with the Princess."[261] This indicates a very high level of inner maturity from the outset.

It is this higher consciousness that sets events of divine providence the prince's way. Because he can see beyond the gruffness of Mine Host, and not take things personally in his feelings, he is led at the appropriate time to the Cook/Little Fat Podger, who can advise him effectively, and to the stable-boy, who leads him into the castle and informs him of all he needs to know about the situation he will face. Because he does not lose heart in the direst of circumstances, he is led to Miss Thomson, who "always helps those who have the courage to ask her." The same is true of Lily. She brings Violet's abilities one stage further. She has more discrimination than her mother. Her wings have been clipped through

---

[259] Barfield, *The Silver Trumpet*, 48.
[260] Barfield, *The Silver Trumpet*, 35.
[261] Barfield, *The Silver Trumpet*, 34.

evil arts from her very birth, through the evil that Gamboy brings into the world. We could say that she has been estranged from her true self from her birth. At the end of the story she has the strength to face the equivalent of death in confronting the strongest fear associated with her moment of birth. She immediately recognizes Prince Peerio as the one her soul has been longing for. And in a sense Lily represents the modern soul, coming to earth with new abilities and longing for spiritual communion but estranged from its heavenly home soon after birth. The Gamboy forces deaden it and put it to sleep, until life circumstances bring it closer to its truer self and awaken it.

Because he has reached beyond original innocence, without losing virtue, Peerio can face Gamboy in a matter-of-fact way. He knows what she is scheming and what is her power, and is confident that he has the resources within himself to withstand her. He can set her back to her place. This is why Gamboy is present on the Sunday of the wedding; she will no longer hurt human beings as she is used to. Peerio is the one who truly sees the world around himself; he sees it differently and more fully. It is the individual who has attained conscious participation: he sees the world from the realm of Imagination.

Because Peerio is so armed in his soul, he can restore Gamboy to her full potential and hold the balance between the sisters of the soul. We are told that in her grave "a look of cunning began to creep into [Violet's] eyes underneath their coverlet of darkness." As Gamboy is tamed, so Violet is wizened. The prince and Lily hold the scales between the two.

Prince Peerio is the one who can do consciously what Prince Courtesy did naturally. Prince Courtesy receives everything he needs through birth and circumstance. He does not have to fight; the path is mapped out for him. Prince Peerio has to overcome at every step of the way; stand against his father's will, travel afar for a long time, devise stratagems, overcome adversities.

In Prince Peerio the qualities that were externalized in the three auxiliary characters, have now very much become the inner soul capacities of clear thinking, balanced feeling, and selfless will. At this new evolutionary stage the Silver Trumpet is no longer threatened. And, quite significantly it is Miss Thomson who brings back the five musicians, whose "magic" reaches one stage higher than the Silver Trumpet itself.

The imagination of the Silver Trumpet seems placed at Barfield's incipient literary career as the herald of things to come. This imagination came to him as he was deeply musing on all the related themes that the tale touches upon. In the years to come Barfield would work at other artistic imaginations, but mostly he would bring the imaginations from the artistic realm into the cognitive and deepen them in his consciousness until attaining not just discrete imaginations but Imagination itself, the imaginative consciousness itself, as he detailed in *Unancestral Voice*.

In *The Silver Trumpet* Barfield also explores microcosmic reality through a story; he highlights the polarities of sympathy and antipathy in ways that he has not used elsewhere. And similarly he hints at the presence and strengthening of the double in the soul. The microcosmic aspects of the human being that Barfield does not explore in cognitive fashion appear here in literary/artistic form.

What *The Silver Trumpet* initiated in 1924 was taken a step further with the imagination of *The Rose on the Ash-Heap* five years later.

THE ROSE ON THE ASH-HEAP

The story, in the tradition of a German *märchen*, or fairy tale with magical/supernatural themes, is the epilogue of Barfield's 550-page early novel *English People*. This placement at the end of a long novel is reminiscent of Goethe's fairy tale of *The Green Snake and the Beautiful Lily* concluding his *Conversations of German Emigrants*.

The story is divided in seven sections. In the introduction to the story, published separately from the novel, a number of themes are announced by Barfield:

- Abdol has usurped the role of Lord of Albion (the rightful ruler of England). Abdol needs no secret police; he uses a highly centralized authority and makes recourse to "*panem and circenses* in a literal sense."
- Abdol's Fun Fest is contrasted with the Circus under the great ash-heap.

177

- Sultan, central protagonist of the story, coming from the East, finds in the West a special master key.
- Sultan will unite with the daughter of the Lord of Albion.

First Section

Sultan, "Lord of all the Asias and hereditary High Priest of all their religions"[262] spends much of his time in a seraglio (harem) devoted to the pleasure of the senses.

In abandonment Sultan finds the perpetual contrast between rapture followed by sorrow and disappointment. Nevertheless Sultan's is still a spiritual quest, for he prays to Shiva. Of late he wants to pursue a beautiful white-skinned dancer he has seen in the Temple. In a dream a distant union is foretold to him. The dream also announces that this union is to bring about many changes, chiefly the expulsion of all the concubines and wives from the seraglio.

The union foretold in the dream brings at first great happiness. Then Sultan awakens to the contrast of his present state, only wanting to dream again. In this state of mind he runs to the Temple, to ask about the dancer. The old man who guards the entrance to the Temple tells him she has taken sacred vows. Sultan indicates to him that he wants to follow the rule of the Temple, adding that in his breast he has long heard the call to the sacred life as much as the call of the blood.[263]

After various entreaties Sultan is promised access to the Temple if he returns on the morrow. However, the next day the Temple appears in great disorder, and Sultan learns that the dancer has fled. The old man seems to indicate that she is fleeing "the [powerful] dreams of a monarch." Sultan still wants to join the Temple, but the old man tells him that this will not help him. However, he also tells him that he had been waiting for the day when Sultan would hear the call of the spirit and that that was also the reason for the presence of the dancer. The old man indicates that the Temple has now only "spinning tops [who] do not make . . . the mistake you made."[264]

[262] Barfield, *The Rose on the Ash-Heap*, 3.
[263] Barfield, *The Rose on the Ash-Heap*, 6.
[264] Barfield, *The Rose on the Ash-Heap*, 7.

Sultan abdicates his throne to pursue the dancer, who has moved westward with the blessing of the old man, without ever being able to overtake her. The dancer precedes him, teaching everywhere music and dances, and these she tailors to the needs of each people she meets. Sultan is touched by the beauty and variety of her teachings. It is said that it was the discipline she followed and the instructions she received in the Temple that have rendered her able to closely discern people's special needs.

In his pursuit Sultan has to overcome the call of the blood, particularly his attachments to a "certain little concubine, whom he had heartlessly abandoned."[265] In his search he arrives to Southern Europe: Greece first, then Spain. Here, while lodging with a noblewoman, he is shown the "new dances." In the dances the courtiers sing to the ladies:

> *Sweet, who dost hold my heart*
> *Fast immured in those eyes*
> *Approach, oh, ease my smart,*
> *Ere thy piteous caitiff dies!*

> *Later the two sing together:*
> *What is eternal? This:*
> *Thou givest me a kiss.*[266]

Sultan experiences this as a moment of bliss, but the next day he is dismayed because his hosts cannot tell with certainty where the dancer has gone. He decides to cross the sea and go to Albion. Sultan promises Shiva not to abandon himself to any other woman than the white-skinned dancer.

In Albion Sultan discovers that nobody knows with certainty about the "Beloved." However, they tell him of the tradition of "a divinely fair woman, a virgin goddess, who, under the name of 'Lady' or, as some said, 'Lucy,' who dwelt secretly in the heart of the country."[267] Sultan now starts to call her "Lady." Then he hears a rumor that she

---

[265] Barfield, *The Rose on the Ash-Heap*, 9.
[266] Barfield, *The Rose on the Ash-Heap*, 11.
[267] Barfield, *The Rose on the Ash-Heap*, 12.

had returned to Asia a while back. Sultan decides to return himself. In Asia it is confirmed to him that Lady has spent three days and nights in the Temple in deep meditation, after which she had departed westward. In great despair Sultan breaks his vows and sleeps with the concubine.

The Beloved has moved in the direction of Northern Europe. Sultan follows her there and finds himself one day on the "banks of the Ister [Danube]." Here Sultan sees beautiful new dances that produce in him an ambivalent reaction; on one hand he knows that these are from her Beloved, on the other hand the languor of the seraglio overtakes his senses. In the midst of this he is led to a "beautiful blonde" who teaches him the steps of the dances and enraptures him, calling him familiarly "Herr Sultan." After he leaves, Sultan carries in his heart the memories of this encounter.

Second Section

Now Albion is introduced and reference is made to "the Princess [whom the Lord of Albion calls Lucy], his newly adopted daughter"[268] and of preparations concerning an incoming threat. Lord Albion is concerned most of all about the preservation of his breed of horses.

Sultan has arrived at this time at the court of the Lord of Albion and demands an audience with the princess, but he refuses to declare his identity. Upon meeting her, Sultan immediately recognizes her and confesses to her of having been very lonely, most of all when he was in the company of the women in the seraglio; he says further "I lost sight of the Eternal's glorious sunlight, lost all sight of the vast concourse of my suffering fellow-creatures and willfully beheld nothing but one pitiful and painted phantom of my desire, which, even so, I struggled in vain to possess."[269] The princess forgives him, but says her father will forgive but cannot forget. Then she kisses him, and asks him to go and return the next day. Of the Lord of Albion we are told that he "is the Emperor of many western lands" but that he leads in freedom.

Abdol is introduced as an "incredibly wealthy and powerful private citizen."[270] He has gained by nook and by crook a great ascendancy and

---

[268] Barfield, *The Rose on the Ash-Heap*, 17.
[269] Barfield, *The Rose on the Ash-Heap*, 18.
[270] Barfield, *The Rose on the Ash-Heap*, 19–20.

is now what many believe to be the true Lord of Albion. Abdol's jealousy and antagonism towards the Lord of Albion derives from the reaction to the latter's desire to raise the best breed of horses as a way to preserve the "legacy from the days when the chivalry was a power in Europe in order that, when the time comes, she [Albion] may be able to distribute it all over the world."[271]

The Lord of Albion has entrusted the nobility with this task, but they soon neglected it, as they neglected their duty towards the common folk. Abdol raised black horses in Arabia, the land of his birth. Though remarkable horses, they are malicious. Knowing this, the Lord of Albion entreated his nobility to keep the two strains separate. But Abdol was a shrewd merchant and managed to outcompete Albion's breed, and even to eliminate Lord of Albion's true stock from the country.

After defeating the Lord of Albion in a large series of horse races, Abdol turned his interest to mineral oils, which rendered horses unnecessary, and to finances in order to gain power over the money supply. Thus he acquired more and more power.

While hearing much of the above from an innkeeper, Sultan falls asleep and has another significant dream. He sees himself united with Lady, completing his wedding day, and being invited in the evening to a grand feast by the Lord of Albion. On the occasion Sultan perceives in the distance the little concubine who still has a hold on his soul. Lady seemed to be unaware of her presence; not so the Lord of Albion. When Sultan goes to the bridal chamber, the surprise awaits him to see his beloved transformed into a monstrously hideous being, who springs upon him, engulfing him in the nausea of her embrace. He awakens from the nightmare to see the Lord of Albion's palace under attack. Ruin has engulfed the palace in a very short time, and Sultan beholds it all around him. It is all transformed in an "enormous heap of grey ashes."[272] Sultan feels unable to pray feeling the bitter taste of ashes in his mouth.

---

[271] Barfield, *The Rose on the Ash-Heap*, 20.
[272] Barfield, *The Rose on the Ash-Heap*, 25.

Third Section

Sultan travels westward to a part of the country that Abdol has not yet contaminated, an area of farmers. One of the peasants advises him "out of the depths of that slow but profound nature-wisdom which was their birthright" to look for the Poet who would be able to assuage his sorrow.

The Poet is described as "elderly and graceful man beautifully dressed."[273] He speaks in analogies referring to the Beloved, and expresses that he knows what it is to mourn for her. Moreover, he indicates that it is this loss that has made him the Poet he is. In comparing all of nature to his Beloved, the Poet can penetrate the mysteries of nature. And he shows Sultan the laboratories and the experiments he carries within them.

In hearing the Poet speak about what that loss meant for him, Sultan can take distance from his own personal sorrows. Sultan cautiously inquires how the Poet lost the Beloved, and the latter reveals to him that it is him who refused her because she did not understand him. The Poet seeks for the all-encompassing dimensions of being in his maiden, "[ennobling] her with the bewildering sense of her own unworthiness." All previous sorrow revisits Sultan, and he asks the Poet whether he has ever tasted the taste of ashes, to which the Poet appears bemused. After this exchange Sultan announces that he will travel further west in search of the Philosopher, for whom the Poet has very little appreciation. Sultan takes leave of the Poet, who first offers him a poem, among whose lines are the following:

> Had they but told me that her name is Sleep.
> How many pangs of sorrow had been saved!
> . . . Had they but told me, none need lie forlorn
> Since icy Death was swallowed up in love. . ..
> Love, love, how many eyes will cease to weep,
> When I shall tell them that thy name is Sleep![274]

In seeking the Philosopher, Sultan travels a long way westward, right into the middle of Abdol's domain and the ugliness that characterizes

---

[273] Barfield, *The Rose on the Ash-Heap*, 27–28.

[274] Barfield, *The Rose on the Ash-Heap*, 32.

it. And the contrast extends from the environments of the two to their appearance. Of the Philosopher we are told that he wears a "shabby old coat and a pair of sagging cylindrical trousers . . . his voice was loud and startling . . . his movements were boyish and awkward."[275] And he continuously smokes a tobacco-pipe.

The Philosopher speaks of his feelings and his private world, in complex and roundabout ways that Sultan often misses. He uses a self-deprecating humor and refers to himself as the most insignificant of all beings. Yet, it seems to Sultan that he conveys a warmer feeling of sympathy towards him than the Poet did. Once Sultan takes the Philosopher seriously and starts commiserating with him, the latter takes to his own persona all the more furiously. When Sultan endures, the Philosopher finally reveals his own story. He married a lady to whom he had been betrothed but who through a turn of fate had turned imbecile, to whom he still devotes great part of his income, and to whom he wants to remain faithful.

The Philosopher indicates that he is not to determine his actions by the pleasure and pain that he derives from them, but through faithfulness to his lot. Sultan feels comforted much more so by the Philosopher than he was by the Poet, and more precisely by the awareness that such a kind of man can exist in such a desolate place. The Philosopher sums up his stand in life by saying "Reason, which amid the many ever holds fast to the One, arises solely out of Constancy and is only to be sustained by that virtue."[276]

However much as Sultan likes the Philosopher, he also realizes his foibles, in particular in relation to his passion for star-gazing. The Philosopher's habit is to expound at length, and in monotonous fashion, about everything he perceives through his telescope. Moreover, Sultan discovers that the Philosopher's chief weakness is his laziness, which justifies his sense of insignificance by way of not having to undertake anything in order to rise above it. However, this sense of insignificance can at times change into its opposite, when he shows his anger towards the vault of the heavens. Then he says "Man is only truly man when he

---

[275] Barfield, *The Rose on the Ash-Heap*, 33.
[276] Barfield, *The Rose on the Ash-Heap*, 36.

can stand four-square to the universe, as I am standing now, and hurl defiance to his icy ruthlessness, even as I am hurling it now."[277]

The Philosopher has changed Sultan's outlook to the extent that when he looks at the night sky, he feels it to be cold and distant. When looking at Sirius, the Dog Star, Sultan sees it change from green to orange and winking at him, but reacts with laughter alone, quite like the Philosopher.

Sultan announces his intention to continue travel westward, to which the Philosopher abduces the excuse that it is not possible to pass beyond the Gasometer, not far from his house, without being sucked into the Fourth Dimension and being sent eastward. Sultan knows this to be a lie and tries to hide his discomfort.

Knowing that he has to leave, partly out of compassion for the Philosopher, Sultan feels moved to tell him the secret of his loss. After hearing him the Philosopher misunderstands him, saying "The Absolute has recently chosen to appear to you . . . in the form of an attractive young female."[278] To which Sultan replies that this is the first time that the Poet gives the same answer as the Poet, referring to the latter's lack of understanding for Sultan's "taste of ashes" experience. Sultan continues to uphold the reality of his loss, of it not being an illusion: "It is not the Absolute that I am missing, at the moment. . . . It is simply Lady."[279] For the Philosopher, Sultan is foolishly confusing a young woman for the Absolute.

Fourth Section

Sultan manages to travel westward with none of the risks the Philosopher has forewarned him about. However, he experiences being more and more alone. He realizes that everybody moves in alienation from anybody else and that nobody is there who can support him. In the process of self-knowledge, achieved partly through the Philosopher, he is now completely divorced from the world of the stars. And yet, as this feeling increases to the point at which he feels like fainting, something reverses, and in a state close to the dream, he senses that the stars are

---

[277] Barfield, *The Rose on the Ash-Heap*, 38.
[278] Barfield, *The Rose on the Ash-Heap*, 40.
[279] Barfield, *The Rose on the Ash-Heap*, 41.

indeed trying to reach him but cannot quite do so. This only makes his mood grow more and more somber the following day.

Sultan now reaches into the thickest and ugliest of Abdol's domain, between factories, gasometers, electric posts and webs of cables, deafening sound, densely populated towns, and people completely alienated. Sultan is on the brink of despair and wishes he could only sing like the Poet. But the Poet cannot comfort him, because his yearning is for Lady alone, and what the Philosopher has taught him cannot revive what has dried up in his heart.

In the midst of this soul agony and the thoughts of what worse things are to follow, Sultan finally finds the strength to sing, something that flows through him to his surprise, speaking of "lost imagination" and of "find[ing] my Lady in [some room's] firelit gloom."[280] The words in the song bring him relief and comfort, and he finds new strength in seeking to go further west.

At the end of his movement west, Sultan reaches "a peninsula on the West Coast, shaped like a triangle and called Delta . . . formed by a single huge triangular mass of crystalline rock that towered high above the Pacific Ocean."[281] Sultan has arrived at Cape Limit, for which the Poet had shown little interest, and of which the Philosopher had talked with dread. When he arrives Sultan can only distinguish clearly the black rock, whereas ocean and sky seemed to merge into each other. He recognizes the round building shape of a hotel with a cupola on its top. He decides to use all the money he has left to spend the night in it, and trust what the future may bring.

To his surprise Sultan discovers that the hotel is Abdol's property, and this is the first time that something of his is graceful in all its details. Sultan is the only guest in the hotel and is given the room at the very top, under the cupola, from which he can survey the vault of the heavens. He tries to sing himself to sleep, but cannot. In a vision he beholds Lady ("the Holy One") coming towards him and holding a scroll, in which he recognizes just as he awakens the poem the Poet had given him before he departed from him. Sultan derives great comfort from the vision and the words of the poem. Lying on his back he can

---

[280] Barfield, *The Rose on the Ash-Heap*, 47.
[281] Barfield, *The Rose on the Ash-Heap*, 47–48.

gaze at the stars, which now seem to draw nearer to him just as they wanted to but could not earlier on. Sultan wants to give "himself up to them with the same mystic abandonment as that which he had once used towards his wives in the seraglio."[282] In the middle of the night he once more sees the Dog Star of Sirius rising and flashing with brilliant violence.

Between waking and sleeping, Sultan witnesses the star singing. The song appears to him both new and similar to what he heard in his distant childhood, telling him "Mortal awake! Thy dawn is near. . . . The time is near. . . . Immortal mortals wake and use your eyes!" Old words he has heard in the past come to him imbued with new meaning, warning him, "Else a great Prince [referring to Sultan!?] in prison dies!"[283]

As the voice of Sirius fades, Sultan beholds the firmament, no longer silent, but in its full glory, revealing its workings in the "violet hue of the interstellar profundity."[284] Now he turns his attention to the seven vibrant stars of the Great Bear, announcing that he shall behold their activity in greater awareness. Sultan finds himself sharing the consciousness of this glorious present with that of his childhood. This movement announces a shift from the "violet hue" to a greater majesty of colors through which shine the constellations of the Zodiac, starting to speak in turns. The movement is announced as a whole first by the whole Zodiac:

> Unturning, His disciples turn
> In mystic dance about the Sun
> (He sent us forth but to return!)
> Weaving the Many into One.
> Though numberless as blades of grass,
> Each part into the Whole doth pass.[285]

---

[282] Barfield, *The Rose on the Ash-Heap*, 50.
[283] Barfield, *The Rose on the Ash-Heap*, 52.
[284] Barfield, *The Rose on the Ash-Heap*, 53.
[285] Barfield, *The Rose on the Ash-Heap*, 54.

Then this vision fades. But now rises before him the constellation of the Virgin in all its glory. Sultan, turning to her in prayer, is answered and "the great lifeless 'Y' [melts] into a breathing woman, a fair woman, a divine woman"[286] who turns towards him, spreading her blessing. This brings back to Sultan the memory of when Lady held him in her arms and kissed him in the town by the Danube.

As the Virgin's voice fades, other voices from the concert of the zodiac rise to imbue Sultan with new courage and strength. Two voices sing first "But my wings folded o'er a heart," then "And he who struggle never fails." Then the Virgin joins again, her voice joined with a fourth one: "Teach it to play the Lion's part!" while the other two voices add "Out of the Scorpion through the Scales."[287] In a crescendo the four voices sing together while others, joined in a choir that seems to engulf the whole firmament, announce Sultan's further task:

> *Oh, traveler through the Zodiac*
> *Pass further on—by turning back!*

The voices and the vision recede, leaving Sultan at peace and strengthened anew, aware of what his next steps must be.

Fifth Section

Sultan is now penniless. Before he leaves Cape Limit, the hotel manager offers him a present, a metal object from "Mr. Abdol's own special orders," a gift offered to all those who stop at the hotel. This, Sultan is told, will give him the means of earning a living. It is in fact a model of the peninsula, representing Cape Limit and the hotel, a steel map that reminds Sultan of a paper map the Philosopher owned. Attached to it is a key, in fact a master-key. And keys are important in Abdol's domain because everybody loses hold of keys to doors and drawers and can no longer find their desired objects. A key of this sort will be very appreciated and allow Sultan to earn a living. Sultan is surprised to receive a gift from such a hard man as Abdol.

---

[286] Barfield, *The Rose on the Ash-Heap*, 55.
[287] Barfield, *The Rose on the Ash-Heap*, 56.

Sultan retraces his steps backward from whence he has come, finding it is not difficult to earn a living with the new key he possesses. He notices that his customers now pay him with a new coin that bears the effigy of Abdol, no longer as was the custom, that of the Lord of Albion. Proceeding in reverse order he passes first by the Philosopher and then the Poet. When he tells them of his stay in Cape Limit, they both refuse to believe him. Not affected by this, Sultan proceeds backwards to Albion, to "the city of the terrible disaster," to the place where the palace had stood. Where the entrance gate has once stood, he now finds a framework covered with light bulbs that forms the gigantic letters of the words "Fun Fair," and beneath it "Abdol's Great Gift to a Great Nation." Passing the gate he witnesses the spectacle of a cacophony of lights, shrieks, hooting, blares of steam-organs, voices shouting advertisements, and litter strewn all over the ground.

Above a concrete building he notices an inscription indicating that this is "Abdol's Palace of Dancing." Sultan enters and finds himself at ease with the ambiance and the décor, finding he is happy to have entered. He notices alcoves, each offering intimacy to a couple, and decorated with a "single romantic red rose." He eavesdrops on the conversation of a couple, speculating on the relationship between love, the "element of intellectual agreement" and the "element of pure appetite." Now Sultan discovers that it is not a rose he saw, but "the two thick lips of an enormous negro."[288] At his instigation the couple now starts rubbing first their fronts, then their backs. Disillusioned, Sultan comes out of the building.

In the fair Sultan continues to see grotesque inventions for allowing all sorts of sensations upon the human body. One is of a carousel in which the horses have been replaced by "great undulating green and purple dragons" and lines and lines of "stereoscopic peepshows" through which men and women can watch tantalizing "pornograms."[289] Beyond these stands a sign that read "Abdol's Automatic Tarts." Within this stand booths and in each one of them a "nude automaton" of either gender, able to repeat simple, endearing sentences. Above the booths stand competing messages, calling the attention of potential customers.

[288] Barfield, *The Rose on the Ash-Heap*, 62-63.
[289] Barfield, *The Rose on the Ash-Heap*, 65.

And among these booths or signs, the name of Abdol, or advertisements of some of his monopolies and activities, are always close at hand.

The most stunning contraption is that of a human figure built up of electric bulbs, hanging on a cross. Under it emerges from the darkness the figure of a soldier, and out of his hand appears the lance-like line from which forms a sponge offered to the crucified one, portrayed in the act of refusing it. When this happens, gradually above the cross appears the inscription "It is not Abdol's" followed a moment later by "Abdol's vinegar."[290]

Tired of this spectacle, Sultan seeks an inn to sleep in. He apparently finds the same one he has stayed in before, with the host as eager as earlier to tell Sultan everything that has happened since the last time, revealing that Abdol has been showering people with his largesse. The old monarchy has been superseded with a republic. The elections, in which all people above eight years old could vote, have rendered Abdol not only President of the Republic, but also First Lord of the Treasury in perpetuity. And one of his first public acts has been that of changing the old palace into an amusement park. Abdol has then revised all labor laws and instigated the use of machines to replace much of labor, allowing those now unemployed to still earn enough to spend their time at the Fun Fair.

Returning to the Fun Fair the next day, Sultan seeks for the place of the old palace and finds that it still lies under ash-heap that has now been turned into a rubbish repository. And this is where Abdol's great "advertisement for vinegar" stands.

Sixth Section

Sultan starts to hear that people no longer need his locksmith services because they now hold their valuables in Abdol's Bank. Day after day Sultan tries to eke out a living with his new trade, but the answer is the same; he is not needed. Every evening he finds himself close to the big ash-heap, bemusedly wondering what he may do next. He contemplates making enough money to go back to the East to retire in a life of solitary mystic contemplation. He starts to hate the Fun Fair, because he also

---

[290] Barfield, *The Rose on the Ash-Heap*, 68.

fears the power it is gaining over him, through his lower impulses. This atmosphere brings back memories of his days in the seraglio.

In the midst of rising desires, Sultan one day notices, growing out of the ashes, a "garden rose." Sultan sees it in the twilight and, after approaching it, notices it is glowing as if animated by some magic. This fills Sultan with wonder and brings back some peace to his heart. He suddenly knows that peace is within reach, and remembers the words of the Poet: "The loss of the Beloved is the finding of the Absolute."[291] He also remembers the Virgin he saw at Cape Limit.

With the vividness of these memories, Sultan still shudders at seeing himself torn in two between great dreams and visions and urgent impulses. In prey to the illusions of his seraglio days, Sultan makes his way towards the center of the ash-heap, shouting shamelessly in spite of himself and of his inner reality: "I have found the Beloved! I desire nothing! I am at Peace!"[292] He then plucks the red rose and presses it against his lips. At the same instant Sultan hears a low voice laughing as if to taunt him, but also the call of the rose now glowing more intensely than before, while all around him it has gotten dark. He hears the rose singing to him:

> *Earth despairs not, though her Spark*
> *Underground is gone—*
> *Roses whisper after dark*
> *Secrets of the Sun.*[293]

Pressing the rose against his lips, Sultan is called, as if from beyond himself, to visit the farther side of the ash-heap. On the other side Sultan can see a big hollow, bordered by a cliff and with a nearly flat surface at the bottom. Descending to the middle of the debris that litters the place, Sultan sees an old door, fitted in a frame, leaning against the cliff. He makes use of his master-key and finds the door opening inward.

---

[291] Barfield, *The Rose on the Ash-Heap*, 73.
[292] Barfield, *The Rose on the Ash-Heap*, 74.
[293] Barfield, *The Rose on the Ash-Heap*, 75.

Seventh Section

Moving into the space behind the door, Sultan enters a circular chamber; at its center he sees a marquee. From one of the entrances of the marquee, Sultan discerns a "tall and dignified man" coming out, and in amiable fashion walking towards Sultan. The stranger tells the visitor that this is a circus, "one of the ordinary side-shows of the Fair."[294] And he further offers that hardly anybody wants to join anymore and that they are only rehearsing for a far future performance; he himself is both Ringmaster and proprietor.

The Ringmaster tells Sultan that he does not depend on Abdol's benevolence since he has title-deeds justifying his ownership, which Abdol cannot overturn, much as he would like to. And Sultan realizes that this is why the ash-heap as not been turned into the Fair like the rest of the land around it.

In order to protect himself from Abdol's customers, the Ringmaster needs a closed entrance to which people can have access only through a key. Abdol is under obligation to deliver the key to the Fair's customers, but most if not all soon lose it. Moreover, the Ringmaster suspects that Abdol has altogether stopped giving out these keys.

When Sultan asks how he can join, the Ringmaster tells him he can start as a Clown (or Motley) and he will have to wear all clothes the master asks him to wear. When Sultan indicates that he has great experience with horses in the East, the Ringmaster reacts angrily, and Sultan desists from further entreaties.

Sultan is shown a cubicle in an underground chamber that will be his future lodging, and the next morning he sees the heap of clothes that he is supposed to wear, of all sizes, both clean and dirty. In deep shame he wears them all, and he is shown the stables where he is asked to choose a horse.

Sultan's eye fall on Abba, a very large Arabian charger. The Ringmaster warns him of the danger in choosing such steed because it is one of the horses of Abdol's breeding.

When Sultan confirms his choice, he notices that the Ringmaster is satisfied too. Sultan embarks on a long and regular practice. The horse

---

[294] Barfield, *The Rose on the Ash-Heap*, 77.

openly dislikes his master and throws him off every chance he can, with resulting injuries for Sultan. One of these leads him to death's door, in a state of complete unconsciousness lasting many days. In his persistence Sultan is helped by the example of constancy of the Philosopher. When on the other hand he has inner doubts and feels mistrust towards the Ringmaster, then in his soul rises the memory of the Poet, and the promises in his poems that help him persevere on the path he has chosen. At last Sultan notices that Abba has turned around, finally convinced that Sultan will be his master. In fact a deep affection arises between the two.

One night Sultan awakens, hearing Abba's whinnying in the stables. He feels called to take some extra hours of night practice with his horse. When he ventures towards the stables, not to his complete surprise, he finds the Ringmaster barring the way. When Sultan starts looking for excuses and asking for privileges, he sees that his master "seemed to grow taller—to tower over the intruder with the fierce threatening gestures of an ogre." And, when Sultan asks for more privileges, the Ringmaster sternly reminds him of how many other vows he has broken. "Suddenly a transitory gleam lit up the master's face. Its expression was dreadful. And the arms which he had raised when he said 'Back!' and which he still held up, as if to bar the way for ever, were like two fiery serpents."[295]

The next day, however, the Ringmaster displays his usual affable self, and in fact offers Sultan to practice by night in a small annex, not far from the marquee. Sultan not only progresses in his art but learns much of what is to befall him. He sees that each Motley, once passed his final test, sheds his pile of clothes and becomes known as a "Godiva."

One of the first tasks of a Godiva is to be sent naked into the world on a special mission. At the end they usually return beaten and wounded, and the Ringmaster acts as their physician, helping them through a recovery lasting many days.

Sultan notices that every time a new Godiva is sent into the world, new recruits join the troupe. Among these now arrive the Philosopher and the Poet. In the new setting the two forget their old rivalry and strike a new friendship with each other and Sultan. Sultan notices that

---

[295] Barfield, *The Rose on the Ash-Heap*, 84.

the Poet progresses very fast, but that, having lived in ease and luxury, he loathes the imposition of all the layers of clothing. Thus it is for Sultan all the harder to understand why he reaches the stage of Godiva relatively easily and faster than Sultan himself. The Philosopher hardly minds the ridicule and the encumbrances. But his laziness and his difficulty in riding the horse without falling are his downfalls. It takes him a long time to discover the night practices. Still, even he "slips his Motley" before Sultan. This is due in part to Sultan having chosen a harder mount, and having been given a larger amount of clothes than all others. Sultan is thus last to pass the Motley test. However, when he passes the test, Sultan does so marvelously, standing on Abba's back running full speed, while he rids himself of all his layers, extolling cheers and applause from all present.

When Sultan finishes, the exultant Ringmaster shows him the way to caves in which surge hot mineral springs. Sultan is welcome to regain his strength, and immediately after to join the Revels as a full Godiva.[296] After his bath Sultan steps across the marquee. The surroundings stand transformed. What had been sand is now a green lawn at whose center stands a fountain pouring its waters into a crystal basin. Across the turf are all sorts of seats and couches. Sultan sees all the people of the circus, naked like himself, resting on the couches, either alone or in couples, accompanied by the sweet sound of music. Many of the Godivas appear different from their ordinary age—the old young, the young old—even in some instances in different gender from their own. Among them he recognizes the Poet and Philosopher.

The next morning Sultan returns to the arena with Abba and the Ringmaster, who asks him to perform an "original turn." While he waits for inspiration, Sultan sees Abba entering the arena with Lady ("the Holy One herself, the White-skinned Dancer, the Darling, the Beloved") standing in poise atop Abba's back. Sultan leaps beside her, embracing her and kissing her. What follows after this episode no longer seems to heed to strict time logic in Sultan's mind. At times he has the impression that his life proceeds as it did before; at other times he feels as if he never leaves Lady from his side, or even that he has never left the seraglio.

---

[296] Barfield, *The Rose on the Ash-Heap*, 89.

On occasion Sultan awakens to the call of "The dragons! The dragons!" He then fights them with Lady as one single warrior out into the Amusement Park where the electric dragons have turned alive and are starting to swallow those who have been riding them.

On the last occasion, after their return underground, the couple notices that an earthquake is causing upheavals and starting fires all around and that the arena and the marquee are rising slowly to the surface of the earth. The Ringmaster, in majestic self-possession, commands the full attention of his troupe.

More events keep unfolding. The cigarette machines spring to action and start firing cigarette boxes to the marquee; other machines are copulating with each other while the generating stations, with their tangles of wires turned into gigantic spiders, electrocute hapless victims they catch in their webs. In the tremendous stampede the circus members are rescuing all those they can, and high on his horse Sultan/Lady are one of the most active.

After this the whole troupe returned to the marquee and are instructed not to leave the space again. When a spark falls on the marquee, bursting it into flames, the arena starts expanding in shockwave after shockwave, while all along the Ringmaster keeps the show going and the horses galloping faster and faster.

The conflagration expands in all directions and cries of woe—"Ah Woe"—rend the air. The horses keep galloping steadily to the alternating rhythms of the woes until a new sound of "Kiss! . . . Kiss! . . . Kiss!" is added. Now the two sounds alternate in chorus with and opposition to each other. While looking at Lady, Sultan beholds the Moon, which seems to be descending over the arena. All along the commanding figure of the Ringmaster still directs his horsemen, and the Moon comes closer and closer, until Sultan can clearly perceive its normally hidden side, formed of "interweaving furious flames." The ground opens under the horses' feet, while Sultan and Lady, embracing one another, merge into a full embrace and "endless ecstasy of desire that was at the same time fruition." The Ringmaster stands augmented in stature at the center of it all, until "suddenly all took fire, melted into one, became a chalice of living flames, the petals of a giant Sun-flower into which the journeying Moon fell with a long sigh of relief."[297]

A Second Look at the Story

The Rose on the Ash-Heap links English history to a variety of themes: chiefly it looks at how the movement of spiritual renewal that has been inaugurated by the Romantics (with the pointed reference to Wordsworth's "Lucy") can be continued with the clear light of thinking into spiritual science. The story also follows wisdom's progress in the form of Lady and Sultan from the East to the West. And last, it clearly connects the above with the Christ impulse.

The tale is articulated in seven archetypal parts, and the pivotal moment occurs at stage 4, at the time of Sultan's dark night of the soul, giving birth to new revelations at Cape Limit. That of Sultan's is both an inner journey and that of a people. We will now look at the story from the perspective of Sultan and Lady, the microcosmic side if you will, then to its relationship to the larger culture, its macrocosmic dimension.

Sultan and Lady

Sultan is "the Lord of all the Asias and hereditary High Priest of all their religions." in essence an extract of all the spirituality of the East. In his breast he has long heard the call to the sacred life as much as the call of the blood. The text tells us that he gives "himself body and soul, in mystic sacrificial delight of self-abandonment."

It is the white-skinned dancer, and the dream of his union with her, that prompts Sultan to seek a spirituality that honors the senses but subordinates them to the call of the sacred life. For her he shows himself willing to submit to the rules of the Temple—though it is too late for it—and to renounce the temptations he has fostered in the life of the seraglio, particularly the appeal of a "certain concubine."

Sultan follows Lady to southern Europe and then to Albion. Here he does not meet her but hears about the Virgin Goddess, "Lucy" or "Lady." This is a knowledge that he has to glean from the margins of society, as it were, while he himself walks in disguise. When his Beloved

---

[297] Barfield, *The Rose on the Ash-Heap*, 98.

returns to Asia for deepening her impulse, Sultan feels sorely tested and betrays his vows, abandoning himself to the concubine.

After this Sultan continues to follow his Beloved's tracks. The future union with Lady is foretold in successive steps. The first is Sultan's encounter with the "beautiful blonde" on the banks of the river Ister (Danube). When he tells her he wishes her embrace and kisses would go on forever, she replies, "That is exactly what you ought to feel."[298]

Sultan feels emboldened to go once more to the palace of the Lord of Albion. He demands an audience from Princess Lucy, the Lord of Albion's newly adopted daughter. The second encounter leads to Sultan's personal confession, not only of his personal weaknesses of the senses, but of his negligence towards his fellow human beings.

Sultan's second Dream clearly announces his pressing challenges. The dream presages union and wedding with Lady. But the presence of the concubine, tugging at Sultan's heart, mars the idyllic scene. In the nuptial chamber Sultan sees the beloved transformed into a hideous appearance. He is now unable to pray and carries the "taste of ashes in his mouth."

Sultan's dream epilogue is mirrored in outer events with Abdol's temporary triumph over the Lord of Albion. And it is in the realm of Abdol that Sultan has to venture in order to wrest something from Abdol himself. This leads him at first into a part of the land that is somehow preserved from Abdol's dominion, but then more deeply into his pervading presence.

The Encounters with Poet and Philosopher form a deep contrast, one that is present in all of Barfield's work. On one hand we have a pristine environment and consciousness for the first; on the other an intensification of Abdol's desolate realm and state of consciousness for the second. The Poet lives in a place where a certain nature-consciousness still prevails. It colors his being and this shows in his beautiful attire and noble-looking presence. The Poet's consciousness harkens to gifts preserved from the past. It is through these that the Poet can give Sultan his most precious gift of a Poem that speaks of Love, Sleep, and Death.

---

[298] Barfield, *The Rose on the Ash-Heap*, 15.

The Philosopher has a neglected appearance, an unpleasant voice, and awkward manners. He offers Sultan the gift of faithfulness, constancy, and individual freedom that comes at the cost of estrangement from the realm of the stars. When the Dog Star/Sirius offers Sultan an unusual experience, he scoffs at it as the Philosopher would. However, the Philosopher is lazy in his thinking; he prefers to see things secondhand through a telescope, which leads to a litany of trite discourses. But inwardly he also rebels against the Gods.

What the two have in common is that neither one can truly relate to Lady and understand Sultan's experiencing a taste of ashes in his mouth. One has elevated a common woman to his ideal of the Beloved, then refused her; the other resigns himself to act the "imbecile" and accepts his lot through the call of duty.

Aren't Poet and Philosopher the two successive stages of humanity's in relation to the spirit? The Poet can still partake of the original human participation in the spirit, which tells him that there is more to life than the call of the senses, because he still can be part of something larger. The Philosopher knows about complete separation, and part of him offers the best response to a call to individual responsibility and sense of freedom from, and rebellion against, the spiritual world. His recourse to the distant telescope rather than direct observation spells the laziness of his associative thinking and observer consciousness.

Taking his leave from Poet and Philosopher alike, Sultan knows he cannot rely on the help of either. He has to face utter loneliness without recourse to telescopes or outer props. He can carry inwardly a newly won sense of freedom and the verses of the Poet. Neither Poet nor Philosopher wants to travel to the farther West. Sultan can only do so by traversing Abdol's landscapes of external squalor and extreme inner emptiness of soul. Everybody around him is immersed in that reality. He has to reach the extreme West of Cape Limit on the shores of the Pacific Ocean.

Sultan is yearning to sing but is unable; he wants to recover his wonder at the stars, but these are unable to draw near. Still, he is closer to crossing the abyss than he can tell. He reaches the extreme West, the peninsula at Cape Limit, and discovers with surprise that here Abdol's domain displays beauty. He shows a supreme trust in the future.

The night under the cupola happens in section 4 of the story, and is the turning point of Sultan's journey. Here he has vision after vision. The previous two dreams of Lady now become a step more conscious; here she carries a scroll with the poem of the Poet. He is rejuvenated. and the stars draw near again.

The Dog Star that he has just recently scoffed at now returns and befriends Sultan with great vividness. It brings back the spirit of his childhood, calls him to awaken, and offers him a long-forgotten warning from his childhood: "Else a great Prince in prison dies!" The Great Bear strengthens the bond between the present illumination and the memory of his childhood. Sultan is meeting with the Guardian of the Threshold at the abyss and now sees the glory of the spiritual activity of the beings of the Zodiac. He knows now that he is a spiritual being coming from the Sun, meant to return therein.

In what Jane Hipolito calls Sultan's passing from Eros to Agape, Lady now gives way to the her counterpart in the constellation of the Virgin, "a fair woman, a divine woman."[299] While the Virgin reminds Sultan of Lady, she also points to and prepares him for a further stage of inner growth, realized at the end of the story. Sultan beholds the activity and instructions of four constellations, "out of the Scorpion through the Scales." And, when this is over he is instructed to "Pass further on—by turning back!"[300] Sultan crosses the threshold and is imbued with new hope, which enables him to retrace his steps with a sense of purpose.

Sultan is as if born anew, and is left completely on his own resources. But he has wrested from the realm of Abdol/Ahriman a key of steel that unlocks new doors and possibilities for him. The hotel manager tells him that ". . . [Abdol's] gift is hard steel. The very hardest. . . . It will stand anything." (59) Sultan has wrested the strength to travel through Abdol/Ahriman's realm and will be at home there, work and make a living, while resisting its temptations.

We are told that Sultan is now penniless. This isn't just a financial statement. Barfield underlines "The whole store of wealth which he

299 Barfield, *The Rose on the Ash-Heap*, xii.
300 Barfield, *The Rose on the Ash-Heap*, 57.

had brought with him from the Asia had given out."[301] Sultan is now to move into the specific Christ-imbued dimension of the wisdom/Sophia.

Sultan first meets the Philosopher and the Poet, both of whom he still appreciates, though neither one of them can momentarily believe that Sultan has returned from Cape Limit. Neither one of them has stood at the abyss. He now has to face the place where he felt "the taste of ashes," the place where both himself and the Lord of Albion had to face defeat.

Sultan has seen the desolation of Abdol's realm, but not the worst of it yet, the place where human beings are enslaved to their passions, mocked and derided in perpetuity: the Fun Fair. He sees the carousel with the electric dragons and all the other attractions. For a moment, it is as if the memories of the seraglio delude him into the illusion of the Palace of Dancing. He finds himself at ease before he realizes that this is a thinly disguised call to pure sexual lust. And this is further confirmed in the stereoscopic peepshows with their pornograms. Sultan, who carries the memory of Lady and the vision of the Virgin, now sees everything that mocks them and counters them in their degraded and fallen versions.

Sultan learns that this is the work of Abdol, the "President of the Republic and First Lord of the Treasury in perpetuity." His derision is not only derision for Lady, but of the Lord of Albion and the one for whom he stands. At the place where Albion's Palace stood, Abdol has also made explicit his mockery of the Risen One, and his attempt to take His place. But it is in this place that the force of the Christ, Lord of the Earth, is hidden, buried but powerful.

Before he meets with the realm of the Christ, Lord of the Earth, Sultan has to withstand the temptation of turning his back to the needs of his fellow human beings by going back to the East and "become a religious, and . . . live alone at peace."[302]

The confrontation happens at the central place where Abdol and Lord of Albion confront each other. And here a rose, rising out of the ash-heap, stands as an apt contrast between the two forces. Sultan has to appeal to his last inner strength, even fake this inner strength, before

---

[301] Barfield, *The Rose on the Ash-Heap*, 58.
[302] Barfield, *The Rose on the Ash-Heap*, 72.

inner voices pulling him for and against the Christ impulse become also external voices tugging at his heart. He trusts the rose and the voice that comes from it: "Earth despairs not, though her spark Underground is gone. Roses whisper after dark secrets of the Sun."[303] This indicates where Sultan is to find the counterimpulse to the Fun Fair. Still, it is thanks to what he has wrested from Abdol's domain—the master-key—that he can seek initiation through the Ringmaster underground. And it is at the center of Abdol's domain that Sultan can overcome his taste of ashes and find the beauty and promise of the rose growing in the midst of utter desolation.

In the most humbling of all gestures, Sultan has to renounce all the glory and knowledge of horse-riding that he carries from the East and start anew as a simple Clown/Motley under the leadership of the most stern/most loving of spiritual masters.

Sultan has to tame his thinking, the horse that we can either lead or be led by, and choses one that has much of Abdol's strain in it. He has to master that thinking that carries malice and is completely fallen. His is a long and humbling path of initiation. He carries the humiliation of all the layers of clothing and the ruefulness of the horse and still harbors the desire to extend his skill, not just to day consciousness but also to night consciousness, until through the redeeming power of the Higher Guardian of the Threshold he can become a Godiva. And the first task of a Godiva is to serve the higher good at no benefit for self, quite the contrary.

The Poet and Philosopher are joined with Sultan again. The Poet has the advantage of more familiarity with the world of the spirit, and his attachment to comfort is only a small impediment; the Philosopher has to overcome the laziness of his thinking before he can lead it to a higher stage. But both their tasks are easier than that of Sultan, who has entered more deeply into Abdol's territory and made use of his tools, his key, and his charger. Sultan is finally received in the presence of the Christ realm, and this also means a stage of timelessness/eternity in which his union with Lady is now uninterrupted. They move, fight, and are but as one.

---

[303] Barfield, *The Rose on the Ash-Heap*, 75.

The Lord of Albion and the Virgin

The story of Sultan's is the journey of the spirit from the ancient East towards the West. And all of this is specific to the Anglo-Saxon spirit, or more broadly the Spirit of the West, coming as it does at the end of a novel entitled *English People*.

The British Empire is the conqueror of Asia and most significantly of India, the cradle of Aryan civilization. And the wisdom of the East made its way to the West in the 18th and 19th centuries. There was a great yearning for it in the Romantic movement. This is what appears in Wordsworth's "Lucy," a name that after all stands for "Light."

The Sophia wisdom makes its way from the East to the West. Historically this wisdom was to serve as a foundation to renew Western and world civilization. We can detect more or less three stages. In a first stage we have the Romantic impulse, which carries old knowledge in an intuitive fashion and tries to rekindle civilization, countering a materialistic science that divorces knowledge of the world and knowledge of the soul. This is what Wordsworth finds emblematically in Lucy who "dwelt among the untrodden ways Beside the springs of Dove; A maid whom there were none to praise, And very few to love." (Wordsworth's 2nd Lucy poem). However, this yearning lives with a touch of nostalgia, and a sense of doom in Wordsworth and the Romantics.

In a second stage the wisdom of the East is brought back to the West through Theosophy, overshadowed by its initial Rosicrucian impulse. Though short lived, this is the transition in which the wisdom of the East can find exposure to the Christ impulse. The old wisdom of the East can only grow from Cape Limit to the Ringmaster's arena through knowledge of the Christ. Theosophy reached in fact the West and the shores of America, establishing its headquarters in New York, to which reference is made through Cape Limit being situated on the Pacific Ocean, far from Albion. And the greatest challenge within Theosophy lay precisely in resisting Steiner's revelation about the Christ in the etheric by wanting to pass on the scepter of Christ to a mere individual.

Finally it is through Theosophy becoming Anthroposophy that access to Lady and the Lord of Albion is made conscious; a new path of knowledge opens that all who want to can take. It leads to the Christ/Ringmaster and to conscious union with the Sophia/Virgin impulse. Here, as Barfield has expressed it in many places elsewhere, is placed this yearning for Romanticism to "come of age" in the form that spiritual science can take for the present, which offers a promise for the renewal of civilization.

Thus we could say the story is charged of all levels of meaning for the future of Albion/Great Britain and the whole of the West. It also points to the future confrontation of the Lord of Albion/Christ with his adversary Abdol/Ahriman for dominion over the earth's future. Of the Lord of Albion we are told that his "dominion . . . is no dominion, but perfect freedom" whereas Abdol has made himself President of the Republic and First Lord of the Treasury in perpetuity. We are offered a view over the civilization of the Anti-Christ spreading over the whole Earth and the response coming from that spirit who is now the Spirit of the Earth, and those who want to follow him.

On one hand stands the spectacle of full human degradation through the fallen nature of sex and all the addictions and dependencies it generates. At the other end of the spectrum we see the beautiful spiritualization of what we experience through the revitalized senses and through the spiritualized intellect. It is aptly portrayed in the Revels in which sensuality is the avenue of, and subservient to, the higher form of spirituality fully honoring individuality. This transformed service to the realm of the senses is placed at the service of our fellow human beings. In the end it is not just the macrocosmic union of opposites in Sultan/Lady that is achieved but a new macrocosmic stage of union of opposites in the Earth's very being (Moon approaching the Sun).

English People was written in 1929, only four years after *The Silver Trumpet*. It is another powerful imagination that complements the earlier one and announces what is to come in terms of Barfield's thinking. Whereas in *The Silver Trumpet*, Barfield looks, broadly speaking, to humanity's history from original participation, to the spectator consciousness, and forward/back again to conscious participation, in *The Rose on the Ash-Heap* this theme is widened and expanded. It is widened to its meaning in relation to the consciousness and history of the West; it is expanded to the future of the confrontation of Christ with the spirit of the Anti-Christ. *The Silver Trumpet* is a pure fairy tale, since it abstracts from any real place or known individuals. *The Rose on the*

Ash-Heap is one step removed, as it were, since it clearly relates to history and, though vaguely, to a place in space (England and Asia) and in time (Romanticism to Anthroposophy) and is also placed in the context of a modern novel concerning England. Nevertheless they share similarities as two imaginations received from the other side of the threshold.

In his last lecture of the cycle *Three Lectures on the Mystery Dramas*, Steiner offers us indications of how fairy tales, even modern ones, come about. A first useful inkling is that of Steiner placing the fairy tale "between the external world and everything that in past times man, with his early clairvoyance, could see in the spiritual world" and calling it a "reflection of true imagination" and also "the purest child of ancient, primitive clairvoyance."[304] Referring to such tales in modern times, Steiner points to their emergence as a result of a longing towards ancient times of humankind. In essence these fairy tales are the first fruits of imagination bestowed upon Barfield through the longing that poetry and his interest in the evolution of consciousness have engendered. They foretell the development of a full imaginative consciousness in their author, as we have seen in the previous chapter.

---

[304] Steiner, lecture "Symbolism and Phantasy in Relation to the Mystery Drama, *The Soul's Probation*," of December 19, 1911, *Three Lectures on the Mystery Dramas*.

Conclusions

Barfield and Tolkien, Comparison and Contrast

Barfield and Tolkien present a polarity that is common in our times, indeed a polarity that is a functional springboard for a new global culture. They are Michaelites of a very different stamp, and for this reason complementary to each other. Integrating their messages can be a very potent way to harmonize our own inner polarities to better meet the challenges of our time.

BIOGRAPHICAL THEMES

Barfield and Tolkien met in their biographies the challenges of the 20th century. They stood at the abyss, each in his own way. Let us see how.

Tolkien was born in the periphery of the British Empire, in the extreme southern tip of Africa. In Bloemfontein the tensions did not just touch between colonists and indigenous people. They split the European population in two with the antagonism and division between Afrikaners and English-speaking people. There the pursuit of wealth deeply affected Tolkien's father and his health.

Tolkien's early life contains all the challenges of British industrialism in a nutshell. Tolkien experienced the ravages over nature after leaving his Sarehole oasis. He knows poverty and comes close to hunger. He sees death face to face through both of his parents, two of his closest friends, and many young men of his generation. He is then brought to the moral abyss of Western civilization in an experience that deeply marked a generation and was reflected in the arts, particularly in painting: the carnage and desolation of the trench war in northern France, Verdun and the battle of the Somme. All of this happens before Tolkien reaches age twenty-one. We could say that Tolkien experiences the full blows of the negative karma of the Consciousness Soul as it is best exemplified in the English people.

Tolkien and Barfield grow in two dissimilar backgrounds as far as religion and spirituality is concerned. Tolkien is immersed through his mother in a deep religiosity of feeling, which is more characteristic of the past than of the 20th century. Christianity, in its Catholic form, will leave a deep imprint on Tolkien's soul.

Barfield on the other hand, is raised in the mood of secularism, skepticism, and alienation that announces what will become the common ground of the future. He is taught to be deeply suspicious of any strong manifestation of feelings, or of any stated certainties concerning the inner life. Only over time does he open up to the mystery of the Christ being. And when he does, this becomes all the more powerful because he has to make it his own with greater inner effort than Tolkien.

Barfield comes to another abyss of Western civilization. He meets inwardly what Tolkien meets through life experience: the death of culture. This is exemplified early on in his infatuation with a young woman, and by contrast with his Sophia experience. In the first experience he has to meet all his inner emptiness. He describes it in a letter as "My self is the only thing that exists, and I wear the external world about me like a suit of clothes—my own body included. . . . Something inside me seems to be so intensely and burningly alive, and everything round me so starkly dead." His Sophia experience indicates to him that he can quell his longings in the whole of nature and in his personal artistic expression.

Barfield also meets his abyss through the experience of stammering, and his way out in the experience of the Word. This leads him to poetry, first and foremost through the Romantics. And the movement forward continues when he meets Anthroposophy, as "Romanticism come of age."

Barfield, who loves the Word, is exposed to the ignominy of the fallen word in his profession of the law. He has to face the inner drudgery of sacrificing his inner creativity in the pursuit of his livelihood. This is essential to Barfield's biography. When he meets the external abyss, he finds it reflected in his inner life in the split between Burgeon and Burden. What almost breaks him offers him the strength to develop imagination and speak with power to his time and his contemporaries.

What Barfield carries in parallel in his own research on poetry and word, and in his pursuit of Anthroposophy, shows him that he can overcome the abyss of modern culture. His position among the Inklings offers him a pulpit from where to speak to his time. He not only learns to order his inner life of thought; he devises how to offer his ideas in a way suitable for his contemporaries. Barfield becomes literally a ladder for knowledge for the Western mind, and a gateway to Anthroposophy.

To sum up, Tolkien meets the abyss in the external world; he meets it as trials of destiny that awaken in him the initiatic qualities of previous incarnations. This is made most apparent in the inspirations that flood his subconscious through the awakening effect of war and trench fever. What he thus receives, Tolkien has to dedicate a lifetime to order and give artistic form. He does this in parallel with an exacting dedication to the Word through his philological work.

Barfield goes another route. His hunger for meaning and truth is met all around him by the aridity of modern thought. He finds refuge in those enclaves of culture that preserved potential for the future: in poetry, where the Word is held at an earlier stage of potential, where it has not completely fallen; in the Romantics, who offered resistance to the modern scientific outlook; and in Anthroposophy. Barfield struggles to reach what we could call¾echoing Steiner¾the wonders of the world. Tolkien's path is that of the ordeals of the soul; the Apollonian way for the first; the Dionysian one for the second.[305]

It is not without irony that both authors had to work at their achievements while facing an additional biographical split within their married lives. For Tolkien this meant taking along Edith, who never felt

---

[305] Steiner, *Wonders of the World.*

at home in Oxford literary and academic circles; for Barfield this found expression in Maud's lasting opposition to Anthroposophy.

Barfield and Tolkien show us two complementary ways of looking at the Word, of confronting the paths inward and outward, and consequently two complementary paths to the Christ in modern time.

MICROCOSM AND MACROCOSM

In *This Ever Diverse Pair* Barfield reveals:

I wanted, above all, to be objective, to write about Nature and events and quite other people, using my own feelings solely as instruments of perception and fountains of diction, sacrificing them like the glass in the window, to let the light and the warmth of the outside world. And now here I am, at it again![306]

Barfield's initial goal of "using his feelings solely as instruments" is challenged by his inner demons, to the point that he risks being engulfed by them. Both the tensions in his marriage and the drudgery of his work push him to the edge of a nervous breakdown, and Barfield has to turn to the understanding of the inner world, not just of nature and objective events. The danger is avoided through the artistic representation of Barfield's soul forces in the personas of Burgeon and Burden. Barfield confronts the inner threshold—of which he speaks but little in cognitive terms—in artistic fashion. We could say the conscious path to the macrocosm is accompanied with an artistic imaginative penetration of the path to the microcosm, leading Barfield to that integration that is essential for Barfield the author—in fact an integration without which there may not have been Barfield the author.

The above movement is continued in what Barfield calls his "long, long love affair with the little book called the *Calendar of the Soul.*"[307] Here quite naturally Barfield tries to achieve a very high degree of integration of the forces of the soul through the power of the Christ being, always present and never mentioned by name in the Calendar, the Christ who holds the balance between macrocosm and microcosm.

---

[306] Barfield, *This Ever Diverse Pair*, 7.
[307] Barfield, *Owen Barfield and the Origin of Language*, lecture of June 21, 1977, 10.

Tolkien proceeds through life in meeting inner trials after inner trials. His inner life reveals the contents of previous lifetimes, whether these be stories he receives or intimations of previous life times, such as in his "Great Wave dream." These he can describe in *The Notion Club Papers* and partly in *The Lord of the Rings*. Tolkien can thus integrate the most shattering life experiences, and these inspire his literary material, though not literally. Tolkien can intuit some of the ultimate levels of spiritual reality, whether these be the encounter with the Lower Guardian of the Threshold or with the Higher Guardian of the Threshold.

Tolkien's challenge lies in educating his thinking. He can achieve this in his specific field of philology with the help of Barfield's *Poetic Diction*; after reading it, he knows that he can no longer go back. Carpenter also reminds us that Tolkien received an honorary degree for his work in philology and that he could have started a new school of thought.

Tolkien's real challenge lies in seeing that there can be such a thing as a truly objective reality expressed through thinking. His faith forms an obstacle to his independent thinking. Had he reached a detached, objective understanding of the Christ being, he could have reconciled his life experiences with his thinking, particularly matters concerning previous lives. Reincarnation would not have been an obstacle to his understanding of the Christ. Had Tolkien fully understood the cycles of evolution as they are retold in Steiner's *Outline of Esoteric Science*, he would have had no need for his futile attempt to reconcile the contents of his *Silmarillion* with the science of his time.

Tolkien can integrate shattering life experiences in an instinctive fashion. What is challenging for him is to discipline the thinking to its ultimate destination. Barfield can integrate ideas with great apparent ease. He has greater difficulty integrating life experiences, and does so mostly in an artistic manner.

It is no wonder then that the two authors proceed from very different artistic perspectives, and that they perceive the objective dimension of the Christ being from diametrically polar opposite sides.

IMAGINATION AND INSPIRATION

Borrowing from Barfield to look at Tolkien we could say that Tolkien had a higher degree of original participatory consciousness than most in his environment and general culture. This seems to clearly point to an overshadowing of one or more previous incarnations. Thus it is that Tolkien is naturally turned towards the past and can naturally look at old mythology with a feeling understanding. He is surprised that people of his age can no longer recognize the truth in myth.

In his *Smith of Wootton Major*, written in later years, Tolkien shows what it means to live out of a clairvoyant inheritance that peters out, one that Smith has to forego and pass on to younger ones. This is also a fitting image of the old Tolkien, who could no longer revive the inspiration of early days and who sought something else, without fully finding it. He cannot become like Alf, the king of Faery, who in the same story travels freely between worlds. He is left conscious of but estranged from faery.

True to his own perceptions, as we will see shortly, Barfield stands at the other end of the spectrum. He is completely immersed in the skeptical onlooker consciousness of his time. However, unlike most people of his time, he has an instinctive recognition of what has made its way into culture through the inspiration of the Romantics, who tried to restore qualities from the past by giving them new meanings. And he knows how to uplift that heritage for modern times.

Speaking of people of old, in whom inspiration manifested¾such as Dante, Shakespeare, and Goethe¾Barfield calls them geniuses, those in whom "the world of spiritual beings has already begun to break through into the conscious self."[308] He underlines that the meaning of the word *genius* itself changes meaning over time; it goes from being an inspiring spiritual being that moves through the individual to something that now fully inhabits the individual.

Barfield calls this movement in time a transition from a "psychology of inspiration to a psychology of imagination." This is a transition from something superindividual via the agency of a spirit manifesting through

---

[308] Barfield, *Romanticism Comes of Age*, 128.

the individual to something "possessed by the individual, though not identical with his everyday personality."[309]

The above final movement is clearly articulated in Barfield's autobiographical *Unancestral Voice*. In the story we see that Barfield has poured a lot of thinking on the matters upon which he later receives the gift of imagination. This is what Barfield has qualified as the individual's activity present in imagination in *Speaker's Meaning*. Though here referred to poetry, it applies to imagination in general: "*an active taking hold of something by* the poet . . . The content of his poetry changes from something that is 'given' to something that has to be actively grasped, or achieved."[310] The whole of *Unancestral Voice* is indeed an illustration of the process through which Burgeon/Barfield attains imagination.

Tolkien's way of operating is more akin to what Barfield sees from the past of humanity. The author sees this activity of pure imagination in some of Tolkien's early paintings, many of which portray polarities. Altogether there are some twenty visionary pictures painted between 1911 and 1913, labeled "Earliest Ishnesses."

We can now turn to the themes that Tolkien could not possibly have elaborated through thought, topics that are "received" as he himself explains in various places in his letters or in his *The Notion Club Papers*. To these belong most if not all of *The Silmarillion*. What the author presented there was truly new material, though it covers something upon which he has turned a lot of his interests and in-depth studies—myths and legends. Moreover, this material was received through exceptional life trials and states of consciousness, as those awakened in the young Tolkien suffering from trench fever. They came out "complete," as Tolkien likes to say on more than one occasion.[311]

---

[309] Barfield, *Romanticism Comes of Age*, 54.
[310] Barfield, *Romanticism Comes of Age*, 56.
[311] As an example, beyond the stories of *The Silmarillion*, concerning *Leaf by Niggle*, Tolkien states "That story was the only thing I have ever done which cost me absolutely no pains at all. Usually I compose only with great difficulty and endless rewriting. I woke up one morning (more than 2 years ago) with that odd thing virtually complete in my head" (Carpenter, *Letters of J. R. R. Tolkien*, 111).

211

What Barfield fails to take into account is the karmic element for a condition that, granted, becomes more and more rare as humanity evolves. He does not consider that in the case of someone like Tolkien the preparation consists in deeply harrowing personal trials awakening memories or inspirations from previous incarnations.

Facet after facet of the two Inklings' personalities form a stark contrast to each other. So does their perception and understanding of the Christ being.

RELATIONSHIP TO THE CHRIST

Barfield recognizes Christ through the Word, particularly how the Christ changed its evolution. Tolkien lived in the Word through an immersion into its qualities. He came to the Christ through the recognition of the Word as it comes from historical sources.

Barfield's cultural background brought in him an innate resistance to the very idea of a supernatural intervention in history, such as the deed of Golgotha. It was through his immersion in the study of words that he detected a qualitative change in man's relationship to the external world of nature and to his inner life in a bracket of time "between on one side Alexander the Great and on the other St. Augustin."[312] The pure phenomena occurring roughly over eight centuries would force a human being, in Barfield's perspective, to seek for a momentous event causing a change of direction in man's inner world, through which the human being went from expressing herself from what she received from the world of nature to being able to give back to nature out of what it had bestowed on her. This he finds aptly expressed in the Greek word *metanoia*, which occurs in the New Testament in relation to Christ's incarnation. On the basis of all of the above Barfield concludes that "if he had never heard of it through the Scriptures, he would have been obliged to try his best to invent something like it as an hypothesis to save the appearances."[313]

---

[312] Barfield, "Philology and the Incarnation."
[313] Barfield, "Philology and the Incarnation."

And the Christ is for Barfield the turning point around which is built his whole understanding of the evolution of consciousness: "Original participation fires the heart from a source outside itself; the images enliven the heart. But in final participation—since the death and resurrection—the heart is fired from within by the Christ; and it is for the heart to enliven the images."[314]

Things stood otherwise for Tolkien, who most naturally came, through his background and inner disposition, to the recognition of the Christ being. For Tolkien, who completely immersed himself from childhood in a feeling relationship to the Christ, the events of the Gospels were myth made history. In other words there was in the Gospels a dimension of historicity, but a history that had at the same time, unique for its kind and its time, a quality of embodied myth. Quite naturally he concludes:

> [The Gospels] contain many *marvels*—peculiarly artistic, beautiful, and moving: *"mythical" in their perfect, self-contained significance*; and among the marvels is the greatest and most complete conceivable eucatastrophe.... The Birth of Christ is the eucatastrophe of Man's history. The *Resurrection is the eucatastrophe of the story of the Incarnation*. This story begins and ends in joy. It has pre-eminently the "inner consistency of reality."[315]

We can also perceive in Tolkien's relationship towards the Christ something else we have quoted in relation to the Mysteries of Hibernia from Steiner: "At the time of the actual events of Golgotha, in Hibernia great festivals were celebrated which portrayed what was to come in great imaginations; however, these pictures were presented as if they were memories of the past." In fact, "These pictures existed on the island of Hibernia before they could be produced from historic memory of the past, but as they only could be produced out of the Spirit itself."[316] The whole of *The Lord of the Rings* can be seen as an imagination of

---

[314] Barfield, *Saving the Appearances*, 172.
[315] Tolkien, *The Monsters and the Critics and Other Essays*, 155–56.
[316] Steiner, *Mystery Centers*, lecture 9 of December 9, 1923.

the Christ deed, and Tolkien vaguely intuited it when he harmonized the dates of events with the traditional dates of Jesus Christ's life. This quality of reversal of the time continuum is likewise perpetually present in *The Lord of the Rings*. Turning points that have just been achieved— the onset of the Fourth Age—evoke the qualities of similar moments of the past—as the end of Atlantis. And events in Tolkien's fictional past also point to future trials of humanity, particularly the meeting with the anti-Christ.

A LITERARY CULMINATION AND ITS IMPORTANCE FOR THE WEST

Barfield shows that he has the greatest of abilities in integrating ideas, more than he does in terms of understanding the forces of destiny. He walks most clearly the path to the macrocosm. Interestingly, Barfield does not speak of the Double anywhere in his opus, other than calling him Burden in two books of a marked autobiographical tenor. And in *The Silver Trumpet* this is further elaborated in artistic terms in the development of the Gamboy twin sister character. In Barfield Spirit Recollection (path inward) is practiced artistically, mostly with the scope of clearing the field for Spirit Beholding (path to the macrocosm).[317] It is important that Barfield can achieve a measure of the former in order to lead his fellow human being clearly into the latter.

Tolkien on the other hand has experienced his Double and the "world Double" at large in all aspects of his life. He had to overcome it through life's trials. He dedicates a great part of his *Lord of the Rings* to an artistic understanding of it in the figure of Gollum and in its relationship with Frodo. He knows most intimately the path to the microcosm. He walks the path to the macrocosm, and its consequent heightening of the thinking faculty, to some degree thanks to the help of Barfield.

When it comes to an understanding of the Christ, once more Tolkien and Barfield offer us two essentially and critically complementary facets

---

[317] For a fuller characterization of these paths, see Morelli, "Spirit Recollection and Spirit Beholding."

of this immense being. And the gestures of this recognition are so clearly archetypal that they reveal the deeper being of the two authors. Tolkien yearns for the Christ and cannot but recognize him in the historical events of the New Testament. He also yearns for the cosmic Christ as the whole of *The Lord of the Rings* testifies. His clinging to Catholicism precludes him from fully arriving at the destination of the journey he so longs to reach.

Christopher Tolkien, based on his father's notes, shows how his father's continuous efforts to revise *The Silmarillion* may have worked against its original freshness. In effect Tolkien was attempting to reconcile his edifice of imaginations with what science has to say about world evolution. And the son concludes, "The old structure was too comprehensive, too interlocked in all its parts, indeed its roots too deep, to withstand such a devastating surgery."[318] This yearning could only have been satisfied by spiritual science.

How different Barfield is from his fellow Inkling. He cannot recognize the historical Christ on the basis of his karmic and cultural heritage. But everything leads him, even before he knows it, to a recognition of that cosmic power which forms the resolution of all polarities he studies. The Christ found in and above the terms of polarities is by essence the cosmic Christ, the being who brings harmony and reconciliation to what seems irreconcilable. Thus one could say that it is just a matter of time before Barfield can recognize the historical Christ, taking his departure from the cosmic Christ.

What is also most remarkable about the two authors, even when we only limit our gaze to the few works that have been explored in this book, is the extent of their understanding of the Christ Mystery in our time. Both authors announce the time of the Christ in the etheric and of the anti-Christ in different ways. In *The Rose on the Ash-Heap* Christ is announced in the figure of Lord of Albion first and in the Ringmaster later, and his opponent in the figure of Abdol. The whole spells the confrontation of Christ and anti-Christ central to our time. And the attainment of the Christ consciousness is sought through the transformation of thinking into imaginative consciousness and beyond.

---

[318] Quoted in Caldecott, *The Power of the Ring*, 195.

In a very different way Tolkien announces the future in a fictional past. The human being has to meet his Double in the realm of Sauron, who plans his complete enslavement. His emissary, Saruman, portrays a modern anti-Christ, a new Inquisitor, capable of charming one and all through the power of his voice, the counter image of the Word. Saruman's power reminds us of Dostoyevsky's Great Inquisitor, he too an image of Anti-Christ.[319] Gandalf and Aragorn point the reader in the direction of those powers the human being can develop at the time of the Christ in the etheric.

Barfield perceives how the anti-Christ plays upon men's lower appetites through *panem and circenses* at the Fun Fair. Tolkien rightly perceives machine magic of modern times as one of the most powerful tools of the adversary. He intuited what Steiner pointed out in terms of "Ahriman [gaining] the possibility of establishing himself as a demon even in the very physical entity."[320]

In summing up, the two authors indicate the path to the Christ in the present in the pursuits of two complementary aspects. In Barfield the movement towards nature clairvoyance is pursued systematically and brought to completion in Imagination. Tolkien treads the path to Inspiration, which could culminate in karmic clairvoyance, though the movement is cut short.

Past and future meet and fertilize each other if one can bring Tolkien to shed light on Barfield and vice versa. Unbeknownst to himself, Tolkien has truly achieved the goal he set himself to reach in his youth, of writing "a body of more or less connected legend . . . which I could dedicate to England."[321] Tolkien revived the early tradition of the West of Hibernia that Great Britain and Ireland lost most thoroughly, according to many and according to Barfield himself. In his *History*

---

[319] See the chapter "The Voice of Saruman" in *The Two Towers*.

[320] Steiner, *The Karma of Vocation*, lecture of November 26, 1916. Steiner refers here to what the human being does in rarefying air (driving air out of space) by creating a vacuum as in the steam machine. What is said of the steam engine is only all the more true when human beings have recourse to electricity or nuclear radiation, or tinkers with the genome, to name but a few of technological possibilities.

[321] Carpenter, *J. R. R. Tolkien: A Biography*, 99–100.

in English Words Barfield concludes, based on his philological studies, "In England the whole Celtic nation and language died early out of the common consciousness, and it died even more suddenly than the persons of Teutonic myth."[322]

Keep in mind that the Celts followed and merged with the civilization of Hibernia, knowledge of which survived but little in later consciousness. And only late in life did Steiner offer us a flavor of these Mysteries in just a few lectures. He did not offer us any insight about the extent of their mythology. This is not to say that Tolkien offered us a precise and uncorrupted idea of what these myths could have been.

In the Inklings the treasure of the past in Tolkien met with the promises of the future in Barfield. Through the latter the human being of the Consciousness Soul can understand what is imagination, why it is important, how it can be pursued. The West, quite rightly according to Barfield, can no longer find a way forward based solely on its cultural heritage. The essential missing part has to be sought from the center, as we will explore shortly.

Through Tolkien and Barfield two inheritances potentize the mission of the West. Tolkien clearly looks to the past that holds the greatest potential for the future of the West. He brings to the surface of consciousness the legacy of Hibernia, which "stands in a certain sense at the starting-point of modern spiritual life, in that it has given impulses to this modern spiritual movement, and yet has taken over much from the older spiritual movements in which the primeval wisdom of man was enshrined."[323] The Hibernian Mysteries are Mysteries of the cycles of time; they continuously interweave past and future.

In Hibernia, a "culture in waiting" preserved the unity of the Atlantean Mysteries in light of the coming of Christ at Golgotha. Here paths to the macrocosm and microcosm stood united, whereas they separated in post-Atlantean civilization at large. The unified Mysteries of Atlantis went two separate ways after the Flood. The Mysteries of the macrocosm went the northern route and inaugurated ancient Indian and Persian civilizations. The Mysteries of the microcosm went the southern route and ushered in Egyptian civilization. In Greece the confluence

---

[322] Barfield, *History in English Words*, 75.
[323] Steiner, *Mystery Centers*, lecture 7 of December 7, 1923.

generated on one hand the Apollonian way to the macrocosm and on the other the Dionysian way to the underworld. Roman civilization marked the severance of the Mysteries from culture at large, and these were preserved at the margins of culture.

In spiritual science the paths that separated over the millennia—from ancient India to Ancient Egypt and Greece—united once more. Rudolf Steiner made these Mysteries accessible to all human beings through his sacrificial deed at the end of the year 1923 at the Christmas Conference. The Mysteries of Hibernia were then revealed for the first time by the highest initiate of the time in the prelude to the Christmas Conference.[324] At this crucial turning point of time past and future intersected and cross-pollinated each other.

In spiritual science once more the totality of the Mysteries is presented to the human soul, most clearly of all in the polarity of Spirit Recollection (microcosm) and Spirit Beholding (macrocosm) that stands out in the first and third panels of the Foundation Stone Meditation, inviting us to truly live and truly think respectively. In between, harmonizing the two, lies the path of feeling of Spirit Mindfulness, which is the most direct path to the Christ.

We could say that Tolkien brings us back the awareness of the Great Mysteries of the West, which stand "in a certain sense at the starting-point of modern spiritual life" and prophetically point to modern times: the Saturn Mysteries that tread the paths to macrocosm and microcosm at whose center is found the cosmic Christ. And Barfield points to the Mysteries that have come from the East to the West over millennia and are now calling to a meeting with the spirit of the West. In Anthroposophy we have the new "Great Mysteries" that join anew paths to the macrocosm and to the microcosm. The West has to turn to Central Europe if it wants to bring renewal to culture out of the fountainhead of the spirit. This is the movement that Barfield completes.

Barfield anchors the future of the West to the cardinal impulses coming from Central Europe in the form of Anthroposophy. This offers him the hope that the modern human being needs. On the other hand it can be surmised why Tolkien's pessimism remained in his old

---

[324] Steiner, *Mystery Centers*, lectures of December 7, 8, and 9, 1923.

age. Close to him lay the answers that could quell a great deal of soul unrest. How can an understanding of destiny be enhanced by a clear idea of karma and reincarnation that does not deny all that Christianity stands for? How can the cycles of evolution indicate a direction towards the Christ, and the new manifestations of his being? Both these central questions would have altered Tolkien's pessimistic outlook for the best.

Barfield's relationship to the spirit of Central Europe is finely nuanced when the author speaks biographically. Knowing German intimately, Barfield underlines his close affinity with the language, which "can express philosophical ideas and thoughts more easily and accurately sometimes than English," thus allowing him to give rigor to his thinking. But he admits, "I am nevertheless English, and tend to bring things down to earth."[325]

Barfield characterizes the contrast between the English-speaking West to Central Europe as that of the Consciousness Soul/Intellectual Soul respectively. The latter still has awareness of link between inner and outer; not so the consciousness soul.

The English people, who carry the Consciousness Soul par excellence, embody the modern scientific spirit to the utmost. And this science applies most and foremost to man's physical body. English outlook is so materialistically founded that it constantly draws the clearest of boundaries between matter and spirit. This means at first the complete severance of microcosm from macrocosm.

The way out of this predicament is to move from a clear understanding of the limits of scientific method to knowing why imagination is true; being able to understand the reality of imagination, when one cannot apprehend it yet, in order to direct one's efforts toward it. This is what Barfield spent a whole life demonstrating: "The consciousness soul will only say 'I know,' when it can add: 'because I have experienced.'"[326] And in practical terms, on order to reach imagination, we must move to a theory of knowledge as was first made manifest in Goethe and then in Steiner.

The above can best be done through the spirit of Central Europe, through the Intellectual Soul that has an instinctive impulse to grasp

---

[325] Sugerman, *Evolution of Consciousness*, 3–4.
[326] Barfield, *Romanticism Comes of Age*, 150.

the meaning of life, best exemplified in the Germanic spirit. The people of Central Europe want to plunge into the abyss to find meaning; this is the abyss from which Faust descends to the Mothers; the abyss in which Goethe discovers the primeval plant; the one from which Freud forged the theory of the unconscious. "One might almost say that the Ego in central Europe lives always at the point of incarnation and the Intellectual Soul is that point."[327] The Intellectual Soul is naturally fashioned for understanding the Mystery of the light in the darkness and the Mystery of the Resurrection.

Barfield leads us then to a clear understanding of how Consciousness Soul and Intellectual Soul—through their English-speaking and German-speaking representatives—complement each other. "It is the function of the intellectual soul to inspire—of the consciousness soul to correct. Only the intellectual soul knows what is the meaning of life—but the consciousness soul knows what is *not* the meaning of life—and therefore either is helpless without the other."[328] The Consciousness Soul serves us as a constant reminder of death; that there is no resurrection without death.

In an image of what the two national spirits have to say to each other, Barfield envisions a dance with two spirits graciously interweaving motions and exchanging words:

> As they meet, the Spirit of the German nation calls across to the Spirit of the English: "Seek life! Know yourself! Go down with Faust to the Mothers, to the Eternal Feminine, go down into the teeming earth and rise again in full certainty, having found both yourself and the world."

The English folk-soul calls back:

> "Seek death! Yes, *know* yourself and the world! Do not merely *believe* in the old way, substituting one creed for another. Rather live in the very breakdown of all

---

[327] Barfield, *Romanticism Comes of Age*, 154.
[328] Barfield, *Romanticism Comes of Age*, 163.

belief. . . . Immerse in the destructive element! And so learn to tear your true self from all thought and all feeling in which the senses echo. Leap, with Hamlet, into the grave, in order to wrestle there. Seek death!"[329]

We could say that Barfield strives lifelong to adapt the message of spiritual science to the spirit of the West; to render it operational, to overcome the tendency to espouse it as a comfortable set of beliefs and/ or a lifestyle.

Barfield and Tolkien were thrown together by destiny in Oxford University's arena, and brought closer through C. S. Lewis into the circle of the Inklings. Barfield had some appreciation for Tolkien's *The Hobbit* but failed to see that his masterpiece is actually *The Lord of the Rings*. Barfield also recognized that Tolkien's idea of sub-creation stands much closer to his idea of conscious participation than any of C. S. Lewis's ideas. Though Barfield could help Tolkien tread new paths of thinking, he did not fully understand Tolkien's being and therefore could not help him go further on the path from Romanticism to Anthroposophy.

When we look at the two individuals, something else appears in retrospective that augments the importance of their meeting. Each karmic path complements the other. The sum total of their work offers the gestures of a "literary culmination." Though incomplete, as we have argued, it is already a monumental achievement.

Tolkien is that soul that carries memories from previous lives, both in concrete memories and in the inspiration of his literary materials. His is a soul turned towards the past. He has a clear memory of an event that has taken place in the distant past: the Flood that brought the civilizations of Númenor/Atlantis to an end. He exudes through his art the content of the initiation Mysteries of the West. He relates most to that art that flourished under the encounter of Paganism and Christianity in England, the one that produced the *Crist* or *Beowulf.* Much of the literature that Tolkien appreciated most was the result of the "two golden centuries" (8th–9th centuries) during which the Celtic Christian missionaries from Iona and Lindisfarne met with the

---

[329] Barfield, *Romanticism Comes of Age*, 166.

Benedictines from Canterbury, York, Wearmouth, and Jarrow. Stratford Caldecott sees this as "a Christian civilization . . . that proved capable of assimilating the best traditions of Paganism and raising them to a new cultural level."[330] We could say that this is the expression of the Platonic School of Chartres in England—bringing together the best of the Mysteries of the past with the message and content of Christianity—though, strictly speaking it precedes Chartres in time.

Tolkien walks first and foremost the inner path, the path to the microcosm. His life is an external repetition of the trials of the Mysteries. And yet in his work, chiefly in *The Lord of the Rings*, he marvelously integrates inner paths of Frodo/Sam with the outer paths of Gandalf, Merry, and Pippin. In Tolkien live the reverberations of a life dedicated to the Mysteries. They speak to him like an echo. These Mysteries span the distances of eons and point the way to the future. Last, Tolkien is that kind of soul who immediately recognizes the Christ and has to place Him at the center of all considerations. In Tolkien we clearly have a Platonic soul, one of those that Steiner also characterizes as an Old Soul.

For Barfield, on the other hand, there is no need to know of his previous incarnations, at least for what concerns his opus. It is in fact quite striking to see the reverse movement. In his imaginations—chiefly the two early tales here explored—his future work is announced and mapped out. The movement here is from the present into the future.

Barfield is in all things the polar opposite of Tolkien. He is clearly fit to challenge the outward-looking culture of our time because he can see what lies in front of the eyes of the modern human being that she most commonly misses. His is the path outward. When he looks to the past, he clearly recognizes Aristotle above Plato. All the more clearly his Middle Ages are those of the Scholastics, whom he can emulate at all levels of thought. He has little to say about the School of Chartres.

Barfield's soul is that of an old Pagan who intuits the coming Christ. He finds himself at home in Anthroposophical cosmology and in the realm of pure thought. He is not just comfortable, but completely versed, in everything that Steiner elaborates in his *Philosophy of Freedom*. He does not yearn to place the Christ at the center of all his inquiries,

---

[330] Caldecott, *The Power of the Ring*, 19.

as Tolkien does. Rather the Christ is at the center of all polarities he studies; but this is the cosmic Christ, not the historic one. In him therefore we have all the traits of what Steiner calls an Aristotelian, and a Young Soul.

In literature as in many other fields of inquiry we find here an example of what qualities the "culmination at the end of the twentieth century"—which Steiner talked about in the final years of his life—could offer to a new culture.[331] At the time of this possible culmination, Aristotelians and Platonists incarnate together for the first time in history. This means both tremendous opportunities and obstacles. The challenges for Tolkien and Barfield to meet in a productive way stemmed from being so bewilderingly different. It is no wonder that they had little to say to each other and that they made recourse to C. S. Lewis as a bridge to their respective inner worlds. And yet there was already a movement of recognition going both ways.

To modern human beings of the third millennium, Barfield and Tolkien still have much to say—witness the number of people who come to Anthroposophy through Barfield, or the worldwide appeal of *The Lord of the Rings*. What the two authors left incomplete¾particularly in their meeting of minds¾we can now bring to fruition by understanding the reasons for their literary success and affirming their differences and complementarities.

---

[331] See Morelli, *Aristotelians and Platonists*, Chapters 7, 8 and 9.

Bibliography

Barfield, Owen. *Angels at Bay*. Edited by Jeffrey H. Taylor and Leslie A. Taylor. Oxford: Barfield Press, 2016.

———. *Eager Spring*. Oxford: Barfield Press, 2008.

———. *English People*. http://www.owenbarfield.org/books/book-reader/index.html#page/2/mode/2up

———. *History in English Words*. Great Barrington, MA: Lindisfarne, 2007.

———. *History, Guilt and Habit*. Three lectures given in Vancouver in October of 1978, introduction by G. B. Tennyson. Oxford: Barfield Press, 2012.

———. *Orpheus*. West Stockbridge, MA: Lindisfarne Press, 1983.

———. *Owen Barfield and the Origin of Language*. Spring Valley, NY: St. George, 1979.

———. "Philology and the Incarnation." *Journal for Anthroposophy*, no. 24 (Autumn 1976). https://www.rsarchive.org/RelAuthors/BarfieldOwen/philology_and_the_incarnation.php

———. *Poetic Diction*. Oxford: Barfield Press, 2016.

———. *Romanticism Comes of Age*. Oxford: Barfield Press, 2012.

———. *The Rose on the Ash-Heap*. Oxford: Barfield Press, 2009.

———. *Saving the Appearances: A Study in Idolatry*. Oxford: Barfield Press, 2011.

———. *The Silver Trumpet*. Longmont, CO: Bookmakers Guild, 1986.

———. *Speaker's Meaning*. Oxford: Barfield Press, 2011.

———. *This Ever Diverse Pair*. Oxford: Barfield Press, 2010.

———. *Unancestral Voice*. Oxford: Barfield Press, 2010.

———. *Worlds Apart*. Oxford: Barfield Press, 2010.

Blaxland-de Lange, Simon. *Owen Barfield: Romanticism Come of Age.* Oxford: Barfield Press, 2012.

Caldecott, Stratford. *The Power of the Ring: The Spiritual Vision behind* The Lord of the Rings *and* The Hobbit. Chestnut Ridge, NY: Crossroad, 2012.

Carpenter, Humphrey, *J. R. R. Tolkien: A Biography.* London: HarperCollins, 2016.

————, ed. *The Letters of J. R. R. Tolkien.* London: HarperCollins, 2006.

Clayton Hunter, Jeanne, and Thomas Kranidas. *A Barfield Sampler: Poetry and Fiction by Owen Barfield.* Albany: State University of New York Press, 1993.

Diener, Astrid. *The Role of Imagination in Culture and Society: Owen Barfield's Early Work.* Eugene, OR: Wipf and Stock, 2002.

Flieger, Verlyn. *Green Suns and Faërie: Essays on Tolkien.* Kent, OH: Kent State University Press, 2012.

————. *Interrupted Music: The making of Tolkien's Mythology.* Kent, OH: Kent State University Press, 2005.

————. *Splintered Light: Logos and Language in Tolkien's World.* Grand Rapids, MI: William B. Eerdmans, 1983.

Hammond, Wayne G., and Christina Scull. *J. R. R. Tolkien, Artist and Illustrator.* London: HarperCollins, 2004.

Helms, Randel. *Tolkien's World.* Boston: Houghton Mifflin, 1974.

Morelli, Luigi. *Aristotelians and Platonists: A Convergence of the Michaelic Streams in Our Time.* Bloomington, IN: iUniverse, 2015.

————. *A Revolution of Hope.* Victoria, BC: Trafford, 2009.

————. "Spirit Recollection and Spirit Beholding." http://millenniumculmination.net/Spirit-Recollection-and-Spirit-Beholding.pdf

Pearce, Joseph. *Tolkien, Man and Myth: A Literary Life.* San Francisco, CA: Ignatius, 1998.

Skogemann, Pia, *Where the Shadows Lie: A Jungian Interpretation of* The Lord of the Rings. Wilmette, IL: Chiron, 2009.

Steiner, Rudolf. *Awakening to Community.* Spring Valley, NY: Anthroposophic Press, 1974.

———. *The East in the Light of the West: The Children of Lucifer and the Brothers of Christ*. Forest Row, UK: Rudolf Steiner Press, 2017.

———. *Geographic Medicine*. Chestnut Ridge, NY: Mercury Press, 1986.

———. *How to Know Higher Worlds*. Hudson, NY: Anthroposophic Press, 1994.

———. *The Karma of Vocation*. Spring Valley, NY: Anthroposophic Press, 1984.

———. *Karmic Relationships*, volume 1. Forest Row, UK: Rudolf Steiner Press, 1972.

———. *Karmic Relationships*, volume 2. Forest Row, UK: Rudolf Steiner Press, 1974.

———. *Karmic Relationships*, volume 7. Forest Row, UK: Rudolf Steiner Press, 1973.

———. *Mystery Centers*. Blauvelt, NY: Garber, 1989.

———. *An Outline of Occult Science*. Hudson, NY: Anthroposophic Press, 1997.

———. *Philosophy of Spiritual Activity*. Spring Valley, NY: Anthroposophic Press, 1986.

———. "Richard Wagner and Mysticism." *Anthroposophy* 5, no. 2 (Midsummer 1930).

——— *Study of Man*. Forest Row, UK: Rudolf Steiner Press, 2011.

———. *Three Lectures on the Mystery Dramas*. Spring Valley, NY: Anthroposophic Press, 1983.

———. *Wonders of the World, Ordeals of the Soul, Revelations of the Spirit*. London: Rudolf Steiner Press, 1983.

Sugerman, Shirley, ed. *Evolution of Consciousness: Studies in Polarity*. Middletown, CT: Wesleyan University Press, 1976.

Tolkien, J. R. R. *The Book of Lost Tales*. London: Harper Collins, 2015.

———. *The Fellowship of the Ring*. New York: Del Rey/Ballantine Books, 2018.

———. *The Lost Road and Other Writings: Language and Legend Before The Lord of the Rings*. London: Harper Collins, 2015.

———. *The Monsters and the Critics and other Essays*. London: HarperCollins, 2006.

———. *The Return of the King*. New York: Del Rey/Ballantine Books, 2018.

———. *Sauron Defeated: The End of the Third Age*. Edited by Christopher Tolkien. London: HarperCollins, 2010.

———. *The Silmarillion*. Boston: Houghton Mifflin, 2004.

———. *The Two Towers*. New York: Del Rey/Ballantine Books, 2018.

West, Richard C. "The Interlace Structure of The Lord of the Rings." In *A Tolkien Compass*, edited by Jared Lobdell. La Salle IL: Open Court, 2004.

Wetmore, James R. "On the Edge of the Unthinkable: An Interview with Owen Barfield." In *Jesus the Imagination: A Journal of Spiritual Revolution*, volume I, edited by Michael Martin, 51–59. Grass Lake, MI: Angelico, 2017.

Zaleski, Philip, and Carol Zaleski. *The Fellowship: The Literary Lives of the Inklings: J. R. R. Tolkien, C. S. Lewis, Owen Barfield, Charles Williams*. New York: Farrar, Straus and Giroux, 2016.

Printed in the United States
By Bookmasters